Topic/Subject

	Date Due	Date Completed

☐ My subject meets the criteria of the assignment.
(pp. 4–6; 34–35)
☐ I have decided on an approach. (pp. 49–55)
☐ Enough sources of information are available.
(pp. 36; 40–41)
☐ My instructor has approved the subject.

Collecting Information

	Date Due	Date Completed

☐ I listed some research questions. (pp. 56–57)
☐ I followed a search strategy. (pp. 58–59; 107–09)
☐ I looked for primary sources. (p. 57)
☐ I looked for secondary sources. (pp. 57–58)
☐ I found information in books. (pp. 69–85)
☐ I found information in periodicals. (pp. 90–98)
☐ I found nonprint information. (pp. 99–107)
☐ I used a computer database. (pp. 85–90)
☐ I used sources outside the library. (pp. 98–99;
100–06)
☐ Each potential source of information is recorded on a
separate card and follows conventions. (pp. 60–69)

Recording Information

	Date Completed

☐ I evaluated each potential source. (pp. 112–15)
☐ Each note is on a separate card. (p. 116)
☐ The source is identified on each card. (p. 117)
☐ I made accurate summaries of information for some
note cards. (pp. 123–24)
☐ I have direct quotations on some cards.
(pp. 126–27)
☐ I used paraphrases on note cards. (pp. 124–26)
☐ Some note cards contain my personal comments,
ideas, opinions, and/or queries. (pp. 127–28)
☐ I have consciously avoided writing notes that might
lead to plagiarism. (pp. 130–32)

Organizing Information

	Date Due	Date Completed

☐ I reevaluated my notes and selected those that allow
me to take a stand on my subject. (pp. 134–36)
☐ I alphabetized the Works Cited cards for sources I
actually used. (p. 135)
☐ I wrote a useful thesis statement. (p. 136–41)
☐ The outline form is correct. (pp. 146–57)
☐ Every item in the outline relates directly to the
thesis statement. (pp. 147–48)
☐ The outline shows an organized progression of
thought. (pp. 143–47)
☐ I received feedback from peers on my work thus far.
(pp. 157; 161)

Writing: First Drafts

	Date Due	Date Completed

- [ ] The opening of my paper leads the audience into the subject. (pp. 165–71)
- [ ] My writing is coherent. (pp. 172–73)
- [ ] Transitions connect ideas smoothly. (p. 188)
- [ ] All assertions are adequately supported. (p. 173)
- [ ] My writing is specific. (p. 174)
- [ ] Every quotation is essential to the text and is properly presented. (pp. 178–81)
- [ ] Resources, references, and quotations are integrated with my own writing in the text. (pp. 174–78)
- [ ] All sources are acknowledged and properly documented. (pp. 194–202)
- [ ] The paper ends with finality. (pp. 182–86)

Writing: Final Revision

	Date Due	Date Completed

- [ ] I have selected the most appropriate words for my ideas. (pp. 187–88)
- [ ] Sentences are the best I can compose. (pp. 187–88)
- [ ] Spelling, punctuation, and capitalization are accurate. (p. 189)
- [ ] All documentation is accurate and consistent with the style selected. (pp. 192–216)
- [ ] Documentation is coordinated with Works Cited. (pp. 194–202)
- [ ] The title of the paper is specific. (pp. 90–91)
- [ ] I am satisfied with this research paper.

Final Presentation

	Date Due	Date Completed

- [ ] I have followed the recommended typing or word processing format. (pp. 146–48)
- [ ] Each page is numbered consecutively and accurately. (pp. 247–53)
- [ ] All illustrations, charts, graphs, tables, pictures, etc., are properly labeled and placed where most relevant to the text. (pp. 150–51)
- [ ] The Works Cited listing (or other statement of resources) is complete and typed in the proper form. (pp. 217–44; 253–54)
- [ ] Any additional sections or materials are completed, properly identified, and put in place. (pp. 248–49; 251–55)
- [ ] I have given my research paper a final proofreading and typographical errors are corrected. (p. 247)

I turned in my research paper on _____ .

Keeping a Process Log lets you see at a glance how much you have accomplished and where you are in the process of preparing your research paper. Read about the Process Log and see an example of one on pages 11–13.

Make your Process Log an ongoing activity. Be sure to write in it whenever you do anything related to your research paper. Each entry should be brief, and the focus should be on what you did.

Here is the format for your Process Log:

Name _____

Class Time _____

Research Paper Process Log

Date	Time	Entry

The Research Paper

Process, Form, and Content

Sixth Edition

Audrey J. Roth
Miami-Dade Community College

Wadsworth Publishing Company
Belmont, California
A Division of Wadsworth, Inc.

Sponsoring Editor: Steve Rutter
English Editor: Angela M. Gantner
Editorial Assistant: Sharon Mason
Production Editor: Michael G. Oates
Interior Design: MaryEllen Podgorski
Print Buyer: Barbara Britton
Copy Editor: Alan Titche
Technical Illustrator: Joan Carol
Compositor: Graphic Typesetting Service,
Los Angeles, California
Cover Designer: Bill Reuter
Cover Photographer: John Clayton

Printed in the United States of America   19

   3 4 5 6 7 8 9 10—93 92 91 90

Library of Congress Cataloging in Publication Data

Roth, Audrey J.
   The research paper : process, form, and content / Audrey J. Roth. — 6th ed.
      p.   cm.
   Includes bibliographies and index.
   ISBN 0-534-09924-6
   1. Report writing. 2. Research. I. Title.
LB2369.R66   1988
808'.02—dc 19   88-39656
                                                                    CIP

To the Teacher

In this new edition, as in earlier ones, I hope to help students understand that writing a research paper is not an impossibly formidable assignment. Rather, it is a series of steps that lead to a documented paper for academic courses; in the future, this same process can readily lead to the kinds of papers and reports that many students are called upon to write in their vocations.

The Process

As in previous editions, this book continues to stress the *process* of preparing a research paper: searching for information in both print and nonprint sources, synthesizing what is learned with original ideas and interpretations, organizing the whole, and then writing and revising. However, even more now than in earlier editions, examples and references throughout the text are to many nonacademic uses of research. My aim in doing so is to give constant enforcement to the truth: that although the formal research paper is a school assignment, many people in all sorts of businesses and professions constantly use the processes of research. Once learned in school, the skills will be available throughout a lifetime.

The Form

Instructors will find a few changes in the form and content of this new edition that make the book even more useful for students than earlier versions.

Those familiar with the form of past editions will find that the overall design is now fresher and more open, thus making reading easier and finding specific information quicker. Subheads will help students locate material by scanning. Visual and verbal illustrations abound; all are easy to see and follow because special attention is paid to their readability and typography.

The Content

New content in this edition is a section called "Managing Your Time" and a "Search Strategy" form. Together with the "Timetable and Checklist," a long-time feature of this book, these new features will help students confront the time management problem that they and their instructors often note.

Another addition to the content of this edition is an enlarged section on integrating resources into the text of the research paper. Although students readily refer to research sources while writing a paper, doing so smoothly while maintaining tone and style in the text usually poses problems; this section will help students overcome such difficulties. Students may even practice such integration with one of the exercises in the *Instructor's Manual* that accompanies this 6th edition.

Revision always gives an author the opportunity to find a better order and make other changes. Therefore, some passages in previous editions of the text have been combined and relocated so students can find more readily what they need to know. For example, explanations of various kinds of print and nonprint sources and how to locate them are now followed immediately (still within Chapter 4) by instructions on how to write preliminary citation cards for *each type* of resource.

The conventions of documentation and works cited in this edition are predominately those recommended by the Modern Language Association in *The MLA Style Manual* (1985) and the *MLA Handbook for Writers of Research Papers,* 3rd ed. (1988), both by Joseph Gibaldi and Walter S. Achtert. Although parenthetical documentation is stressed, one section of the text explains and illustrates endnotes and another is about other documentation systems. The conventions of APA documentation and reference forms, as shown in the *Publication Manual of the American Psychological Association,* 3rd ed. (1983), are also included (in Chapters 8 and 9) so students who need to use them in future research work or in papers for other courses can readily make the transition.

Because computer-use has become more ubiquitous since the last edition of this book, attention to computers continues in this edition. Readers will find that besides cognizance of the increasing number of CD-ROM and other computer search aids now in libraries, there is still material on how students can use microcomputers in taking notes, organizing ideas, writing, revising, and proofreading.

Another strength of the present edition is one that reviewers have consistently told me about in past editions: the emphasis on helping students narrow topics to subjects suitable for research papers. I continue to believe, and students in my own classes who use this text continue to reinforce my certainty, that to begin researching too broad a topic leads to disaster but working with a suitably narrow subject will, with support and care during the research process, yield a good research paper.

Teachers may want to note that the ten chapters of this edition follow the format already used successfully by many students and their teachers; what has been reported as particularly useful is retained and, where possible, reemphasized. These include the continuing emphasis on audience, from selecting a subject to incorporating that knowledge into writing and revising.

Again, students are shown how to avoid plagiarism, even during the note taking stage. And again, persuasive writing is stressed, so the sample research paper in Chapter 10 is in that mode. That sample paper contains *marginal notes in two colors*: those in *turquoise* point out characteristics of the research paper *form*; those in *black* make note of the *content* of the sample research paper. Students can use these notes as quick guides and summaries of the text.

The Instructor's Manual

Although once I believed that following the process method of the textbook was all the practice students needed to produce their own research papers, now I know that practicing some of the skills taught in the text helps students produce better papers. Therefore, an *Instructor's Manual* was introduced some years ago. The *Manual* for this sixth edition is revised, updated, and enlarged. It contains exercises for student practice, answers for the teacher, variations on the exercises for students who need a little extra practice, and a long list of activities coordinated with each chapter in the text. In all, instructors will find ample material to choose from, depending on student requirements and on time available. Exercise pages in the *Manual* may be duplicated readily and distributed to students.

And Thanks. . .

Books take a long time to write and revise and revise again, but authors who are lucky—as I am—have many people that help the book through to publication. To my students over the years who have worked through this material, and especially to those who permitted me to include their work, I am grateful. They teach me more every time we start the process! Susan Byrd, of the Miami-Dade Community College South Campus library, has been most helpful. Working again with Steve Rutter was a delight—and I thank him for setting impossible deadlines but helping me meet them. Michael Oates is absolutely wonderful at handling all sorts of unusual details having to do with production and Alan Titche was an understanding copy editor. A special note of appreciation to MaryEllen Podgorski for her design and to Bob Kauser for his aid.

Thanks go, also, to the many colleagues whose comments and suggestions have helped me to continue improving this book. Those who assisted most recently are: Jennifer L. Bailey, California State University–Dominguez Hills; Patricia C. Barney, Citrus College; Joseph T. Barwick, Central Piedmont Community College; Arnold J. Bradford, Northern Virginia Community College; Patricia E. Connors, Memphis State University; Joanne B. Detlef, Indiana University–South Bend; Patricia Ferrara, Georgia State University; Harriet Herliney, Glendale Community College; Linda T. Humphrey, Citrus Community College; Fred Rue Jacobs, Bakersfield College; David H. Katz, Community College of Philadelphia; Michele Moragne e Silva, St. Edward's University; David L. Murphy, Sandhills Community College; Michael G. O'Hara, Muscatine Community College; Dorothy Raffel, George Mason University; Janice Reid, Clark County Community College; Mark Reynolds, Jefferson Davis Junior College; Al Starr, Essex Community College; Henrietta S. Twining, Alabama A & M University; and Brenda R. Williams, University of Hartford.

Books also take a lot of an author's time away from the family. Fortunately, mine is an understanding one. And Ray deserves a special medal! Six of them, in fact!

> Audrey J. Roth
> Miami, Florida

To the Student

Preparing and writing a research paper is an active and individual process—an ideal learning process. It can lead you beyond texts, beyond a library, and encourage you to investigate on your own. It provides a structure, but within it you can make exciting discoveries of knowledge and of yourself that are basic to education.

The research paper also gives you a chance to individualize a school assignment, to tailor a piece of work to your own inclinations and abilities, to show others what you can do. Writing a research paper is more than just a classroom exercise. It is an experience in searching out, understanding, and synthesizing that forms the basis of many skills applicable to both academic and nonacademic tasks. It is, in the fullest sense, a discovery, an education. So, to produce a good research paper is both a useful and a thoroughly satisfying experience!

In this new edition I have continued to give you help in ways that many students have already found useful—and added a few that students in my classes have said to include. "Managing Your Time" is a new section in Chapter 1 because it addresses a problem students often voice. The new "Search Strategy" form and the "Timetable and Checklist" at the front of the book will also help you make the best use of your time. And many students say that keeping the "Process Log" lets them see how they are progressing.

An expanded section in Chapter 7 of this edition is on integrating resource information with the text you are writing so your paper doesn't look like a cut-and-paste job.

Students have found that taking time to focus on a subject narrow enough to work with also helps them produce a successful research paper. That's why there are two chapters on this early part of the process. I hope you will use the varied suggestions in them, if you have free choice of a subject, to explore the possibilities open to you before making a final choice.

Because I know that few of you will spend the rest of your life in academe, examples and illustrations throughout the text are drawn from a variety of businesses and professions (as well as from different academic disciplines). As you read them, bear in mind that although you are using this text for a school research paper, the skills you are learning and practicing will be eminently useful to you long after this particular course is over.

You will find that the design and typography of this new edition makes it easy to use and to find what you're looking for. For example, samples of preliminary works cited cards appear right after the text sections about each different source of information you can consult. Among these are many nonprint resources—material you might recall at some time when your job requires you to search for information.

Use the many subheads to scan for specifics. Make the graphics that show spacing and other details of conventions a quick reference source. Look carefully at the marginal notes on each page of the sample research paper (pages 257–78): those in turquoise call attention to forms you need to follow in your own paper; those in black are remarks about the content of the sample research paper and can serve as a guide for writing your paper. These special aids, along with the very detailed index, are all here to help you!

If your library has computer facilities, you will find references to using them in this text. If you have access to a microcomputer, you will find in this book many suggestions about using it for taking notes, organizing information, and writing and revising your paper.

This book doesn't guarantee to rid you of genuine concerns or to provide a magic formula that makes everything easy. It *does,* however, offer a procedure to follow and a framework to use in preparing a research paper. It will guide you through the entire process, from choosing a subject to submitting a written paper of good quality in acceptable form. You can use it as a guide in many courses, even if you are left completely on your own to write a research paper. (The examples of several kinds of documentation systems makes it applicable in a variety of academic areas.) You will probably also find this book a valuable permanent addition to your personal library.

In short, I hope this book will make research a useful part of your education and preparation for the future. I also hope that as you learn increasingly to work on your own and trust your own abilities, you will often make those personal discoveries that are the *real* bases of learning.

A. J. R.

Contents

Chapter 1
Starting the Research Paper 1

Chapter 2
Choosing a General Topic   15

Chapter 3
Narrowing the Topic   39

Chapter 5
Recording Information   110

Chapter 6
Organizing Ideas *134*

Chapter 7
Writing Your Paper   *162*

Chapter 8
Documenting Your Paper   192

Chapter 9
Preparing the Works Cited   *217*

Chapter 10
Final Presentation   *245*

Chapter 1

Starting the Research Paper

You have been doing research all your life. If you have ever done a careful, serious, and systematic investigation to find information you wanted—before you bought a VCR or chose a school or decided on a favorite pizza parlor—you were doing research.

Other people do research, too. Congress makes investigations, such as the Iran-Contra hearings, in order to gather information that will help them make laws. The people who design entertainments at Disney World have an on-site library from which they can research such subjects as mechanics, robotics, and costumes—all needed for their work.

There are several different kinds of research:

- **Pure research,** usually associated with the natural sciences, aims at adding new knowledge to what people have already been able to learn, even if such knowledge doesn't seem to have any immediate or practical use. It might be done in a laboratory or by a landing vehicle scooping up surface samples from Mars.

- **Scholarly research** is similar to pure research, except that the searcher works with materials already in existence. You do scholarly research when you write a paper for a course; your teachers do it when they write journal articles or prepare speeches to give at their professional organizations.

- **Applied research** is the practical application of what has already been discovered or theorized. For instance, after nylon was developed in the laboratory, people in applied research found ways to use it in thousands of products from hosiery to carpets and fishing line.

- **Technical or business research** is one form of applied research. People who must make such practical decisions as choosing a new location for a manufacturing plant rely on this kind of research.

- **Market research** is the study of what consumers want. We have roll-out refrigerators, snowmobiles, nonstick zippers, dog walking services, and uncounted other products and services because market research showed people would use them.

The English word *research* comes from a prefix and a root word that mean "to seek out again." Most **academic** or **scholarly** research is, indeed, a matter of seeking out ideas and materials already found or developed by others. But then the researcher puts them together in new ways—and makes discoveries, achieves new insights. That is what you will be doing as you use this book to write a research paper.

You may have been given an assignment called a "term paper," a "library report," an "investigative report," a "documented paper," or a "research paper." The names are often used interchangeably. Whatever the name, the assignment requires you to locate information on a given subject from a library (and often from other sources) and write conclusions based on your findings.

Differences Among Research Papers, Documented Papers, and Reports

Perhaps in elementary or high school you did some library work or even wrote a library paper—recording the facts you discovered and handing in the results. If you only compiled information without making evaluations or interpretations about those facts, you were actually preparing a **report.**

Reports can be on a single subject: whales, direct-mail advertising, presidential party platforms. They may be (and often are) book-length. But reports have many practical applications in addition to fulfilling school assignments. They are so much a part of business, industrial, and governmental practice that courses are given in business and technical report writing.

A good report must be documented, must acknowledge the sources of information from which it's compiled. For academic purposes, the term **documented report** is often used. It requires that you find and record a series of facts or other information which you present *without* including your own evaluation, interpretation, or ideas. Although no truly unbiased work is possible, in a documented report you should try to present the results of your research in as "objective" a manner as you can. In order to do so, you must take notes meticulously, ascribe sources accurately, and be sure summaries and paraphrases are thorough.

Several kinds of documented reports are possible. You might *trace* the history of something, such as how windsurfing came to be accepted as an Olympic sport or how attempts were made to keep the California condor alive as a species in the wild. Or, you could *explain* a notion such as flexible working times, perhaps illustrating the explanation with examples of how this concept has been implemented in various businesses or industries. You might *present comparative information,* such as descriptions of a movie that has been remade several times over a period of years. You might *examine* (and report on) some single feature, such as how robots are being used for difficult or dangerous jobs in the auto manufacturing industry.

A **research paper** differs from a report or a documented report in one major way: *you are expected to evaluate or interpret* or in some other way add to and participate in the information you gather and write about. In a research paper you are expected to develop a point of view toward your material, take a stand, express some original thought.

You can do that by first narrowing down a general area and then taking a specific approach to the material. Later, that approach will be reflected in the thesis or underlying idea of the research paper. So, instead of writing about "whales" in general, you might examine how available evidence on whale sounds has led to theories of animal communication. A direct-mail advertising campaign could be linked to other media campaigns, and a research paper on presidential party platforms could be developed by comparing those platforms in the last presidential election year. Censorship might be linked to choices about what school libraries buy (which is, in fact, related to the subject of the sample research paper in Chapter 10).

Length Is Variable

Length has nothing to do with whether a piece of work is a report or a research paper. Content makes the difference! The length of a research paper may be

- specified in advance (by an assignment)
- related to an instructor's expectations for course work
- determined by the complexity of the material
- governed by a student's willingness to work
- controlled by the time a student has available.

Most undergraduate college-level research papers are expected to be from 1,500 to 3,000 words (from six to twelve double-spaced, typewritten pages of text). This book is written on the assumption that you will be working on a research paper of that length.

What a Research Paper Is

A research paper is an entirely new work, one you create, one that can only be found on the pages you write. If it is the kind of research paper this book is about, it will have a number of qualities that reflect *you,* that make it your own special creation.

1. *The research paper synthesizes your discoveries about a topic and your judgment, interpretation, and evaluation of those discoveries.*

    Your discoveries consist mostly of the ideas, knowledge, and actual words of people who have written, spoken, or made pictures about the subject you investigated. They are likely to come from both print and nonprint sources. But all that collected material only has value because *you weighed your discoveries and drew conclusions from them.* Your involvement is evident because the entire research paper reflects your own ideas as much as those of anyone else who has worked on the subject.

    Selecting information to use is a personal process. Deciding how to approach this information, developing a point of view toward it, and, finally, choosing your own words to present it are all highly personal activities. Therefore, the more you involve yourself in these activities, the more the resulting research paper will be your own!

2. *The research paper is a work that shows your originality.*

    The paper resulting from your study, evaluation, and synthesis will be a totally new creation, something you originate. True, you will have put many hours of thought and much effort into a work that takes only a short time to read. But that is the nature of any creative endeavor. Moreover, it's a real art to make the difficult appear easy, not to let an audience be aware of preparation and practice. What you read most easily is often a result of the most work. In a carefully crafted research paper, your own hand and thought—your originality—are evident.

3. *The research paper acknowledges all sources you have used.*

    Documentation and acknowledgement of what is not original is so basic to research papers that a whole series of customs or conventions has developed for crediting what you borrow from other people. Chapter 8 explains these customs and shows you how to document your own work. Chapter 9 augments that information.

Ethical behavior also demands that you acknowledge the sources that contributed to your work. Finding information and making it available to others, whether in writing, orally, or in film, is hard work. Just as you do these tasks for a research paper, so others have done the same (or similar) tasks for what became your sources. So although your research paper is a new and original work, none of it would have been possible without the various sources you consulted to prepare it. Acknowledging that debt to others is only right and fair!

What a Research Paper Is Not

If you accept the definition offered so far in this book—that a research paper is a synthesis of your thought applied to the material supplied to you by others, that it is original, and that it acknowledges source material—you will never make the mistake of attempting to hand in what is certainly *not* a research paper.

1. *A summary of an article or a book (or other source material) is NOT a research paper.*
    A summary can't fit our definition of a research paper for two reasons: 1) a single source doesn't allow you to select materials or to exercise your own judgment and 2) the organization can't be your own because a summary must follow the structure of the original source.
    Summaries of written, visual, or audio materials have their uses—and they are important ones—but substituting for a research paper is not one of them.

2. *The ideas of others, repeated uncritically, do NOT make a research paper.*
    By definition, the research paper has to reflect something about yourself—a synthesis, an interpretation, or some other personal involvement. To repeat, uncritically, what others have said is merely to report information already available elsewhere. For example, no amount of reading *about* a novel can substitute for reading the work yourself, any more than reading about a musical group can substitute for hearing the musicians perform.

3. *A series of quotations, no matter how skillfully put together, does NOT make a research paper.*
    Quotations have an important place in a research paper because they are the words of experts in the field—or of those who are experts with words. But if your paper is nothing more than a series of quotations, the "you" of the synthesis is missing; you, yourself, are not involved in such a paper, and the work certainly gives no evidence of your originality.

Furthermore, each quotation is likely to have an individual style. To organize dozens of quotations from different people into a coherent whole is impossible!

4. *Unsubstantiated personal opinion does NOT constitute a research paper.*
Individual beliefs and attitudes are valuable in certain kinds of writing assignments, but the research paper is not one of them. For one thing, the "search" aspect is entirely lacking. For another, a research paper topic is not one that lends itself to opinions without extensive and factual bases.

5. *Copying or accepting another person's work without acknowledging it, whether the work is published or unpublished, professional or amateur, is NOT research. IT IS PLAGIARISM.*
It is morally wrong to pass off as your own any writing you did not do. To present such work without acknowledging the source—and therefore let someone assume it is yours when, in fact, it is not—is plagiarism. Turning in as your own a research paper done by someone else is indefensible, whether you accepted it from a friend trying to help you out or you bought it from a company that supplies research papers. There are laws against plagiarism, and in many schools any student involved in plagiarism (including the supplier of such a paper) is automatically dismissed.

On the most literal level, perhaps no word or thought is completely original; you learned it somewhere. Often only the finest line of distinction separates what must be credited in a research paper from what you can safely present without documentation. What requires crediting or documentation to avoid plagiarism and what doesn't is discussed on pages 130–32.

Students who respect themselves and their work will certainly not be tempted to copy from anyone. Instead, they will always extend proper credit to others for ideas, as well as for specific wording. (See Chapter 5 for more about plagiarism.)

Five Steps to a Research Paper

Research papers are as likely to be assigned in nursing, forestry, or accounting as they are in English, history, anthropology, or chemistry. Whatever the school course or the subject of the paper, your **goals** will be the same:

- to learn from a study you undertake
- to present your material competently
- and to earn as high a grade (and as much personal satisfaction) as possible.

You can achieve these goals most readily if you **follow an orderly procedure from the time the paper is assigned until you turn it in.** Instead of looking for shortcuts (which often turn out to make your work more difficult), concentrate on doing each of the following steps carefully and completely. If some parts of this process seem difficult or tedious at first, don't worry. You'll find them easier as they become more familiar. And if some of the instructions sound unnecessary at first, remember that many people have found them the best of several possibilities.

The completed research paper, whatever its length or whatever its subject, will be the result of your having taken only five steps.

Step 1. Choosing the Subject

Choose the right subject and you have a good chance of producing a good (or excellent) research paper. Choose the wrong subject, and you probably *can't* write a good research paper. So important and basic is this step to everything else you do that Chapters 2 and 3 are devoted to helping you with this task.

If you have the option of choosing your own subject, remember that specific subjects make better papers than very broad ones. "The Importance of Economics" could be everything or nothing. "International Cooperation as Exemplified by the World Bank" is more specific and likely to make a better research paper. "Surgery" sounds like the title of a series of books. But "The Growing Scandal of Unnecessary Surgery" is specific and lets you be a participant in writing what you discover from investigation.

Step 2. Collecting Information

You might do most of Step 1 at your desk. For Step 2 you need to get outside your usual study area. Your first stop will probably be a library, where you will find relevant (or not-so-relevant) materials. But plan on going beyond this limited research source. Query people. For instance, you might interview the manager of a shopping mall if you were writing about how architecture affects people's lives. Also, think of videotapes, films, the radio, computer programs, and your television set as valuable sources for information.

To complete this step, you will

a. find varied sources of relevant information
b. read, look at, or listen to what the sources contain
c. keep a record (that is, write notes) about what you learn.

You may already have some knowledge of your chosen subject and can certainly incorporate that into your paper. But you will undoubtedly have to seek out specifically most of what you eventually want to write for any research paper you do. Chapters 4 and 5 will help you in this second step, the one in which you will be concerned mostly with the *search* in *research*.

Step 3. Evaluating Materials

A good research paper reflects a critical attitude toward the information you collect. Evaluating information—that is, judging and weighing the usefulness of the material you've collected and its relevance to your subject—takes place as you formulate your own ideas about your investigation and develop an attitude toward what you have been learning.

Not every piece of information you collect is equally important. As the paper begins to take shape in your mind, you may even realize that some of your notes are no longer relevant. Or, you may change your outlook about an author's veracity and find you need to do a little more research. Chapter 5 will give you some help in this step. However, much of this evaluation takes place as you work with your subject and aim toward the next step.

Step 4. Organizing Ideas

A collection of facts, quotations, summaries, and ideas can be either meaningless or purposeful. Just as a collection of musical notes can be either random noise or a top-selling record, the work of the previous three steps can be either a hodgepodge or the foundation of a successful research paper. The difference depends on how well you put together the materials you have.

If the material you collected and evaluated is coordinated and arranged to lead logically to a conclusion, if it all makes a point that is supported, you will have a good research paper. Therefore, putting your notes together in an organized way, such as an outline, before you begin writing the paper is crucial. Chapter 6 will help you organize material so you can begin to write.

Step 5. Writing the Paper

Writing your research paper is easier if you carefully and thoughtfully complete all the preparatory work of the previous four steps than if you try to plunge into writing without really being ready. In this step you finally put down on paper what you have learned and what you believe about your subject. The process you follow in doing so is the same you have undoubtedly used in writing (especially in school and college) for many years; it's the process all writing goes through. Many of the elements of writing noted below happen simultaneously. (That is, you may revise as you draft or even when you proofread.)

Draft a copy of your research paper as the starting point for this step. Follow your outline or other organizing guide and the aids in Chapter 7 to write out your paper. If you can use a computer word processing program, you will find it most helpful to do so for this step.

Document your paper as you draft (and be sure to keep the documentation straight when you revise). Because documentation is most likely to be parenthetical, as explained in Chapter 8, it is easy to incorporate into this early writing stage. When you finish the paper, you can prepare the list of Works Cited as explained in Chapter 9.

Revise what you have written. Take a hard look at what you've said and how you've presented it. You may decide that one idea works better in a different place from where you originally put it; move it. See if you can get a better flow of thought by moving some text. (With a computer you can move a block of text, then send the text back to its original location if you don't think it works better.) Even if you're not using a word processor, be willing to make changes in what you've written. Cut and paste sections of your draft if you want to try out rearrangements.

We know that most writers do some revising as they draft; confident ones may make many changes as they write. If you are *really* revising and not just prettying up punctuation and spelling, you will want to allow plenty of time to do so. Don't move away from revision until you're satisfied that you have said everything you want to say in the most effective way you know.

Edit your writing for spelling, punctuation, capitalization, and adherence to required research paper forms during the last stage of revision and before you prepare the final copy of your work in the presentation form recommended in Chapter 10.

Why a Research Paper Is Important

All the skills you have just been reading about in this sketch of the research paper process—making decisions about a subject, developing an inquiring attitude, gathering information, examining it critically, thinking creatively, organizing effectively, and writing convincingly—are crucial to academic success. They are also basic to success in business, professional, and private life.

Air conditioning specialists, flight engineers, fashion designers, and nurses use these same skills daily and follow this same process. Business people use these skills in deciding whether or not to promote a worker or buy new merchandise. Attorneys use the sequence whether they are preparing a murder case for courtroom presentation or incorporating a new business.

Learn these skills now, in preparing a research paper. You will find yourself using them again and again in many ways and in different circumstances, both in and outside of school.

Teachers don't assign research papers capriciously. Nor are they anxious to spend personal time reading research papers. Several reasons, in addition to sharpening the skills noted, commend the research paper as a popular and valuable assignment.

1. Many kinds of writing—from essay tests to investment brochures—require you to gather and process factual information on a specific subject, just as the research paper does. Though you may not be interested in becoming a published writer, you are bound to become

a more perceptive reader for being able to handle this particular writing process.

2. There is an enormous sense of achievement in working *independently* to follow through on a task and fulfill a goal—as you must in completing a research paper. You will also take satisfaction in knowing that you've done a job to the best of your ability, that you've written something well, and that you're well informed on a specific subject. Students often say that accomplishing a task they felt shaky about undertaking was particularly important to them. And not the least of personal satisfactions, of course, is having your efforts rewarded by a high grade on the assignment.

3. Doing a research paper offers you a chance to find out about something you have wanted to know about, or to find out about a subject you think you *may* be interested in, or to look at something related to a course you would like to take but have no time to schedule at the moment.

4. You learn how to use the facilities of your school and community to support your work. Certainly, you gain confidence using the library when you do a research paper.

5. You establish yourself as an individual, even in a very large class, when an instructor reads your paper. Then, the teacher's concentration is entirely on you and your work.

6. Writing a research paper requires you to exercise that form of judgment called *critical thinking*. So many elements enter into critical thinking—the ability to weigh words, to discriminate among ideas, to separate fact from opinion or assumption, to find and select relevant materials, to draw conclusions, to synthesize results—that many people believe the phrase describes *all* of education. Certainly, all this is what you do when you engage in the process of writing a research paper. So completing such a paper is practice in developing skill in critical thinking, perhaps the most important, the most desirable goal of education.

Who Reads Research Papers— and Why

Before you begin work on your research paper, you should know your audience—who is going to read it. Will it be just the instructor for whose class you are writing the paper? Will other students in the class be reading it? Will you want to show it to your visiting relatives? Smart writers know in advance for whom they are writing in order to **choose a subject of interest to the reader** and in order to **write in a way that will get the information to the reader.**

Although you will certainly need to choose a subject that interests you enough to work with, you will also want your prospective audience to be interested in what *you* have to say. Be less concerned that the reader is interested initially in the subject you choose because your good work on the paper and thoughtful writing will make your work interesting reading. Besides, if you care about your topic and what you write about it, chances are the audience will care, too.

Many research papers are read only by the student's instructor, the person who assigned the work. Therefore, you can assume your reader has an interest in a topic related to the field of study in which the paper was assigned. But if you have a free choice of topics, consider whether the instructor will want to read a paper on, for instance, ballet or auto racing. Don't make the mistake of assuming lack of interest on any topic. You might learn of an instructor's preferences during a conference on your research paper topic. Or, you might ask outright about topic preferences. However, most teachers will be glad to read about any topic, provided that the research paper is well written!

If you know that classmates will be working with you during the research paper process, you will probably have a chance to discuss your proposed subject choices with them. You may also help each other with drafts of your work in progress. Or, you may be asked to make an oral or written presentation for classmates based on your research paper. Knowing your audience will help you choose a subject of interest to them. It will also let you know what level of vocabulary and sentence complexity to use.

You may also write a research paper for someone else, perhaps for a family member or an employer. Fix a specific picture of that audience in your mind—not only the face or physical appearance but also that reader's concerns, interests, education, language choices or customs, usual type of reading, and so on. Keep that person in mind all through the various steps of the research process.

Finally, think about *why* you are going to write this research paper. For a grade, of course. But it's possible that friends, relatives, or future teachers may want to read your paper—or an abstract of it. Some students have found that a paper written in one course and subsequently shown to the instructor in another course served as the basis for further study or a springboard to new ideas and perspectives. You may even decide that you want to write a research paper for yourself because you want to learn something in particular!

Keeping a Process Log

In preparing and writing a research paper, you follow a process (the Five Steps you have already read about). So it's easy to keep a **Process Log,** a record of **what you do starting now and ending with the completed research paper.**

A *log* is a record of performance, of what happened and when. The Process Log you will keep now, however, should include a bit more than just what you did. Write in it, also, some brief, personal comments as you record more mundane matters. Even though entries are brief, one look at the Process Log will show you (and your instructor) what you have accomplished and where you are in the research process. When your research paper is finished, you will also have a memento of your work—something on which you can look back proudly!

Here are some kinds of entries you can put in your Process Log:

- **Thinking time**—This is really working time because you need to think before you can work (or while you're working)

- **Study time**—This book certainly contributes to helping you through the process of writing a research paper, so be sure to record the time you spend reading assignments in it and give a brief summary of what you accomplished during each study period.

- **Reminders to yourself**—Use the Process Log to note a follow-up you want to make or a source you want to check—so that you can relate the information to what you have already done.

- **Difficulties you encounter**—No sustained work is without its difficulties or problems. The Process Log is not meant to be record only of sweetness and light. If you have difficulty with any aspect of your work (such as all the books on your subject being out of the library or a periodical microfilm you needed being damaged and therefore difficult to read), record it in your Process Log.

- **Solutions to problems**—Don't be afraid to blow your own horn. If you solve a problem, write about it in your Process Log!

Begin keeping your Process Log **now**. The form is simple. Use the example below. (You'll also find the Process Log format just before the title page of this book.)

Date	Time	Entry
Write the date of the entry.	Record the time you began and ended doing what you did.	Tell what you did that was part of the research paper process. Be detailed and specific.

Copy the format into a notebook, repeating it as you need additional pages. If you have access to a duplicating or a photocopying machine, make a master page from which you can make copies. Or, set up the format on a computer and print out copies as you need them.

The following sample is from the actual Process Log kept by the author of the sample research paper in Chapter 10 (pages 257–78). It illustrates the sort of entries you can put in your own Process Log.

Date	Time	Entry
May 10	1– 1:15 pm	I looked for some of the books on my Preliminary Works Cited cards. Half the books I wanted from the school library show as being charged out + the librarian is afraid at least one of them is lost. Discouraging!
	2:30 – 2:35	This was "seriously thinking time" about how to get some of that material I need. I will call the downtown library + see if any of the things are there. It's too late to change the topic! Besides, I will be looking for information in periodicals + there is a film in the media center. Maybe I can set up some interviews.
May 11	1–1:30 pm	Getting this computer search certainly saved hours of work! Now I will have to see if some of the likely-looking titles are in the library.
May 23	7– 10 pm	Writing this paper is easier than I expected it to be! I still have some trouble in putting all the citations at the ends of sentences, but now I understand better how to integrate the notes with the text.

Managing Your Time

Make your Process Log an ongoing activity. Get in the habit of writing in it whenever you do anything related to your research paper. If you wait to record one entry, you are likely to wait to record another—and another. Then it will be difficult and time-consuming to try to reconstruct your activities and pinpoint times. It's far easier, and more productive, to make short notes as you work.

Use the **Timetable and Checklist for Preparing Your Research Paper** at the very beginning of this book to keep you on track and on time during the research process. If your instructor doesn't give you due dates for the various steps in the research process that are listed on those front pages, set your own schedule. And stick to it!

Don't procrastinate!   Work that is put off is often work never done. Or, it is done sloppily and hastily. Instead of delaying what you need to do, get the work done on time—and then maybe take a break or give yourself a treat as a reward.

Choose a set working place and time. If you don't feel like working on a research paper after football practice, give yourself a morning work time. Just make it regular. And pick the place you want to use for working. If the library is too noisy to suit you, set your working time somewhere else. If you work better at night than early in the morning, take that into account.

Discipline yourself.   Most students have several courses to prepare for in a term; the course for which you are writing the research isn't your only one. Or, you may have a job that takes up a lot of your out-of-school time. You have to find time to fit the steps of the research process into your schedule— and make yourself do them.

Try to work regularly rather than sporadically. All-night, last-minute rush sessions don't work for most people. Not if you want to produce a research paper you can be proud of! Rather than two six-hour sessions, rearrange your time to allow six two-hour sessions. Aim at building your research paper activities into your schedule regularly and unspectacularly; you will find you can do them more effectively!

Chapter 2

Choosing a General Topic

Most research papers are assigned at the beginning of a school term and are due shortly before the term ends. Therefore, you have plenty of time to gather information, mull over ideas, write your paper, and revise it several times before turning it in. If you start when you get the assignment, and don't procrastinate, you will be able to do a good job. (If you have interim due dates for various parts of the process, write them on **The Timetable and Checklist for Preparing Your Research Paper** at the very beginning of this book. If you instructor doesn't give you such dates, set them for yourself.)

Research paper topics will be one of three kinds:

1. **Assigned Topics** are selected by an instructor and presented to you. Often, these appear as an actual list of writing subjects to choose from.
2. **Field-of-Study Topics** are those that you select, but your assignment stipulates that the topic must relate in a specific way to the course for which the research paper is assigned.
3. **Free-Choice Topics** give you broad rein to investigate any area you choose.

A good topic is the beginning of a good research paper. So the rest of this chapter is about selecting a topic you can research. Chapter 3 then shows you how to narrow a topic into a subject suitable for a research paper. **In this book, the word *topic* refers to a broad range or general field** of interest, and the word *subject* indicates that part of a topic that is narrow enough to investigate and write about.

EXAMPLE: "Literature" is a *topic*.
                "Time Travel as a Literary Device in the Novel *Slaughterhouse Five*"
                is a *subject*.

The subject is derived by narrowing the topic.

Sometimes topic and subject selections seem to telescope so the two processes meld into one. But in the explanations that follow, they are considered separately.

Assigned Topics

Often an "Assigned Topic" is really a subject—an idea that has already been narrowed and is ready for investigation. Examples of such topics (or subjects) are the mathematical contributions of Leibniz or lie detector tests as a prerequisite for employment.

An Assigned Topic is not stifling and you should not view it as limiting. Rather, consider that it makes your beginning work easier yet provides you with many opportunities for personal expression. You will still have plenty of leeway to develop a project that depends heavily on what *you* discover and what *you* have to say on a subject.

Field-of-Study Topics

If the broad field for which you have to write a research paper is familiar to you, finding a topic to write about will be easier than if the field is entirely new. Even if the field *is* unfamiliar, you can cope if you follow an orderly procedure.

1. **Take stock of what you already know.**
2. **Use printed aids to help:** your textbook
                                   other course materials
                                   encyclopedias
                                   the library card catalog (or an on-
                                       line catalog)
                                   periodical indexes
3. **Build from your own interests.**

Taking Stock of What You Know

If you have taken a course prerequisite to the one for which you have to write this research paper, you already know something about this field of study. If the field is new to you, think about what the instructor has said in giving you an overview of the course. Maybe you know something about the field from talking with friends about the class or about the field. You can use all that prior knowledge as a starting place.

List some of the broad categories of information in this field of study that you already know. Suppose you have to work within anthropology. If you already know that archaeology is a branch of anthropology, or that one unit in the course is about cultural anthropology, you have a good beginning.

Or, **write down some of the information** you were particularly interested in from a prerequisite course. Don't worry about organizing what you write and don't worry about spelling and punctuation; just get the ideas down on paper. By doing so, you use one method of taking stock of what you already know, and you will get a start at choosing a Field-of-Study Topic about which to write your research paper.

Using Printed Aids: Your Textbook

Your class textbook is a most convenient place to begin looking for a Field-of-Study Topic for your research paper. The **Table of Contents** will tell you a lot about the course and give you an overview of the field, even if you won't be studying the entire text in one term. Read through the contents, keeping alert for ideas that might interest you. Circle those you think might be interesting to pursue. Suppose you are in a beginning sociology course for which the textbook is *Sociology*, 2nd ed., by Rodney Stark (Belmont: Wadsworth, 1987). Figure 1 shows a portion of the Table of Contents of that textbook with possible topics circled. For example, you might decide to investigate occupational prestige or cults.

Look through the **index** of the textbook, too. An index gives the specific page location of key ideas in a book. If you see a topic of interest listed in the index, circle it for possible Field-of-Study research (see Figure 2).

A **glossary** lists and defines key terms used in a book. From the words listed you can get a great deal of information about what's important in a course even before you take it, so you can get a head start on your research project by selecting one such term. (In the textbook *Sociology* used as examples in Figures 1 and 2, the glossary is combined with the index.)

The **bibliography** of your textbook is another place to look. You may find in it a book title intriguing enough to encourage you to look into that particular subject.

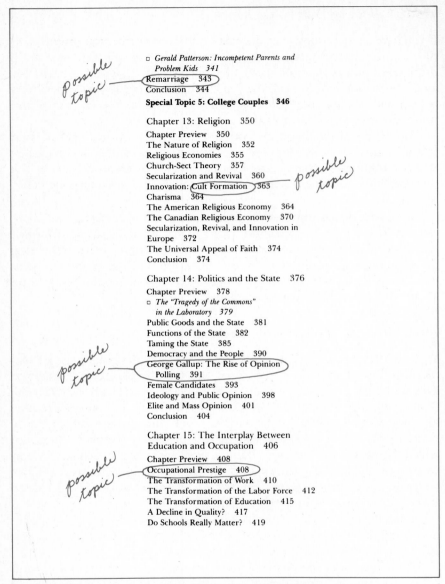

possible topic

possible topic

possible topic

possible topic

Fig. 1. Example of a contents page used to select a topic.

If the **preface** or **introduction** of your textbook contains more than a summary of the contents, you may also be able to use the ideas in it to suggest a topic for research.

Finally, if your textbook is an anthology, the **authors included** in it may be people whose work bears investigation for a Field-of-Study Topic.

Divisional system *(continued)*
functional, 524–527, 534–536
geographical, 524
Divorce
in modern families, 336–339
patterns of, 349
rate in North America, 321
and remarriage, 343–344
Domesday Book Pronounced "dooms-
day" book, this is an outstanding
medieval census conducted by
William the Conqueror following
his takeover of England in 1066.
456, 458
Downward mobility A lowering of
level within the stratification system. 35
Dropouts, cognitive development of,
421, 423
Du Pont, 534–537, 541
Dyad The smallest possible group,
consisting of only two people. 8,
10

E

Ecology and social change, 440
Economic conflict, 292–295
Economic development of minority
groups, 303, 309
Economic status and integration,
511–513
Education, 406–429
correlation with occupational status, 268
economic benefits of, 423–424
functions of, 425–427
impact of school on, 419–423
international differences in, 423,
424
as measure of status, 235, 426–427
quality of, 417–419
by race/ethnicity, 299
role of, in modernization, 452–453
and socialization, 426, 427
summer vacations and, 420–421
See also Mass education
Elite movement, spaceflight as example of, 568–573, 575
Elites in politics, 401, 403
Elitist state A society ruled by a single
elite group; such states repress
and exploit nonelite members.
387–388
Emotional development, 145
Empires as command economies, 448
Environment
manipulation of, 133–134
and pressures on societies, 100
and Viking society, 440–441
Environmental suppressors
of human growth, 122
of intellect, 128
Environmental theories of behavior,
114, 147–152

Epidemics, 467
Equilibrium A state of balance
among system parts that is the
result of interdependence.
96–97
Erie Railroad, 524
Eskimos, 255, 440–441
Ethnic groups Groups that think of
themselves as sharing special
bonds of history and culture that
set them apart from others.
278–280
economic conflict and, 292–296
economic development of,
303–304
geographic concentration of,
301–303
intergroup conflict of, 279–280,
511–513
and middle class, 304
sports and, 314–315, 317
in urban neighborhoods, 509–513
Evolution, theory of, 278
Evolutionary theory of stratification
A theory that holds that because
culture accumulates in human societies, eventually it happens that
no one can master the whole of a
group's culture. At that point,
cultural specialization, or a division of labor, occurs. Since some
specialties will be more valued
than others, inequality, or stratification, will exist. 246–247
Exchange mobility Mobility that occurs because some people fall,
thereby making room for others
to rise in the stratification system.
239
Exclusion of immigrants, 294
Expansive population structure An
age structure in which each
younger cohort is larger than the
one before it; such a population
is growing. 463–464
Experiment A research design in
which the researcher has control
over the independent variable;
that is, the researcher can manip-
ulate when and how strongly the
independent variable occurs and
has the ability to determine ran-
domly which subjects are ex-
posed to which level of the independent variable. 75–79
Experimental controls Methods to
ensure that nothing varies in an
experiment except the independent variable, thus ensuring non-
spuriousness. 77–79
Exploitation All profit in an exchange
in excess of the minimum
amount needed to cause an exchange to occur. 247
Exponential increase A rate of

growth (or decline) that speeds
up as an increasingly larger number of units is added (or sub-
tracted) each cycle, as in 1-2-4-8-
16. 468–469
Extended families Those families
containing more than one adult
couple. 97–98, 324

F

Facial expression, 115
Factions in primitive societies,
102–103
Fad. *See* Craze
False consciousness A term that Marx
applied to members of one class
who think they have common interests with members of another
class. 230
Family A small kinship-structured
group with the key function of
nurturant socialization of the
newborn. 320–345
child care in, 326–330, 332, 335,
339–343
crowding in, 327–328
decline of, 320, 322
extended, 97–98, 324
functions of, 322, 324–326
median income of North American, 227
modern, 333–339
nuclear, 97, 324
one-parent, 339–341
as primary group, 12, 13
traditional European preindustrial,
326–332
Famine as check on population,
465–466, 469
Feral children The name often applied to children who, because of
severe neglect, act as if they were
raised in the wild (*feral* means un-
tamed). 136–137
Fertility rate The total number of
births for a year divided by the
total number of women in their
child-bearing years (the U.S.
Census bases this rate on all
women from age 15 to 44).
460–461
and baby boom, 486–487
and cultural lag, 478–479
decline in, 335–336, 339, 480
future projections of, 480–482
impact of modernization on,
473–476, 481
and infant mortality in Europe, 475
and life expectancy rates, 481–482
in Malthusian theory, 469
in North America, 457
and thresholds of modernization,
474, 476
Feudal societies, 274–275

Fig. 2. **Example of an index page with possible topics circled.**

Using Printed Aids: Course Materials

Some courses are not taught from a single textbook but from several books
that are either assigned or recommended. Or, you may receive a suggested
reading list. You can use any of the books on such lists in the same way you
can use your textbook to help you choose a broad Field-of-Study Topic.

If you are given a course syllabus (whether or not the course has a textbook), look through it, also, at the beginning of the term and draw information about what the course will cover. Use the syllabus as an additional start in deciding on a topic for your research paper.

Using Printed Aids: Encyclopedias

The principal value in reading an encyclopedia article on the field of a course (or on a related field) is the overall view it will give you. Don't expect detailed information but, rather, a broad perspective from which you can make choices.

You might look in one or more encyclopedias for topics related to one idea you start with. For instance, the entry on Foods in *The World Book Encyclopedia* (1988) is only eight pages long but contains many cross references (that is, listing of related articles). (Figure 3.) Some of them may be topics you want to look into—or which suggest still other topics to you.

Another way to use an encyclopedia article to help you find a topic for research is to consider its major divisions as a starting place. For example, the entry on "Environment" in the *Encyclopedia Americana* (1985) is divided into these sections: Assaults on the Environment, Environment and Human Well-Being, The Risk of Environmental Collapse, Protecting the Future. Any of these sections might suggest a topic for you to research.

Finally, a bibliography at the end of an encyclopedia entry (see Figure 4) will introduce you to still more ideas. Sometimes these books, or others by the same authors, will be in the library you are using, or they can be obtained through an interlibrary loan system. You can either use the titles in this bibliography as topic ideas, or you can use the books as additional sources, drawing ideas from their tables of contents, introductions, indexes, or other features.

Using Printed Aids: The Card Catalog

The library you will be using for your research may have the familiar card catalog drawers, a printed catalog, or an on-line computer catalog. The catalog may be divided and therefore have one set of entries by subject alone, or it may be in dictionary form and thus have all holdings listed alphabetically according to card headings. Whichever the form, you can use the catalog to help discover a Field-of-Study Topic.

As libraries of all sizes begin to acquire computers and the materials they can store, you will find more on-line catalogs. At a computer terminal, then, you can call up on screen titles, authors, and subjects of books you seek. The on-line catalog is generally a faster way to look for information because you don't have to go from drawer to drawer and flip through catalog cards. However, a library usually retains its card catalog and thus this book is predicated on the notion that you have access to such cards.

Foods of the New World. In 1492, Christopher Columbus sailed west from Spain. He was seeking a short sea route to the spice lands of the Indies. But Columbus landed in the New World, America, not the Indies. And although Columbus did not find spices, his voyage led to a new world of food for Europeans. American Indians introduced Europeans to avocados, chocolate, corn, peanuts, peppers, pineapples, sweet and white potatoes, squashes, and tomatoes.

The American colonists enjoyed many of the Indian foods. In fact, the Indians taught them how to raise corn, which became the most important crop of the early colonial period. The Indians also taught the colonists how to cook lobsters and wild turkeys. The colonists, in turn, brought their seeds and such livestock as cattle and hogs to the New World.

Recent developments. In the United States today, people's food habits are changing in numerous ways. For example, snacks have become part of the daily diet of many Americans. At the same time, others worry about becoming overweight and watch what and how much they eat. Many health-conscious Americans believe that food additives and other chemicals used in producing and processing foods harm the body. They also are concerned that many important nutrients are lost during processing. These worries have led to the popularity of so-called *health foods.* Health foods include many unprocessed foods as well as foods grown without the use of chemical fertilizers and pesticides.

Many health-conscious people also try to include more fiber in their diet. Fiber is thought to help prevent certain intestinal diseases. Fresh fruits and vegetables and whole-grain foods supply dietary fiber. Some people avoid butter, eggs, fatty meats, and other foods high in a fatty substance called *cholesterol.* Too much cholesterol in the bloodstream may contribute to hardening of the arteries.

Another trend is the rising popularity of cooking as a hobby. In contrast, more people eat many of their meals in restaurants. Fast-food restaurants, especially, have become increasingly popular.   Margaret McWilliams

Related articles. See various country articles in *World Book* in which local foods are discussed, such as **Mexico** (Way of life). See also the following articles:

Kinds of food

Bread	Cheese	Grain	Nut	Sugar
Candy	Egg	Meat	Poultry	Vegetable
Cereal	Fruit	Milk	Spice	

Nutrition

Carbohydrate	Digestive system	Health	Protein
Diet	Fat	Lipid	Vitamin
Dietitian		Nutrition	Weight control

Preparation and processing

Artificial sweetener	Dehydrated food	Freeze-drying
Canning	Fishing industry	Meat packing
Cold storage	Food, Frozen	Packaging
Cooking	Food additive	Refrigeration
	Food preservation	

Special food dishes

Barbecue	Chili con carne	Pemmican
Bird's-nest soup	Haggis	Trepang
Caviar		

Beverages

Alcoholic beverage	Chocolate	Maguey	Soft drink
	Coffee	Mate	Tea

Other related articles

Agriculture	Flower (Other uses)	Kosher
Christmas (Christmas feasting)	Food and Agriculture Organization	Marketing
Climate (Food and climate)	Food and Drug Administration	Plant
		Prehistoric people (Food)
Easter (The lamb; Other foods)	Food poisoning	Restaurant
Eskimo (Food)	Food supply	Salt
Fast	Green Revolution	Supermarket
	Home economics	Thanksgiving Day

Outline

I. Sources of food
  A. Food from plants   B. Food from animals
II. How the body uses food
  A. Producing energy
  B. Building and repairing tissues
  C. Regulating body processes
III. Why diets differ around the world
  A. Geographic reasons   C. Religious reasons
  B. Economic reasons   D. Customs
IV. The food industry
  A. Production   E. Marketing
  B. Processing   F. Government regulations
  C. Packaging   G. Food research
  D. Transportation
V. Food through the ages

Questions

What were some foods that the American Indians introduced to Europeans?
How does the physical environment help determine what the people of a region eat?
What are the most important foods from plants? From animals?
What are *food additives?* What do they do?
How does packaging help keep food from spoiling?
What is *curry? Shish kebab? Smörgåsbord?*
Why is it important to have a well-balanced diet?
What are some reasons diets differ in developed and developing countries?
What are *health foods?* Why are they popular?
Why are proteins essential to good health?

Reading and Study Guide

See *Food* in the Research Guide/Index, Volume 22, for a *Reading and Study Guide.*

Additional resources

Level I
Adler, Irving. *Food.* Harper, 1977.
Berger, Melvin and Gilda. *The New Food Book: Nutrition, Diet, Consumer Tips, and Foods of the Future.* Harper, 1978.
Burns, Marilyn. *Good for Me! All About Food in 32 Bites.* Little, Brown, 1978.
Pizer, Vernon. *Eat the Grapes Downward: An Uninhibited Romp Through the Surprising World of Food.* Dodd, 1983.
U.S. Department of Agriculture. *What's to Eat? And Other Questions Kids Ask About Food: The 1979 Yearbook of Agriculture.* U.S. Government Printing Office, 1979.

Level II
Coyle, L. Patrick. *The World Encyclopedia of Food.* Facts on File, 1982.
Gelb, Barbara L. *The Dictionary of Food and What's in It for You.* Paddington Press, 1978.
Powledge, Fred. *Fat of the Land.* Simon & Schuster, 1984. Tells how food is processed and marketed in the United States.
Ritchie, Carson I. A. *Food in Civilization: How History Has Been Affected by Human Tastes.* Beaufort Books, 1981.
U.S. Department of Agriculture. *Will There Be Enough Food? The 1981 Yearbook of Agriculture.* U.S. Government Printing Office, 1981.

Fig. 3. Last page of the "Food" entry in *The World Book Encyclopedia.* In the left column, the head "Related articles" leads the reader to further topics, as does the material listed under the head "Additional resources."
© 1988 World Book, Inc.

Bibliography

Baldwin, Alfred L., *Theories of Child Development* (New York 1967).

Hoffman, Martin L., and Hoffman, Lois W., eds., *Review of Child Development and Research*, vol. 1 (New York 1964).

Hunt, Joseph McV., *Intelligence and Experience* (New York 1961).

Kessen, William, *The Child* (New York 1965).

Mussen, Paul H., Conger, J. J., and Kagan, J., *Child Development and Personality* (New York 1963).

For Specialized Study

Bandura, Albert, and Walters, R. H., *Social Learning and Personality Development* (New York 1963).

Bronfenbrener, U., "Soviet Methods of Character Education: Some Implications for Research," *American Psychologist*, vol. 17, pp. 550–564 (Washington 1962).

Bruner, Jerome S., and others, *Studies in Cognitive Growth* (New York 1966).

Dollard, John, and Miller, Neal E., *Personality and Psychotherapy* (New York 1950).

Flavell, John H., *The Developmental Psychology of Jean Piaget* (Princeton 1963).

Harlow, Harry F., "Love in Infant Monkeys," *Scientific American*, vol. 200, pp. 68–74 (New York 1959).

Hunt, Joseph McV., *Intelligence and Experience* (New York 1961).

Kagan, J., and Moss, H. A., *Birth to Maturity: A Study in Psychological Development* (New York 1962).

Kendler, H. H., and Kendler, T. S., "Vertical and Horizontal Processes in Problem-solving," *Psychological Review*, vol. 69, pp. 1–16 (Washington 1962).

Lenneberg, Eric H., *New Directions in the Study of Language* (Cambridge, Mass., 1964).

Scott, J. P., "The Process of Primary Socialization in Canine and Human Infants, *Monographs of the Society for Research in Child Development*, vol. 28 (Lafayette, Ind., 1963).

Sears, Robert R., Maccoby, E. E., and Levin, H., *Patterns of Child Rearing* (Evanston, Ill., 1957).

Yarrow, L., "Maternal Deprivation: Toward an Empirical and Conceptual Re-evaluation," *Psychological Bulletin*, vol. 58, pp. 459–490 (Washington 1961).

CHILD GUIDANCE CLINIC. See CHILD WELFARE.

Fig. 4. The extensive bibliography that ends the discussion of "Child Development" in *Encyclopedia Americana*.
© 1985 Grolier, Inc. Reprinted with permission.

The card catalog (familiar to most students and therefore the one illustrated in this book) contains at least three card entries for every nonfiction book in its collection: one filed by author, one by title, and one by subject.

Begin by looking in the catalog for subject headings having to do with the content of the course for which you will be writing the research paper. Whatever you find will, of course, be very broad: accounting, space, pollution, censorship. Then look at some of the books you identify through the catalog under the subject headings; go through them as already suggested in the section above on using your textbook as a source of ideas.

Don't overlook the potential of "see also" catalog listings to help you even more. These cards refer you to related subject headings where you can find even more books to consult. (Figure 5 shows several "see also" cards for

```
        Censorship
            See also subdivision Censorship
        under specific subjects, e.g.
        Radio - Censorship


    Censorship
        See also
    Expurgated books
    Liberty of the press
    Condemned books
    Prohibited books
```

Fig. 5. "See also" catalog cards for the entry "Censorship."

the topic of censorship.) Following the leads of topics on a "see also" card will surely yield enough books to help you select one field of study.

Using Printed Aids: Periodical Indexes

Many million more words are printed in periodicals than in books, so you will find periodicals very helpful in choosing a topic for your Field-of-Study research. *Education Index*, *Chemical Abstracts*, and *Book Review Index* are just three specific indexes in various fields; many others are listed in the "Selected List of Reference Works Available in Libraries" beginning on page 279. Such general indexes as the *New York Times Index* or the familiar *Readers' Guide to Periodical Literature* will also help you find topics to get started.

Suppose you must find a research paper topic for a social science course that includes economics, psychology, anthropology, and sociology. You might look under one of those general headings in a periodical index—*not* for the titles of articles but to get ideas for a topic by seeing what related topics or subdivisions are in the index. For example, Figure 6 shows a page from *Readers' Guide to Periodical Literature* showing the "see also" listing for Investments as well as some of the related headings. Check several volumes of an

Laws and regulations
Fund shopping gets easier [SEC rules] C. Yang. il *Business Week* p87 F 15 '88
Great Britain
See also
Cambrian & General Securities
INVESTMENTS
See also
Bonds
Bonds, Government
Brokers
Capital investments
Coins as an investment
Computers—Investment use
Hedging (Finance)
Information storage and retrieval systems—Investment use
Interest (Economics)
Investment newsletters
Investment trusts
Real estate investment
Securities
Stocks
Workout investments
Caution is the watchword. J. J. Curran. il *Fortune* 117:127-8+ F 15 '88
Interest-rate woes: where should you put your savings now? M. Daly. il *Better Homes and Gardens* 66:64-5 Ja '88
Investments: all we need is a good smokin' dollar. il *Money* 17:40 F '88
Pit bulls and pussycats of investment year 1987. il *Money* 17:27 F '88
INVESTMENTS, AMERICAN
Foreign stocks: one more thing we can't seem to export to Tokyo—the crash. il *Money* 17:42 F '88
Mexico
High tech goes third world [U.S. auto plant in Mexico] H. Shaiken. il *Technology Review* 91:38-45+ Ja '88
INVESTMENTS, ASIAN
United States
The 'eastern capital' of Asia. J. Schwartz. il *Newsweek* 111:56-8 F 22 '88
INVESTMENTS, BRITISH
United States
How long can Farmers keep the British at bay? [BAT Industries bid for Farmers Group Inc.] N. Easton. il por *Business Week* p26-7 F 8 '88
INVESTMENTS, CANADIAN
United States
Campeau strikes again [bid from R. Campeau for Federated Department Stores] D. Jenish. il pors *Maclean's* 101:42-4 F 15 '88
Federated gets healthier—and becomes a target [bid from R. Campeau] S. Phillips. il por *Business Week* p25-6 F 8 '88
INVESTMENTS, FOREIGN
See also
Debts, External
Japan
Wall Street is handing out pink slips in Tokyo, too. A. Borrus and B. Buell. il *Business Week* p43+ F 8 '88
United States
America at auction: going . . . not gone [views of M. and S. Tolchin] E. Pomice. il *U.S. News & World Report* 104:68-9 F 22 '88
Restoring American independence. F. G. Rohatyn. il *The New York Review of Books* 35:8-10 F 18 '88

Fig. 6. **Portion of a page from *Readers' Guide to Periodical Literature*. Under the heading "Investments" are the "see also" entries as well as related topics.**
Copyright © 1988 by H. W. Wilson Company. Reprinted by permission of the publisher.

index or look at one or more related topics within an index to be sure you get a broad range of ideas to work with.

Be sure to check of the "see also" listings for an index entry; they, too, may suggest additional Field-of-Study Topics.

Using Your Own Knowledge

One of the most satisfying ways of selecting a Field-of-Study Topic is to relate the field you have to work with to what you already know or have special interests in, either vocational or avocational. Then you can study something you already care about or something you may find useful.

A personal inventory.   Begin by making a Personal Inventory. On a piece of paper, make four columns with the following headings, and under each write as many individual items as you can.

> **Know and Care About** (Include hobbies, clubs, special events, scouting badges earned, favorite kinds of music, previous school courses, and so on.)
>
> **Special Concerns** (Things you think about, ideas that intrigue you, and so on.)
>
> **Vocational Interests** (Include a satisfying job you now have or careers you are considering)
>
> **Like to Learn More About**

EXAMPLE:

Know & Care About	*Special Concerns*	*Vocational interests*	*Learn About*
motocross racing	acid rain	nursing	gun control
hair styling	amateurs in	aviation	ocean
astronomy	sports		pollution
	space travel		destruction of
	driving laws		rain forests
			sailboating

Be honest with yourself on these lists; they're for your own use. Make each list as long as you can. Use memories, free association—whatever techniques you can to add items to each of the four lists. Don't be selective or judgmental; just concentrate on filling as much paper as you can with these lists. Obviously, you won't be able to use many items (nor will they all make sense with what you're going to do next). But think of the store of resources you'll have for other courses, for writing assignments, for your résumé!

Making relationships.   Using your Personal Inventory to make relationships that help you arrive at a topic for your Field-of-Study research paper is the next step. At the top of a sheet of paper write the name of the field or course for which you must write the research paper. Then draw a vertical line down the center of the page. Choose a word from one of the lists you just made and write it on the right side of the line. Now you are ready to start making relationships to help you find a Field-of-Study Topic. On the left side of the line, make a list of words related to the course for which you need to write the research paper. Use words from the table of contents of a textbook, special terms you know, or words arrived at from free association (explained on page 44) with the material in the course.

EXAMPLE:

Literature [course for which you will write this research paper]
[literature-related words
arrived at by free association]

1. authors	
2. novels	
3. nonfiction	
4. plays	airplanes
5. eras	[special interest]
6. poems	
7. countries	
8. adventures	

By combining each word in the left column with the word on the right, you can arrive at related ideas that will serve as general topics for the research paper.

EXAMPLE:

1. authors + airplanes = pilots who have written books
2. novels + airplanes = novels about flying
3. nonfiction + airplanes = developments in aviation industry reported
                            in nonfiction books
                            special-purpose aircraft (speed, spying, war)
                            as reported in nonfiction books
4. plays + airplanes = plays or movies about flying or flyers
5. eras + airplanes = flight in mythology of ancient cultures

6. poems + airplanes = poetry about flying or by pilots
7. countries + airplanes = stories of flying, true or fictional, from different countries
8. adventures + airplanes = great adventures undertaken by pilots

If one word doesn't work out for you, try another from one of the lists in your Personal Inventory. Be creative, be inventive, be imaginative in making relationships!

Free-Choice Topics

If you have your free choice of topic, suddenly all of human knowledge is open to you! The trick is to pinpoint just one part of it to work with, and the best way to do that is to examine systematically several possibilities before choosing what is most appealing to you. The six possibilities described in this section and the "Qualities of a Good Topic" in the next section (pages 34–35) will help you make that choice.

1. ***Expand on a familiar area.***
You might choose a topic or area about which you already know something but would like to know more. Instead of breaking completely new ground, you have a chance to increase your learning, in an organized way.

EXAMPLES:

You learned about the Mayas in a history course but would like to know more about them.

You did some reading on medieval beliefs about witchcraft on your own and want to know about contemporary attitudes to it.

2. ***Look to an area new to you.***
Now is the time to take out the name, topics, ideas you tucked away in memory but never got around to investigating.

EXAMPLES:

Grimmelshausen is such an unusual name. Who was that person?

An article about the future mentioned cryogenics. What is it all about?

You've always meant to find out about the history of jazz.

When friends talked about the hazards of computer manufacturing, you couldn't join in because you didn't know anything about the subject. Now's your chance to learn.

3. Try a textbook.

Look through a textbook (either one you own or one in the library) in some subject you care about or that holds special interest for you. Look through the table of contents, glossary, bibliography, or preface. Use the same methods described on pages 16–25 about choosing a Field-of-Study Topic.

4. Work from your strengths.

Take stock of your strengths and abilities so you can use one of them as the basis for your research paper. If you haven't read the section on making a Personal Inventory on page 25 (because you knew you had a Free-Choice Topic), look at it now. Use this listing for your categories:

- what you know and care about
- special concerns or intriguing ideas
- vocational interests
- what you want to know more about
- outstanding or significant personal experiences
- things you do well

List words and phrases (never mind about complete sentences here!) under each of those headings. Don't stop to evaluate what you write; just get the ideas down on paper.

Every item on each list represents a personal strength because each is prompted by you. Use the items as starting places to find topics you care enough about to study further.

5. Become a browser in the library.

Walk around and see what's available to you—but within a structure you set up in order to save time and wandering. You might decide to look at periodicals that are out on open shelves and scan the titles of articles in them for topic ideas. If *Omni, Ms, Ebony,* and the *Saturday Evening Post* are already familiar to you, try looking through titles that are new to you. Perhaps in *American Crafts, Modern Healthcare, Changing Times, Journal of Atmospheric Sciences,* or *Mental Retardation* you will find articles whose titles suggest research topics to you.

Another kind of purposeful browsing is to take a cue from the "Selected List of Reference Works Available in Libraries" (Appendix A, pages 279–93). The library you are working in may not have all the works listed there, but you can check off the titles that seem of interest, and if the volumes are available you can skim through them on the lookout for topics you care to investigate further.

6. Try brainstorming.

Write down all sorts of names, subjects, places, events, or whatever else comes to mind. Or, enlist the aid of a friend—because people often generate more ideas for themselves when they work with somebody else—and both of you speak such words into a tape recorder. Then, either check off likely research prospects on your written list or write down research possibilities when you play back the tape. Narrow the list to two or three topics before heading for the library to find books on them. Examine book titles and leaf through those that seem most interesting. Perhaps that's the way you will arrive at a research topic.

7. *"Get inside" the library catalog system.*

If you want to understand most completely the riches available to you in a library—and therefore available to you as Free-Choice Topics—you should understand the system by which books are catalogued in a library.

You can "get inside" your library catalog system by examining it to find a topic idea. If the library you use has an open-shelf system, you can then look through that particular section of books until you find a topic that strikes your fancy for research. If the library you use doesn't have open shelves, you will have to do your browsing for titles in the catalog and then request books that seem likely prospects for topic ideas.

Whether the library you work at has its books catalogued on cards, on microfilm or microfiche, in a print catalog, or on a computer, all are cataloged by either the **Library of Congress** or by the **Dewey Decimal** classification system. Both systems classify books—and, thus, knowledge or topics—in broad categories, each of which is then subdivided into progressively smaller or narrower groups.

The Library of Congress Classification System	The Dewey Decimal Classification System
A General works and polygraphy	000–099 Generalities
B Philosophy and religion	100–199 Philosophy and related
C History and auxiliary sciences	200–299 Religion
D History and topography (except America)	300–399 The social sciences
E–F America	400–499 Language
G Geography and anthropology	500–599 Pure sciences
H Social sciences	600–699 Technology (Applied science)
	700–799 The arts

continued   *continued*

The Library of Congress Classification System	The Dewey Decimal Classification System

The Library of Congress
Classification System

J Political science

K Law

L Education

M Music

N Fine arts

P Language and literature

Q Science

R Medicine

S Agriculture and plant and
  animal industry

T Technology

U Military science

V Naval science

Z Bibliography and library
  science

Note that there are only 21 groups in this system; the letters I, O, W, X, and Y are omitted.

The Dewey Decimal
Classification System

800–899 Literature and
        rhetoric

900–999 General geography
        and history

This system was developed by Melvil Dewey. Note that each class is identified by a three-digit number.

Each classification system is further divided. The Library of Congress system is divided by letters, and then subdivisions are identified by a numerical range. Figure 7 shows how these two levels are identified—and you can readily see how ideas for topics can evolve from this system.

In the Dewey Decimal system, each division is subdivided into groups of ten numbers (see Figure 8) and each of *them* is further divided to accommodate books of greater specialization (see Figure 9). Therefore, you can help yourself focus on a general area of study just by looking at this third level of classification.

Remember, though, that browsing through a library or making a topic decision on the basis of the secondary or even the tertiary Dewey Decimal classification will not yield workable topics without the narrowing process explained in Chapter 3. "South American History" or "Reptiles and Birds" may be suitable books, but certainly not suitable for a student paper. What these broad cataloging areas *can* give you is the start you need to decide on a Free-Choice Topic, which you can then narrow to a single subject you can handle successfully.

H

SOCIOLOGY

HM   Sociology (General and theoretical)

    101–121   Civilization.   Culture.   **Progress**
            Cf. CB

    201–219 Social elements, forces, laws

    251–299 Social psychology

HN   Social history.   Social reform

    30–39   The church and social problems
          Cf. BR 115.S6

  Social groups

HQ   Family.   Marriage.   Home

     16– 471   Sex relations

     750– 799   Eugenics.   Child culture, study, etc.

    1101–1870   Woman.   Feminism

    1871–2030   Women's clubs

HS   Associations: Secret societies, clubs, etc.

HT   Communities.   Classes.   Races

    101– 381   Urban groups: The city

    401– 485   Rural groups: The country

    851–1445   Slavery
        Works on slavery in the United States of America are
        classified in E441–453.

HV   Social pathology.   Philanthropy.   Charities and corrections

    530– 696   Social welfare

    697–4630   Protection, assistance and relief of special classes
           according to age, defects, race, occupation, etc.

    4701–4959   Protection of animals

    4961–4998   Degeneration

    5001–5720   Alcoholism.   Intemperance.   Temperance reform

    5725–5840   Tobacco and drug habits

    6001–6249   Criminology (General)

    6251–7220   Crimes and offenses

    7231–9920   Penology

    7551–8280   Police.   Detectives.   Constabulary

    8301–9920   Prisons.   Penitentiaries.   Punishment and reform

HX   Socialism.   Communism.   Anarchism.   Bolshevism

    806–811   Utopias

[8]

Fig. 7. Page 8 of the *Outline of the Library of Congress Classification,*
showing letter combinations with numbers for further
subdivision.

Second Summary *
The 100 Divisions

000	Generalities	500	Pure sciences
010	Bibliography	510	Mathematics
020	Library & information sciences	520	Astronomy & allied sciences
030	General encyclopedic works	530	Physics
040		540	Chemistry & allied sciences
050	General serial publications	550	Sciences of earth & other worlds
060	General organizations & museology	560	Paleontology
070	Journalism, publishing, newspapers	570	Life sciences
080	General collections	580	Botanical sciences
090	Manuscripts & book rarities	590	Zoological sciences

100	Philosophy & related disciplines	600	Technology (Applied sciences)
110	Metaphysics	610	Medical sciences
120	Epistemology, causation, humankind	620	Engineering & allied operations
130	Paranormal phenomena & arts	630	Agriculture & related technologies
140	Specific philosophical viewpoints	640	Home economics & family living
150	Psychology	650	Management & auxiliary services
160	Logic	660	Chemical & related technologies
170	Ethics (Moral philosophy)	670	Manufactures
180	Ancient, medieval, Oriental	680	Manufacture for specific uses
190	Modern Western philosophy	690	Buildings

200	Religion	700	The arts
210	Natural religion	710	Civic & landscape art
220	Bible	720	Architecture
230	Christian theology	730	Plastic arts Sculpture
240	Christian moral & devotional	740	Drawing, decorative & minor arts
250	Local church & religious orders	750	Painting & paintings
260	Social & ecclesiastical theology	760	Graphic arts Prints
270	History & geography of church	770	Photography & photographs
280	Christian denominations & sects	780	Music
290	Other & comparative religions	790	Recreational & performing arts

300	Social sciences	800	Literature (Belles-lettres)
310	Statistics	810	American literature in English
320	Political science	820	English & Anglo-Saxon literatures
330	Economics	830	Literatures of Germanic languages
340	Law	840	Literatures of Romance languages
350	Public administration	850	Italian, Romanian, Rhaeto-Romanic
360	Social problems & services	860	Spanish & Portuguese literatures
370	Education	870	Italic literatures Latin
380	Commerce (Trade)	880	Hellenic literatures Greek
390	Customs, etiquette, folklore	890	Literatures of other languages

400	Language	900	General geography & history
410	Linguistics	910	General geography Travel
420	English & Anglo-Saxon languages	920	General biography & genealogy
430	Germanic languages German	930	General history of ancient world
440	Romance languages French	940	General history of Europe
450	Italian, Romanian, Rhaeto-Romanic	950	General history of Asia
460	Spanish & Portuguese languages	960	General history of Africa
470	Italic languages Latin	970	General history of North America
480	Hellenic Classical Greek	980	General history of South America
490	Other languages	990	General history of other areas

* Consult schedules for complete and exact headings

Fig. 8. Page 472 of the *Dewey Decimal Classification and Relative Index*.

(Edition 19, 1979. Reproduced by permission of Forest Press Division, Lake Placid Education Foundation, owners of the copyright.)

Summaries

Language

400	**Language**	450	**Italian, Romanian, Rhaeto-Romanic**	
401	Philosophy & theory	451	Written & spoken Italian	
402	Miscellany	452	Italian etymology	
403	Dictionaries & encyclopedias	453	Italian dictionaries	
404	Special topics of general applicability	454		
405	Serial publications	455	Italian structural system	
406	Organizations	456		
407	Study & teaching	457	Nonstandard Italian	
408	Treatment among groups of persons	458	Standard Italian usage	
409	Historical & geographical treatment	459	Romanian & Rhaeto-Romanic	
410	**Linguistics**	460	**Spanish & Portuguese languages**	
411	Notations	461	Written & spoken Spanish	
412	Etymology	462	Spanish etymology	
413	Polyglot dictionaries	463	Spanish dictionaries	
414	Phonology	464		
415	Structural systems (Grammar)	465	Spanish structural system	
416		466		
417	Dialectology & paleography	467	Nonstandard Spanish	
418	Usage (Applied linguistics)	468	Standard Spanish usage	
419	Verbal language not spoken or written	469	Portuguese	
420	**English & Anglo-Saxon languages**	470	**Italic languages Latin**	
421	Written & spoken English	471	Written & spoken classical Latin	
422	English etymology	472	Classical Latin etymology	
423	English dictionaries	473	Classical Latin dictionaries	
424		474		
425	English structural system	475	Classical Latin structural system	
426		476		
427	Nonstandard English	477	Old, Postclassical, Vulgar Latin	
428	Standard English usage	478	Classical Latin usage	
429	Anglo-Saxon (Old English)	479	Other Italic languages	
430	**Germanic languages German**	480	**Hellenic languages Classical Greek**	
431	Written & spoken German	481	Written & spoken classical Greek	
432	German etymology	482	Classical Greek etymology	
433	German dictionaries	483	Classical Greek dictionaries	
434		484		
435	German structural system	485	Classical Greek structural system	
436		486		
437	Nonstandard German	487	Postclassical Greek	
438	Standard German usage	488	Classical Greek usage	
439	Other Germanic languages	489	Other Hellenic languages	
440	**Romance languages French**	490	**Other languages**	
441	Written & spoken French	491	East Indo-European & Celtic	
442	French etymology	492	Afro-Asiatic (Hamito-Semitic)	
443	French dictionaries	493	Hamitic & Chad languages	
444		494	Ural-Altaic, Paleosiberian, Dravidian	
445	French structural system	495	Sino-Tibetan & other	
446		496	African languages	
447	Nonstandard French	497	North American native languages	
448	Standard French usage	498	South American native languages	
449	Provençal & Catalan	499	Other languages	

Fig. 9. **Page 477 of the *Dewey Decimal Classification and Relative Index*.**

(Edition 19, 1979. Reproduced by permission of Forest Press Division, Lake Placid Education Foundation, owner of the copyright.)

Qualities of a Good Topic

A good research paper depends so much on a good choice of topic that you need to make this selection carefully. Remember, too, that the term "topic" in this book describes a broad and general area of knowledge, *not* the specific subject that you narrow it to and the one you actually investigate.

However, you know you are on the right track if your proposed research topic meets the following qualifications:

1. *The topic will enable you to fulfill the assignment.*

Since you are probably doing a research paper as an assignment, be sure that what you propose will do what you've been asked to do. Can you find enough information to meet the specified length? If you are choosing a Field-of-Study Topic, is it really related to the course for which you are writing it? If your instructor will deal with the topic in class, how will your research augment what is included in the course?

If you aren't sure about a topic choice, check with your instructor, even if such approval isn't required.

2. *The topic interests you enough to work on it.*

You commit yourself to a lot of time and energy when you start a research paper. If you don't think you are sufficiently interested in a topic or don't feel a commitment toward it, don't even start on it. Choose another one!

3. *The topic will teach you something.*

A research paper is not busywork. You should be able to learn something new from the content of the topic you are investigating. If you don't think you will learn, choose another topic.

4. *The topic is of manageable scope.*

Narrowing down an initial topic choice is the ultimate key to manageability. Even at the initial stages, a research paper isn't the only demand on your time, so you can (and *should*) impose your own limitations on it. "American Foreign Policy" and "Religion" are obviously too broad, as is any topic about which you can find a book in the library. No matter how interesting or exciting a topic seems, work with it *only* if you can give it the kind of time it will require of you. Otherwise, choose an alternative.

5. *You can bring something to the topic.*

You have already read (on page 4) that a research paper "synthesizes your discoveries about a topic and your judgment, interpretation, and evaluation of those discoveries." That is, you put something of yourself and your ideas in the research paper, together with the material you discover. A good topic *lets* you do that.

6. **Enough information on the topic is available to you.**

Most of the information for your research paper may have to come from a library. So if you haven't looked through a library (because you didn't need to use resources there in selecting a topic), you should go to the library now. You need to ascertain that there will be enough print information available for your research paper.

If you select a topic recently in the news and are required to use both books and periodicals as reference sources, you may have to *change* your proposed topic because books are not yet available. There is an informational time lag. Although weekly periodicals are timely, the editors of other magazines and journals often select the contents many months in advance. Books take even longer for publication, often a year from submission of a finished manuscript. Therefore, while books may supply the background for current newsworthy topics, their usefulness may be limited—or there may be nothing available in any book on a very current topic.

Furthermore, if you plan to do most of your library work at a neighborhood branch rather than in a school library, you will have still another reason for getting to the library quickly. Libraries select their holdings to best serve their users. A community library will tend to have holdings that reflect the interests of its constituents and therefore have more general than scholarly sources. You may have to change libraries or change topics.

7. **The topic is suitable for your audience.**

Remember that you are writing this research paper for one or more readers. The prior knowledge of that audience, their reading ability, concerns, age, educational background, and known leanings or beliefs should enter into your decision about the suitability of a topic. For example, if you propose writing on a specialized technical topic, the teacher will understand material that beginning students in the field could not cope with.

8. **The topic lets you demonstrate all your abilities that a research paper is meant to show.**

A topic too broad, too restrictive, too mundane, or too esoteric might not let you show off the extent of your ability to develop ideas, find information, evaluate and organize it, make reasoned judgments, present them convincingly, and support your statements. Be sure that the topic you decide to research will let you demonstrate all these skills.

Topics to Avoid

To avoid wasting time and effort, you ought to know that certain kinds of topics are unsuitable for research papers. The following list (some of which are the obverse of *good* qualities you've just read about) is a guide to help you avoid potential problems when choosing your topic.

1. Do not reuse a paper you have written for another instructor.

Repetition doesn't produce new learning. Besides, to pretend you have done new work when, in fact, you have not done any is dishonest.

However, some instructors are willing to let you continue studying something you have already investigated, provided the topic warrants further research. Or, they will let you examine another aspect of a topic about which you have already written a paper. Neither of these situations is the same as handling in to an instructor a paper you have already presented to someone else. Should you want to use a previously submitted research paper as the *basis* for a new one, it is safest to discuss the matter frankly with your present instructor.

2. Do not choose a topic on which you do not plan to do all the work yourself.

If anyone else does the research or any of the writing on this assignment, the work is not your own and is, therefore, not acceptable. Using material from someone else without proper acknowledgment is **plagiarism.**

3. Do not choose a topic that is too broad for a research paper.

Topics that are the titles of books may be a starting place, but not a stopping place; you must go on to the second step of narrowing. After all, if a published writer needs a whole book to deal with a topic, you can't say much of substance about it in ten or fifteen pages!

4. Do not choose a topic for which a single source will provide all the information you need.

You can *only* develop an individual viewpoint, use investigative skills, evaluate materials, and organize your findings in an original way when you consult several sources for information. In short, you can follow the procedures for scholarly research *only* if you read and study widely.

5. Do not choose a topic about which your conclusions will be irrelevant.

A paper on how Ford should have designed the Edsel (an automobile Ford manufactured only briefly) is not fruitful because it doesn't matter now. Shift your thinking. If the Edsel is really a love of your life, another sort of investigation about the car might have some value. Or, the subject might be relevant to special kinds of design or marketing courses.

6. Do not start work on any topic unless you think it will hold your interest long enough to complete the paper.

Research is a difficult enough assignment in itself. If you have to fight boredom with your own topic along the way, it becomes impossible.

7. Be wary of choosing a topic so neutral that you cannot express an attitude toward it.

Unless you plan a documented report, and not a research paper, you will need to express some views or opinions about your material. A topic such as

"Commercial By-Products of the Fishing Industry" may be suitable for a documented paper because it is essentially reportorial—but it will not make a good research paper topic. Many teachers discourage biographical papers for the same reason. Unless you have the time and energy to consult primary sources (explained on page 57) or do original investigative work, such papers often become a compilation of what others have written.

8. *Do not pursue a topic that seems to go nowhere for you.*

If you have great trouble narrowing a topic to a manageable subject or finding an approach to a subject (both are explained in the next chapter), perhaps that topic will prove unproductive for you. If "The Beatles" is a topic you are determined to research but you flounder and can't seem to make progress beyond that decision, ask your instructor for help. Or drop that topic and go on to something you can work with. Another person might be able to narrow that topic and make it workable, but if you can't you are better off making a complete change and starting something more productive.

9. *Consider avoiding a topic that has been particularly popular among students.*

Unless you can give a special slant to the study or you have a particular interest in pursuing such a topic, your teacher (and others who make up the audience) may be just plain bored reading yet another paper on abortion, drugs, or pollution. Check with your instructor if in doubt about the advisability of researching a particular topic. Or ask a research librarian; that person receives requests for help constantly and thus often knows what topics other students have been working on.

10. *Consider avoiding a highly controversial or emotional topic unless you think you can bring something new and special to it.*

You may find that time and length limitations on the research paper won't let you present sufficient material to cover a controversial topic satisfactorily. Similarly, avoid choosing a topic to which you have a deep emotional commitment, such as a particular religious belief, because you might not be able to be sufficiently objective or critical toward it to produce a good research paper. If you have any doubts about the advisability of working on a topic, discuss the matter with your instructor.

11. *Do not choose a topic unsuited to your audience.*

Some topics may offend the sensibilities of the instructor or other readers. For example, reading about various ways to investigate gory murders may not be the way your audience wants to spend its time. Writing for an audience means that you conform in some way to your audience's expectations or interests. So no matter how clever or sensational you think a topic is, don't hesitate to abandon it—or change the way you plan to treat it—if you suspect the topic may not suit your intended audience.

An Addendum:
Double Submissions

A topic that might be submitted for assigned research papers in more than one course during the same term is not necessarily a topic to avoid, but one you may be forced to consider carefully. Teachers who know you have research papers due for two courses may prefer that you do a top-notch job on one paper rather than a half-hearted or hurried job on two papers. For example, a paper for a psychology class may be on a topic that is also acceptable for an education course; one that is done for an English class might be on a topic suitable to fulfill a research assignment in electronics or art history. Both teachers, therefore, may permit the same paper to be submitted to them.

If you consider a dual submission, **consult your instructors,** explain your reasoning, and **get permission** for a dual submission before making any final topic choices. Realize, however, that in a dual submission you may have to use different forms of documentation (depending on the standards of the academic discipline) and you will have to adhere to the grading criteria of two different people—all the more reason for planning ahead with your instructors.

Chapter 3

Narrowing
the Topic

Once you have decided on a topic for study, you need to narrow—that is, limit—it to a **specific subject** before starting to gather information. It would be foolish and a waste of time to start searching for material on "advertising," for example, before deciding what you want to know about it. The topic is a good starting point, but you need to focus on a single aspect of it before you can move ahead through the research process.

Some Limitations You Work Within

Every task has some limitations, some framework within which it is to be accomplished. Every research paper has three such limitations that are "givens" and within which you must work:

1. The required length of the paper you will write.
2. The source material available to you.
3. The audience who will read your paper.

Length

You can choose a broader subject for a 2,500-word paper than you can for one of 1,000 words. Since you will want to deal *adequately* with whatever subject you choose, the length you expect the paper to be is a good guide to making a selection.

If your assignment for the research paper doesn't include a statement of expected length, you will have to use your own judgment. Be guided by the sort of work you expect of yourself, the time available to fulfill the assignment, and the importance you and your instructor put on the individual research paper. (As you already read on pages 3–4, this book assumes you are preparing a research paper of 1,500 to 3,000 words, or about six to twelve double-spaced, typewritten pages. Use your judgment, based on time and expectations, for papers of the same or other lengths.)

The subject you decide on, after narrowing a topic, should have sufficient range and depth to show your work as that of a serious student. Don't choose a subject so broad that you must be superficial in order to fit it into the required length. A literary research paper on Arthur Miller is too much for you to work with. (Check the library and see how many books and articles have been written about him!) But the narrower subject of "Biographical Elements in Arthur Miller's *A Memory of Two Mondays*" could be handled in a class assignment. Similarly, "Developments in Geriatrics" is too much to write about, but "How Pets Can Help Older Citizens" is sufficiently limited.

Although many people seem to have trouble limiting the range of a subject, it's also possible to choose a subject so specialized or esoteric that you need to devote several pages of background information to accommodate your audience before you begin to write about the subject itself. Then you don't have enough space (or time) left to say anything substantial in your research paper.

Materials Available

You must have sufficient research sources readily available for your study. Since school libraries try to have materials for the work of their students, your school library is probably your best source of information. However, not all libraries are suitable for all projects. Highly specialized libraries, new ones, or those unable to make adequate new purchases because of budget limits may hamper your research. Or, a school where engineering and natural science courses are primary may not have enough materials on art or music to make extensive research on those subjects possible.

You may also find that you can't *conveniently* locate enough information for a paper you want to write. For instance, if you were interested in the location of nuclear power plants within earthquake zones, you might not be able to find enough information *readily* unless you lived in California. And even then, material you needed might not be immediately available.

Therefore, before you decide definitely on a subject for your research, **go to the principal library you plan to use.** Look through the card catalog and check the holdings of the library against one or two of the most relevant periodical indexes to make sure enough information is available to you. (See Appendix A for a list of some of the many kinds of library resources available.) If you find a great many books on your proposed subject, skim through some of them to get ideas for further information. If you have trouble finding information in the library, check with a librarian; each is a specialist in helping students locate materials. If you still can't find the right kind of information, adjust the scope of your proposed subject so you can work with the available sources.

Also, investigate the availability of **nonprint materials** before you make a final decision about your subject. Not all research sources are in print or in a library (as explained in Chapter 4, pages 57–59). Unless you are asked to do just a library search, most instructors are happy to have you demonstrate your ability to find and work from varied sources. Interviews may be useful. What you hear on radio or see on television may be relevant. You may even plan to write letters of inquiry if you have enough time to wait for answers. And if a requirement of your research paper is that you include nonprint as well as print sources, you must *certainly* ascertain their availability before making a final decision on your subject for investigation.

Audience

Research papers are written to be read. Therefore, at the very beginning of the research process, you need to consider who will read what you write. In some classes, students work collaboratively at various stages or make an oral presentation about their final research papers. If yours is such a class, you will get help from other students or perhaps classmates will be your audience. In Chapter 1 (pages 10–11) you read about some basic considerations of audience; you will be reading other reminders about audience on the pages to come. Suffice it to note here that your initial considerations of narrowing a topic to a workable subject should be done with your readers in mind: who they are, what they know, what they'd be interested in knowing, and how they will respond to what you write.

Focusing on a Subject to Research

Occasionally the topic you choose will immediately bring to mind a specific subject, a part of that broad category you want to investigate. If that happens, you're lucky. Finding a specific subject is crucial to a successful research paper, and many students have trouble narrowing a topic to workable proportions. If you are such a person, you should try one (or all) of the five methods explained here. All have proved helpful to others:

> **freewriting**
> **subdividing**
> **free association**
> **clustering**
> **the five Ws**

Each will help you find a focus for your work that you feel comfortable with or that you will find sufficiently intriguing to pursue.

Freewriting

Sit down with a blank sheet of paper in front of you, take pen or pencil in hand (or sit before your typewriter or computer keyboard), and start writing whatever comes into your head about the topic you selected. Don't plan or try to think ahead; don't worry about spelling or punctuation. Just write without stopping. That's freewriting.

Doing some freewriting (perhaps having somebody time you for ten minutes) is a good way to get thoughts down on paper—thoughts you don't have to organize or evaluate but can just get out of your system. Writers often use the method to find out what they know or think about a subject, for freewriting taps sources of information deep within you.

After you finish a short writing session, look back over what you've written and see if you have begun to come to terms with your topic and have written something that will help you limit it to a workable subject.

If what you put on paper doesn't yield a subject, choose a word or phrase you put down that is narrower than the topic. Then use that as the starting point for another freewriting session. The second—or third—time may be the charm and you find a subject to work from.

Subdividing

Another way to narrow a topic is to write down what you've selected and then divide it into progressively smaller units. Continue this subdividing until you reach a subject you are interested in researching. See example on facing page.

EXAMPLE OF SUBDIVIDING:

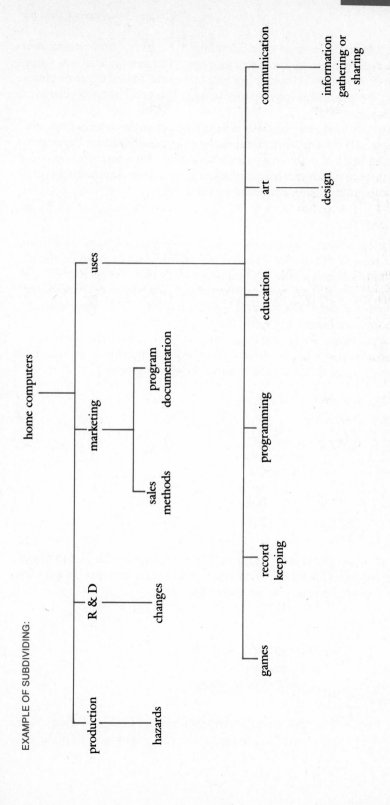

Notice how the first level of subdividing the topic of home computers yielded areas still too broad for a research paper. The second level was somewhat better. For example, "Production Hazards in the Manufacture of Home Computers" is a possible research paper subject. But other areas needed even more narrowing.

Sometimes several real possibilities for a research paper emerge only after a few levels of subdividing. You could explore the possibilities of developing and marketing original programs written for home computers. Or you could investigate ways in which our lives might change as home computers are used increasingly for information gathering and sharing.

Free Association

Free association is used in many problem-solving situations—and narrowing a topic to a suitable subject for research is certainly a problem to be solved. Free association (sometimes called brainstorming when you do it orally and with other people) is the practice of writing down words or phrases that occur to you just as they come to mind—without worry about order, spelling, usefulness, applicability, or any other matter of judgment.

Begin by writing down the topic you selected, and underneath it list everything that comes to your mind. Make the list as quickly as you can just by letting your mind rove over every idea the topic suggests.

EXAMPLE:

Crime

police	laws
riots	deterrents
prevention	big cities
white collar	growing rates
punishment	penal system
repeat offenders	death penalty
citizen activities	

From this list you could choose a subject, but it would probably be too broad. So another listing made by free association is in order; this time begin with one of the words or phrases on the above list.

EXAMPLE:

White-collar Crime

offices	department stores
perpetrators	internal security systems
deterrents	

You might decide that "Internal Security Systems to Prevent White-collar Crime" is a subject you want to investigate. Or, you might have to make still more associations—memories triggered by something you wrote on the above list. For example, thinking about deterrents to white-collar crime may make you think about having been asked to take a lie detector test when applying for a sales job—and bring you to a research paper topic on "Lie Detector Tests as a Prerequisite for Employment."

If the free association method doesn't produce a subject suitable for your research paper, you might go to the library with an "almost" subject and refine or limit it after browsing through some books and periodical indexes.

Clustering

Clustering is another narrowing technique that makes use of your ideas by asking you to write them down in a way that shows their relationships. Begin by putting your topic in the center of a page, enclose it in a small circle, and then start your imagination or "stream of consciousness" working. As ideas occur to you, arrange them in relation to one another with more circled words and more lines showing which ideas stem from which others.

The Five Ws

Asking questions is still another way of narrowing a topic to a subject you can work with. You might simply ask yourself (or write down) those questions that occur to you about the topic you start with. You could assume the role of someone who knows nothing about the topic and ask questions to elicit information you'd like to have.

Or you can develop questions in an organized way by adapting the journalistic tradition that good reporting means covering the five Ws of a story: **who, what, where, when, and why.** These key words lead to the complete coverage of a subject being reported, so if you use them as guides, they can help you find a useful research subject.

> **Who**—people
> **What**—problems, things, ideas
> **Where**—places
> **When**—past, present, future
> **Why**—causes, reasons, results, conditions

To use these five Ws as a help in finding a research subject, write your topic at the top of the page and under it write each of the five W words as headings across the page. Then use brainstorming or free association with each of the words in a column heading, writing down your ideas as lists.

EXAMPLE 1:

Television   (the broad topic)

Who?	show hosts
	power structure
	directors
	Johnny Carson
What?	violence
	news
	religious networks
	commercials
	technical developments
	home VCR tapes
Where?	satellite transmissions
	remotes
	studio requirements

Television   (the broad topic) (*continued*)

When?	commercial beginnings
	future of cable
Why?	importance in elections
	persuasive power
	education
	selling to children

Some of the words in the above listing are still too broad for a ten-page paper and need further narrowing. Use the same five Ws method again, as in the following example:

EXAMPLE 2:

Television Violence   (taken from "What" list)

Who?	actors
	audience
What?	effects
	types of
Where?	cartoons
	news
	series
	specials
When?	prime time
	Sat. A.M.
Why?	realism
	audience
	psychology

On the basis of this further narrowing, you might decide that an appealing subject to investigate is the audience psychology of wanting to see violence on television programs, or you might decide to study the effect of violence in cartoons on children.

Combined Method

The subject of the sample research paper in this book (Chapter 10, pages 257–78) was actually arrived at by a combination of the methods you have been reading about. The student, Ms. Matz, became interested in censorship and started by brainstorming that broad topic in this way:

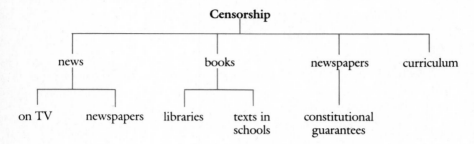

At this stage, it was apparent that still more narrowing was in order. Although Ms. Matz was interested in book censorship, she decided to combine some of the subtopics. Textbooks didn't interest her particularly, but libraries did.

Libraries

public	choices of content
private school	sources of information
public school	grade levels
personal	

The train of thought seemed to be about school libraries as a workable limitation because Ms. Matz had read a news article about certain books being removed from a school library at the order of a local school superintendent. Therefore, she decided to investigate book censorship in school libraries. The title of her paper, "School Libraries Should Not Ban Books," evolved later.

Finding an Approach

If you don't want to read *everything* written about your subject, you should decide on an approach to it before you start the actual research. Then, you can make intelligent decisions during the information-gathering stage about what you should read carefully (and perhaps take notes on) and what you can safely skim.

Sometimes the approach to a research subject is defined for you by the assignment. For example, many instructors require a persuasive or argumentative paper. But the choice may be up to you. If you decide at this stage which approach you will use, you will have three advantages:

1. You will be able to exercise your critical thinking abilities to **select information more carefully.** That is, you will have an advance idea of what information needs to be included.
2. You will know what kind of **support** you need to find for the ideas you will deal with.
3. You will start to develop some notions of **how to present your information.** That is, you will begin to get a feel for how to organize your paper.

Deciding on an approach to your subject **does not mean** deciding on a thesis statement *before* doing the research. To do so would mean you'd already decided what to say and therefore didn't expect to learn anything from this whole process!

Rather, the early choice of an approach is a matter of focusing energy and ideas, so you can do good work with greater ease. For example, the author of the sample research paper beginning on page 257 selected censorship as it applied to school library books as her subject. Since Ms. Matz is a person who often takes stands for what she believes in (whether they are popular ones or not), she chose to argue either for or against such censorship. Although she has not generally been a supporter of censorship, Ms. Matz *didn't really know* in advance which side she would take on this issue because she didn't feel sufficiently informed to make that decision without some study.

Deciding on an Approach Before Being Well-Informed About Your Subject

If you aren't already familiar with the subject you are going to research, get a quick overview of it by looking at an encyclopedia article, by consulting at least one periodical index to find the titles of articles people are writing about it, and by looking through some books on your subject. Skim, but don't read these sources closely yet. (The skill of skimming for ideas is explained on page 111.) When you have this fuller sense of what you will be working with, you can make an intelligent choice of approach.

Five Approaches to a Research Subject

1. You can **examine** or **analyze** it, looking at various aspects of the subject and viewing it from more than one perspective.
2. You can **evaluate** or **criticize** it, thus making a judgment about the quality of your subject.
3. You can **compare and contrast** things or ideas, showing how both similarities and dissimilarities exist or are evident when you look closely at the subject.
4. You can **establish relationships** among ideas, showing how they may have drawn from each other or how they are related in other ways— or to other ideas.
5. You can **argue for or against something** or try to **persuade** readers to agree with you.

As you will note in the following explanations and examples, it is not always possible to make clear-cut distinctions among the five ways of approaching a topic. A paper that is concerned with *examining* a subject may also involve some *comparison*. *Comparison and contrast* are essentially types of *relationships*. However, if you decide on a primary approach to your subject at the outset, you will find it easier to work purposefully and to gather only related material—and thus save yourself time and effort.

Examining or Analyzing

Examining a subject is like putting it under a microscope so you can see its details and look at them individually. You can examine anything from a single event to an entire political system or scientific theory, looking at it closely enough to see what its components are and how it is put together.

Here are some kinds of examinations you might undertake and examples of titles of papers that might result:

- **Stylistic devices** in a work of literature. Examples: "*Tom Jones* As a Picaresque Novel" or "*Gulliver's Travels* As Political Satire"
- **Intellectual, scientific, or sociological background** of a person or an historical period. Examples: "The Labor Union Movement in Golda Meir's Youth" or "Pre-Sputnik Space Exploration"
- **Variations or revisions,** especially of a work of art or a philosophical idea. Examples: "How Picasso Developed *Guernica*" or "Versions of 'Sailing to Byzantium'" or "Communism to Marx and to Mao"
- **Evolution** of a business practice. Examples: "The Phenomenon of Record Sales Promotions on Television" or "Solar Heaters As a Growth Industry"

A word of warning if you choose to examine a subject in your research paper. Don't fall into the trap of just enumerating a series of pieces of information, thus ending with a report rather than with a research paper. For instance, "The Anthropological Films of Robert Flaherty" could turn into little more than an annotated filmography unless you took an approach that forced you to look at the qualities or structures of such films.

Evaluating or Criticizing

An *evaluation* is a judgment about something; it is made after the subject has been studied and examined at length. *Criticism* means weighing or judging the quality of something; it should include both positive and negative commentary. (Contrary to popular belief, criticism is *not* just fault-finding.)

Some kinds of evaluative or critical approaches you might take and sample titles of research are:

- **Evaluate individuals, works, or ideas** in order to make judgments about them. Examples: "The Effectiveness of Seat Belt Laws" or "Rachel Carson's Writing and Ecological Awareness" or "Computer Games As Learning Tools"
- **Criticize works or ideas.** Examples: "Practicality of Space Shuttle Experiments" or "The Ethics of the Death Penalty"

Comparing and Contrasting

To compare is to find similarities; *to contrast* is to find differences. The two words define different approaches, but they are generally used together to give a fuller view of a subject than either can provide alone. Another reason for the usual linkage is that there must be some similarity established before contrast is possible. For instance, though Republican and Democratic platforms during national election years are obviously different, they can be compared and contrasted because, with varying specifics, each sets forth the party's philosophy on national and international issues.

Some examples of this approach, together with sample titles, are those that look at:

- **Works of art.** Examples: "*1984* at Publication and in the Year 1984" or "*High Noon* and *Shane* As Archetypal Western Films"
- **Views of an individual.** Examples: "How Four Political Columnists Saw Harry Truman During His Presidency" or "Mayoral and City Managerial Governments"
- **Ideas.** Examples: "Various Buddhist Sects" or "The Need for Underwater Oil Exploration" or "Nutritional Values in Three Popular Diets"

- **Events.** Examples: "Fiction and Nonfiction Accounts of D-Day Land-ings" or "Reporting the Attica Affair"

Note that comparison and contrast doesn't have to be limited to two elements.

Relating

People learn by establishing relationships between what they already know and what is unfamiliar. Therefore, if you decide to undertake a research project that establishes or explores relationships, you are undertaking a challenging but rewarding study from which you can learn a great deal. In fact, if you think back over what you have just read about comparison and contrast (and, to a lesser degree, about examining and evaluating as approaches), you will see that the ability to perceive and establish relationships permeates much of what you do in deciding on any sort of approach to a research paper assignment.

If you set out specifically to approach your subject as one of establishing relationships, you might select one of the following kinds of relationships:

- **A theory and its practical application.** Examples: "The Psychology of the Underdog in 'Peanuts' " or "Mendelian Theory in the Selective Breed-ing of Cattle" or "Chimps Learn Language Like Children" or "The Influence of Numerology on Medieval Church Architecture"
- **A person's work or thought and life.** Examples: "Martin Luther King, Jr. as an Effective Leader of Civil Rights Activists" or "What Cesar Chavez May Have Learned from Gandhi"
- **Specific events or attitudes.** Examples: "The Impact of ZPG on Mar-keting" or "The Death Penalty as a Deterrent to Crime" or "What an Election Year Means to PR Firms"

Arguing or Persuading

When you try to persuade someone to believe or act in a particular way, you are arguing your case. One school of thought is that as soon as you take a stand on a subject—as you must do to make yourself part of a research project and to determine an approach toward a subject—you automatically begin persuading your audience. However, argumentation and persuasion are rhe-torically (that is, organizationally) different from the other approaches you have been reading about. If you are now taking or have ever taken a course in composition or in public speaking, you may be familiar with exposition and argumentation as rhetorical forms; the four approaches you have already read about would be considered exposition.

At the heart of argumentive or persuasive writing is a thesis or over-riding principal idea that is logically supported by evidence. "Logic" is a reasoning process without fallacies (that is, without errors). Evidence of your own critical thinking ability is that you can convince a careful reader by choosing what you need to include in an argument and then unfolding the material in an orderly arrangement.

Although you will not generally want to take a position in deciding on an argumentive or persuasive approach until *after* you have done some research on the subject, you should know that several kinds of possibilities exist. You could:

- **Defend a position** that has already been taken. Examples: "Secession Was the South's Only Solution" or "Money Spent on Space Exploration is Well Spent"

- **Justify an action.** Examples: "Frequent Auto Design Changes *Are* Necessary"

- **Prove or support a belief.** Examples: " 'Scholarships' to College Athletes Should Be Called by Another Name" or "Space Exploration Is No Longer Needed" or "Tests Don't Measure Learning" or "Horror Movies Are Needed in Our Society"

Because illustrating the argumentive or persuasive approach, no less than the others shown here, is easiest with a title, the bias is evident in each of these examples. However, as you will read in a moment, the title often doesn't emerge until after an outline or a draft of the research paper is written.

Wording Your Approach

When you find an approach to your subject, you are focusing on a principal idea that you might develop in your research paper. Rather than depend on remembering the wording, **write it out and put in in front of you when you work.** Memory is short and too many things demand your time and thoughts during the several steps of this process. It's easy to forget what you haven't written down, but you'll stay on track with your approach written out.

Make your approach statement a two-part phrase. Use the subject as one part and the approach as the other part.

EXAMPLES:

Approach	*Subject*
examine ways an individual can overcome	obesity

or

    argue for or against self-help programs
      to overcome .... obesity

    compare and contrast the book, ballet,
      and film of .... *Peter Rabbit*

    compare a quota system to .... immigration by "boat people"

or

    argue for or against stiffer laws about
      who should and shouldn't be
      allowed to enter the United States
      in light of .... immigration by "boat people"

Note that *none of these sample subjects or approaches is in the form of a question*. You will have plenty of questions to ask yourself as you begin to collect information, and you should save questions until then. Therefore, if you find yourself thinking in terms of a question, simply rephrase it into a statement:

EXAMPLES:

Question	*Rephrased as Statement*
How was Richard III been depicted in different eras?	Richard III as depicted by Shakespeare and by twentieth-century historians (approach: comparison & contrast)

You wouldn't know before finding information on the subject whether that depiction was similar or different, so the wording of this approach would have to remain general.

A Word of Caution

Once you have decided on a subject and an approach, you commit yourself to a direction for the research paper. If you've taken the time to perform all of this part of the process, including skimming some related print materials (as described on page 111), you have probably chosen an approach you can work with. But you *may* find that you have misjudged in the approach. Or, you may discover as you start collecting information that the approach you expected to use isn't feasible. Rather than stick with something that won't work out well, find another approach based on your early information gathering or on a conference with your instructor.

Choosing a Final Title

Sometimes the wording you select for your approach will sound very much like the title for a paper. It may even end up as the title, though you don't need to make that decision until the end of your writing. However, if you feel more comfortable working from a title rather than from a subject stated as an approach, by all means write one down so you don't forget it. Many professional writers say they work best when they start writing from a title.

Titles for research papers don't have to be clever or provocative. In fact, since your paper will be an academic one, and since most academic writing has descriptive titles, you should probably follow suit. The advantage of a descriptive title for this sort of paper is that it immediately signals the audience what to expect. The titles used as examples of approaches in this chapter are good guides to the variety of wording possible. So is the title of the sample research paper on pages 257–78: "School Libraries Should Not Ban Books."

Chapter 4

Searching for Information

A library is an exciting place. Yet, it can be intimidating. New books are added to the shelves almost daily, and the magazine you looked at last week may have been sent to the bindery this week. A crowd around each computer terminal makes you feel you can never get your turn to use it for finding information. Students carrying thick stacks of 4 × 6-inch cards and busily taking notes may make you feel uncomfortable about even *beginning* to search out information for your own research paper. You may be anxious to start working on the paper because you've spent a lot of time finding just the right subject— or you may be worried because a deadline is approaching and you've procrastinated about starting your research.

Once you've decided on an approach to your research subject, searching for information sources gives you a starting place because you have some ideas about what to look for.

Asking some questions—role-playing the part of your audience—will give even more focus and thus help you know what kind of information to seek. Suppose you were going to argue the subject of school library censorship (as does the sample research paper in Chapter 10). Some questions the author asked herself at this stage were: Who wants censorship? Where do they get ideas about what to remove from libraries? How successful have censors been in removing books from school libraries? What efforts have been made to uphold or strike down such censorship? Are there legal precedents I can check? What do librarians feel about the subject? When did such censorship start? Is it still going on? To what extent?

Make a similar list of questions for your own research subject as a prelude to looking for information. If you need an aid to think up questions, put the five Ws to work again; ask who, what, where, when, and why.

Primary and Secondary Sources

Primary sources come straight from the people or works you are researching and are therefore the most direct kinds of information you can collect. Your research paper should rely on them when they are available, because they are firsthand observations and investigations. Examples of primary sources are Neil Armstrong's report of his moon walk or President Nixon writing or speaking about his decision to resign.

Diaries, notes, letters, interviews, and autobiographies are often primary source materials. If you are writing about literature or the arts, the works of art are your primary source: *novels, short stories, poems, plays, films, paintings, sculpture, librettos, and musical scores.*

Many other kinds of print and nonprint sources are primary. *Interviews with workers* about their jobs, *observations of an astronomer,* the recounting by a music historian of the *discovery that person made* of a previously unknown Mozart manuscript—all these are primary sources. *Recordings of radio broadcasts* by President Reagan, a *reporter's observation* of a student rally, and the *words of a student participant* can also serve as primary sources. Many *public documents* also qualify as primary sources: the *Congressional Record,* publications of the Bureau of the Census Statistics, and others.

Use your ingenuity to locate primary sources for your research subject. For instance, to find out about the psychological strain of living with AIDS, primary sources would be interviews with AIDS patients themselves.

Naturally, primary sources may not always be available. Or the limited time you have for some research assignments makes obtaining certain primary sources difficult or even impossible. Thus, you may be forced to depend in varying degrees on secondary sources.

Secondary sources are one step removed from the original and are often an examination of a study someone else has made on a subject or an evaluation of, commentary on, or summary of primary material.

Critical reviews, biographies, journal articles, and second-person reports are secondary sources. Helpful as they are, consider them on their own merits: as the words and thoughts of another person on the subject. Therefore, they will probably show the biases of the author—just as your own research paper will reflect your own bias. Consider that when you read or take notes from secondary sources.

EXAMPLES:

Primary Sources	*Secondary Sources*

about Abraham Lincoln

Lincoln's letters, speeches	Carl Sandburg's books

about Carl Sandburg

his books about Lincoln	a biography
his letters and notes	

misuse of government funds

reports and records of	newspaper stories about the
disbursements	issue

Although secondary sources are useful, there is danger in relying too heavily on them, especially if you ignore the materials on which they are based. You should check on them carefully by going back to the original (primary) source when possible. Never rely solely on a book or play review; always read the work yourself. View materials skeptically and critically. Learning something about an author is also a way of judging veracity, reliability, and bias. (See Chapter 5, pages 113–115, for suggestions on how to evaluate source materials.) Then you will have a clearer picture of the usefulness of secondary sources in your own information gathering.

A Search Strategy

A library is not the only place to look for information, but it's the best starting place. (Later in this chapter, beginning on page 99, you will read about sources of nonprint information.) The most productive way to search out material on your subject is to make a plan in advance, to **have a search strategy**. That is, you should decide in advance which sources of information you will consult (this chapter will suggest many to you, and librarians will know of others) and the order in which you will consult them.

On the next few pages you will read an overview of some of the most useful resources. The remainder of the chapter will detail some places to find information and show how to make preliminary Works Cited cards for them. At the end of this chapter is a form that you can use as a guide to an organized search strategy by filling in the appropriate dates and information. Use it to keep your research moving and to keep you on target!

Involve a **librarian** at an early stage of your search strategy. Nobody knows more about the resources of a library than the men and women who have been specially trained to help students use those resources. In fact, at most colleges and universities the librarians have faculty status, thus attesting to their function as teachers.

The most effective search strategy begins with finding **general reference information** before moving to more specific studies. For most people that means starting in the reference room or section of the library. There, you will find encyclopedias, general and specialized dictionaries, almanacs, handbooks, maps, atlases, directories, bibliographies, indexes, and biographical reference books. Your search strategy should include consulting

- **Encyclopedias** for the overviews they offer.
- **Bibliographies** to find volumes and other sources, sometimes unexpected, on your subject.
- **Handbooks** to give you additional general information.
- **Card catalog**, whether on-line (computer) or in the familiar boxes of cards. Generally, look under subject headings to find relevant books and read the description on a card to get a better idea of contents.

  A follow-up to the **book shelves** (if you have access to them) where promising titles are located may yield additional titles of books you overlooked or that were cataloged under a different heading.
- **Computer databases** because they give access to a wide variety of subjects and special interests, mostly in periodicals but also in books and newsletters. Most libraries now subscribe to one or more of these services.
- **Periodical indexes** for sources of up-to-date information on your subject.
- **Newspaper indexes** for both recent and not-so-recent materials.
- **Abstracting services** to find many sources not listed elsewhere.
- **Nonprint sources** such as slides, movies, records or tapes (both video and audio), and filmstrips. Sometimes they are listed in a general card catalog, sometimes at a media center.

  Decide now—as part of your search strategy—if you want to use such other nonprint resources as interviews, questionnaires, or letters.

Most of this chapter contains specific information about the various stopping places in your search strategy so that you can be familiar with what's available and thus do your work most expeditiously. Additional suggestions are in the "Selected List of Reference Works Available in Libraries" in Appendix A, page 279.

Preliminary Citations

Preliminary citations give information about the sources you can consult to get information for your research paper. They are "preliminary" because they only give you the *potential* sources of information; some materials will not be available to you, and some will not be relevant to what you seek. However, you need to write them now—while you are following your search strategy. Later you will use them

1. **to find the specific materials** you want to read (or view or listen to) in order to record information for your paper.
2. **to prepare the Works Cited list** at the conclusion of your research paper.
3. **to simplify documenting the text** of your research paper.

To have useful preliminary citations:

- **write on 3 × 5-inch cards,** preferably in ink.

- **follow proper citation form,** including hanging indentation and proper punctuation of entries (illustrated in the following section).

- **record the complete name of each author,** but omit titles and degrees. If only initials are shown, find the name each represents when you look at the source later; then record it on this card.

- **write out the complete title of the work,** using the punctuation shown in your search source but with conventional capitalization, even though the search source does not follow it.

- **note all publication information accurately,** but follow the conventions of citation rather than those used in your search source.

- **record the call number of books** so you can locate them when you need to.

- **record the location of other materials,** especially if they're not in the library.

- **note special elements in a source** (such as maps or diagrams).

- **make a card for each proposed interview;** fill in the date if you've already made an appointment.

Reasons for Preliminary Citations

The main reason for preliminary citation cards is to see what information is available and to help you **locate the research materials.** Once done, you will not have to retrace your steps or spend additional time.

A second reason is to help you **decide if you've chosen a usable subject.** Too many preliminary citation cards means you probably ought to narrow the subject further. For instance, forty-five cards (that is, forty-five separate places containing information) gathered readily for a 2,500-word paper indicate you should be more selective. Too few cards means you will have trouble finding information and probably ought to enlarge the scope of your subject or the approach.

A third reason for preliminary citation cards is to let you know that you have **followed instructions for this assignment.** If you can only find articles in popular magazines but are required to include professional journals as source material, you should probably make a shift in your subject. If a requirement is to include nonprint resources, the preliminary citation cards will either show that you have some to consult or that you will need to be inventive enough to find such sources.

Content of Preliminary Citation Cards

Accurate citation is one of the hallmarks of a good research paper. By recording complete information carefully on your preliminary citation cards, you ensure accuracy both in the textual documentation and in the Works Cited listing at the end of your paper.

If you know that your instructor will require an annotated citation (explained on page 253), leave room on each card for the notes you need in order to write this brief comment about the content of the source.

The citations of various sources—books, magazines, TV programs, interviews, films, and so on—vary. Therefore, sample preliminary citation cards appear in each section of the "Sources of Print Information" and of the "Sources of Nonprint Information" that follow.

Three units of information appear on all citations: **author, title,** and **publication information.** They are recorded in that order.

The **author, or authors,** of a work always appears first. (However, authors or editors of reference works such as dictionaries and encyclopedias are omitted on preliminary citation cards and in the Works Cited list.) If no author is given for a source, begin the citation with the title. Also, be sure to distinguish between an author (who actually writes the words of a piece) and an editor (who compiles and organizes materials written by other people). The latter may or may not appear first; consult page 223 for specific examples.

The **title** of a work must be recorded accurately, even to the punctuation. If a colon is included, the wording both before and after it is part of the title. Other special problems, such as one title within another, are explained on page 64.

Publication information tells where, by whom, and when a document was published. Even though nonprint materials are not actually "published" in the traditional sense of the word, you must give information about them. For example, the producer of a film, the director of a television program, or the catalog number of an audio recording qualify as publication information for those items.

Details and examples of the content of specific kinds of information sources, and the models of preliminary citation cards for them, appear later in this chapter and also on pages 220–39.

Conventions of Preliminary Citation Cards

The research paper follows many conventions of format, spacing, punctuation, and other details. Nowhere is that more evident than in the citations. You will be expected to adhere to all such conventions, so it's a good idea to follow them when you write the preliminary citation cards. Such conventions are listed below; those for nonprint materials and special situations are given in Chapter 8.

1. **General Conventions**

    1.1 **Using hanging indentation form.** That is, the first line of each entry begins at the left-hand margin and continues to the right-hand margin; each succeeding line is indented five spaces from the left margin and also continues as far as needed to the right margin.

    1.2 **End the author, title, and publication units by placing a period after each.** But if the title of a work ends with a question mark or an exclamation mark, let it substitute for the period. Allow two spaces after the author and title periods, just as you do after periods in typing regular text.

    1.3 **When there is a comma or a colon in the citation, allow one space after it,** also as in regular typing.

    1.4 **Periods after initials or abbreviations that end units suffice for the period that would normally conclude the unit.**

    1.5 **Long poems appearing in book form, such as *Paradise Lost* or *The Rime of the Ancient Mariner,* are treated as books.**

    1.6 **The Bible and the names of books within it are not underlined.** The King James Version is assumed unless you state otherwise.

2. **Conventions About Books**

    2.1 **Do not distinguish between a hardbound and a paperbound book.** The work itself is the subject of the citation; the kind of cover it has is irrelevant.

    2.2 **Alphabetically arranged entries in familiar reference books do not need either volume or page numbers noted.** Anyone who wants to look up the source you cite will approach the task alphabetically, just as you did.

    2.3 **Only special information about the edition of a book ("rev.," "alt.," "6th ed.," and so on) is noted.** Otherwise, it is assumed to be a first edition and you do not record that fact.

3. **Conventions About Authors**

    3.1 **The author's surname appears first, followed by a comma, then the given name and a period.** A catalog card may give an author's complete name (including a middle name), or a periodical index may give only an author's initials; copy the name as the source indicates—but check the actual publication you use and change the preliminary citation card to conform to the author's preference in print.

3.2 If an author uses a *middle initial,* the period after it suffices for the period ending the unit.

EXAMPLE: Poet Wystan Hugh Auden was customarily known by his first two initials, so a preliminary Works Cited card for him should read `Auden, W. H.`

3.3 If there are *two or more authors,* only the name of the first one is reversed; the others are in normal first-name then last-name order. The names are joined by the word "and" preceded by a comma.

EXAMPLE: `Altshuler, Thelma, and Richard Paul Janaro.`

3.4 If a work has *three authors,* put a comma instead of the word "and" between the first and second persons' names; use the "and" with a comma before the second and third persons' names.

EXAMPLE: `Heertje, Arnold, Francis W. Rushing, and Felicity Skidmore.`

3.5 If a work has four or more authors, record only the first person's name and use the Latin abbreviation "et al." to signal the others.

EXAMPLE: `Maimon, Elaine P., et al.`

4. Conventions About Titles

4.1 Titles of books, pamphlets, magazines, newspapers, radio or TV programs, videotapes, full-length films, plays, operas, and computer software are underlined. Subheads of books are considered part of the title.

EXAMPLE: <u>Film: Reel to Reel.</u>

4.2 Titles of poems, short stories, essays, articles in newspapers or magazines or journals, individual radio or TV episodes in a series, songs, lectures, and speeches are enclosed in quotation marks. Put the period ending the title unit *inside* the quotation marks.

4.3 **Capitalize the first letter of each word in a title (except articles, conjunctions, or prepositions), even if all lowercase or all capitals appear in the information from which you get the title.**

4.4 **Special cases of titles:**

  a. If *a book is a revised edition or some other variation,* end the underlining, put a comma after the title, then abbreviate the special information. Some common designations, used alone or in combination as required, are: rev. (revised), alt. (alternate), ed. (edition). The period signifying the abbreviation substitutes for the period at the end of the entry.

  EXAMPLE: The Research Paper, 6th ed.

  b. If a title that is usually underlined is part of a book title, underline the title of the book but neither underline nor put quotation marks around the second title.

  EXAMPLE: Rashomon, the feature-length film, is the subject of a book for which it's also part of the title. It would appear this way on a preliminary citation card: Focus on Rashomon.

  c. Titles normally put in quotation marks are so recorded if they appear within titles that are underlined.

  EXAMPLE: Sourcebook for "Snows of Kilimanjaro."

  However, if they appear within titles usually enclosed by quotation marks, they are enclosed in single quote marks.

  EXAMPLE: "The Scapegoat in 'The Lottery' and in Life."

5. Conventions of Publication Information —Books

5.1 **Publication information for books consists of the city where the publisher is located, the publisher's name, and the copyright date.** Put a colon after the city and a comma after the publisher's name. (The unit ends with a period, of course.)

5.2 **Only the city of publication for books is noted;** omit the state where it is located. However, add an abbreviation to identify a province in Canada or one for the name of a foreign country (other than Canada).

5.3 **If you cannot find a place of publication, write "n.p." where the city would ordinarily appear.**

5.4 **If several cities appear for a publisher's location, use the first one or the featured one in the list.**

5.5 **The names of book publishers are recorded in abbreviated form, usually only the first word.** See "Streamlining Publishers' Names" at the end of this section.

5.6 **If no publisher is given, write "n.p." after the colon where the publisher's name would ordinarily appear.**

5.7 **If no publication date is given, write "n.d." after the comma where you would ordinarily put the copyright date.** There is no need to put another period at the conclusion of that abbreviation.

5.8 **If several copyright dates are given, record only the most recent one.**

5.9 **Do not confuse the date of a printing with a copyright date.** Some books are reprinted a number of times and you may see something like "5th printing, 1985"; but the copyright date is earlier.

6. Conventions of Publication Information—Magazines

6.1 **Publication information about magazines consists of the title (underlined), the date of publication (followed by a colon) and the pages on which the article appeared.** Leave one space after the title and one space after the colon. Magazines that number pages annually rather than by individual issue are recorded in a slightly different way that is explained on page 68 in the section titled "Differences in Periodical Page Numbering Systems."

6.2 **All months except May, June, and July are recorded in the traditional three-letter abbreviation.**

6.3 **If the article is on successive pages, record the first and last pages with a hyphen between.**

6.4 **If the article is *not* on successive pages, record only the first page followed by " + ."** Articles that have advertising matter or other articles separating their pages are not on successive pages.

6.5 **If the pages of the article begin and end with three digits and the first one is the same, no repetition is needed.**

EXAMPLE: 229–85.   or   106–08.

7. Conventions of Publication Information—Newspapers

7.1 **Publication information about newspapers consists of the name of the paper (underlined), the day, month, and year of publication (followed by a comma), the name of the edition (followed by a colon), the section of the newspaper, and the page on which the article appeared.**

EXAMPLE: <u>Miami Herald</u> 5 May 1988, final ed.: B1.

7.2 Omit an article that is part of the name of a newspaper, even if it appears on the masthead.

EXAMPLE: Although the name of the paper is *The Miami Herald,* record it on a preliminary citation card as <u>Miami Herald</u>

7.3 If the name of the city is not part of the name of the newspaper, supply it in square brackets.

EXAMPLE: <u>Times—Picayune</u> [New Orleans]

7.4 You may need to add the state as further identification for some newspapers. If you do, use the two-letter postal abbreviation.

EXAMPLE: <u>Monitor</u> [Concord, NH]

7.5 Articles not on successive pages are noted with a " + " after the beginning page number.

EXAMPLE: 2 +

Many other conventions cover your recording of both print and nonprint preliminary Works Cited. If you don't find the information you need in this chapter (either in this section or the two sources of print and nonprint information), check the examples on pages 220 – 39 or use the index to find a description that covers what you want to find.

Streamlining publishers' names. In the interest of streamlining publication information, the Modern Language Association [MLA], upon whose documentation conventions this book is based, adopted a shortened form for names of publishers. Therefore, instead of using a long name and such abbreviations as "Co." or "Inc." or "Ltd." you may now use just one word to indicate most companies.

In each list below, the column on the left shows the full name of a publisher and the column on the right shows how that information should appear on a preliminary Works Cited card—and on the Works Cited page of your research paper.

The first name or word suffices to identify a publisher whose company title may include several names or words. Anyone who doesn't know the complete name of the company can easily find it out from a reference book, a librarian, or anyone familiar with publishing companies.

Farrar, Straus & Giroux, Inc.	Farrar
Harper & Row, Publishers, Inc.	Harper
St. Martin's Press, Inc.	St. Martin's
Pocket Books	Pocket
The Free Press	Free

If the *publisher's name is that of one person* (the first and last name or initials and last name), *record just the last name.*

R. R. Bowker Company	Bowker
Alfred A Knopf, Inc.	Knopf
G. P. Putnam's Sons	Putnam

Omit business abbreviations (such as Co., Inc., or Corp.), *articles, and descriptive words* (such as Press or Publishers) that are part of the publisher's full name.

Wadsworth Publishing Co.	Wadsworth
Clark Boardman Co., Ltd.	Boardman
George Allen and Unwin Publishers, Inc.	Allen

A book published by a university press is recorded by the *name of the university together with the initials "U"* (for University) *and "P"* (for Press or Publishers).

Oxford University Press	Oxford UP
Princeton University Press	Princeton UP
University of Chicago Press	U of Chicago P
The Johns Hopkins University Press	Johns Hopkins UP

Use standard abbreviations for words that are part of the publisher's name.

Harvard Law Review Association	Harvard Law Rev. Assn.
Academy for Educational Development, Inc.	Acad. for Educ. Dev.

Use familiar capital letter combinations if that is how the name of a publisher is customarily shown.

U.S. Government Printing Office	GPO
National Council of Teachers of English	NCTE

However, if you believe readers may not know the acronym or letter combination, use abbreviations in preference: Mod. Lang. Assn., rather than MLA.

Differences in periodical page numbering systems. The page numbers in magazines and journals follow one of two conventions: paging is either by issue or by volume year.

Paging by issue means that every time the magazine is published, the page numbering system begins with 1 and continues through until the end of that issue. Most general magazines are paged this way: *Time, Newsweek, Ebony, Car and Driver,* and many more.

Magazines and journals plan their publishing (and their finances) on an annual basis, and the publications of a year are called a "volume." Usually the volume year is the same as a calendar year (that is, running from January through December), but a volume year may be the same as a customary academic year (September through June) as it is for some academic journals, or even the same as a company's fiscal year (perhaps from July through June). Issues of a magazine that come out during its first year of publication are usually called Volume 1 and succeeding years of publication increase accordingly. So if you see "Volume 30" on a magazine or journal, you are fairly safe in assuming it is the thirtieth year of publication. (That *doesn't always* hold true, however. The May 9, 1988 issue of *Time* is volume 131—and the magazine certainly hasn't been in print for 131 years!)

Paging by volume year—also called continuous pagination or successive pagination—means that Page 1 of that magazine or journal will only appear in the first issue of a volume. Thereafter, the pagination or page numbering will continue throughout the volume year.

EXAMPLE:

Suppose a quarterly journal is paged by volume year:

Volume 16	published in January	contains pages 1 through 128
	published in April	contains pages 129 through 256
	published in July	contains pages 257 through 390
	published in October	contains pages 391 through 578
Volume 17	published in January	contains pages 1 through 134
	published in April	contains pages 135 through 289
	and so on.	and so on.

Why do you need to know about this difference between paging by issue and paging by volume? Because the magazine citation is different for each—and you have to record that difference when you make preliminary citation cards.

EXAMPLE   (Paging by issue):

Moore, Sally. "Adventure in Autumn." <u>AAA World</u> May/June
       1988: 6–7.

EXAMPLE   (Paging by volume year):

Sloan, Gary. "Relational Ambiguity Between Sentences."
    College Composition and Communication 39 (1988): 154–
    65.

Note that if the publication is paged by volume year, you record the volume number (here, "39") and the year of publication. If paging is by issue, even though the publication has a volume number, omit the volume number in the citation.

Since most magazine indexes show both volume number and page number for each entry (Example: *Pers Comput* 9:33), how do you know whether or not an individual issue is paged singly or successively? The answer is that you usually can't tell—but you can make a good guess. With rare exceptions (*National Geographic* is one), popular or general reader magazines are paged by issue, so the page number shown in an index will probably not be too high. On the other hand, if you see an index entry with page numbers in the hundreds (*College English* 50: 454-57), you can be pretty sure that publication is paged by volume year.

Sources of Print Information

Almost all the printed information you will need for your research paper will be found in a library. Print, however, may take more than the traditional book or newspaper form. When you use an on-line computer database, the result of the search will be a printed message. Other computer-stored information will appear to you on-screen as print. This section details some of the sources you can use in your search strategy.

Encyclopedias

A **general encyclopedia** will give you a broad, general picture of the subject you're researching. If you want to know whether a particular encyclopedia covers the subject you're looking for, consult the index (which is usually in the last volume of a set.) However, the contents of most of encyclopedias are arranged alphabetically, so you could also look under the appropriate heading.

The *Encyclopedia Americana* and the *World Book Encyclopedia* are familiar to most students and are good for background information; there are also bibliographies with most entries. The *Academic American Encyclopedia* is known for its fine graphics that supplement the print entries.

The *Encyclopaedia Britannica,* though a general encyclopedia, has always been considered strong in the humanities. Since it is arranged differently from other encyclopedias, a special word about it is in order. The *Britannica* has three units. The *Micropaedia* is ten volumes, indicated by roman numerals, containing ready reference material and an index. Use it first when you look up information because it will either give you all you are looking for or tell you where to find more information in the *Macropaedia.* The nineteen volumes of the *Macropaedia,* each designated by an arabic numeral, give knowledge in depth. The one-volume *Propaedia* gives a general outline of knowledge; its entries are probably too broad for you to consult for the kind of research paper this book is about, but they provide a good overview and direction for more specific sources.

Consult **subject encyclopedias** (if there are any in the field you are working on) for a more detailed and restricted discussion of a subject. They, too, usually have their contents arranged alphabetically.

The Encyclopedia of Crime and Justice, The Encyclopedia of World Art, the *McGraw-Hill Encyclopedia of Science and Technology,* and the *New Grove Dictionary of Music and Musicians* (actually a twenty-volume encyclopedia, despite its title) are examples of the kind and range of subject encyclopedias available. Others are listed in Appendix A, "Selected List of Reference Works Available in Libraries," pages 279–93.

Preliminary citations from an encyclopedia.   An encyclopedia *is not* a place from which to get a whole paper (although, unfortunately, some people believe it is). But it *is* a source of material that will give you enough of a general view of a subject to start from in your research and in your understanding of the subject you selected. As you read in Chapter 2, many encyclopedia entries also have bibliographies, and by consulting additional books and articles shown there (if they're available to you), you enlarge your search for information.

Be sure you find the *author* of an encyclopedia entry so you can record that information on your citation card. Most encyclopedia articles are either signed or have the author's initials at the end; the full name of the person whose initials are given can usually be found within the volume.

Figure 10 is a sample of a preliminary Works Cited card for an encyclopedia article to use as a model. Note the spacing, marked for you in color. Note also that volume and page numbers are unnecessary because the work is organized alphabetically.

Should you use the *Encyclopaedia Britannica,* that part of the set used is considered part of the title, this way: Encyclopaedia Britannica: Micropaedia. 1985.

Other Reference Books and Indexes (Bibliographies, Handbooks, Biographical References, the Vertical File, Government Publications, and more)

When librarians look for information on a given subject, they often go first to Eugene Sheehy's *Guide to Reference Books.* You can, too. Sheehy identifies

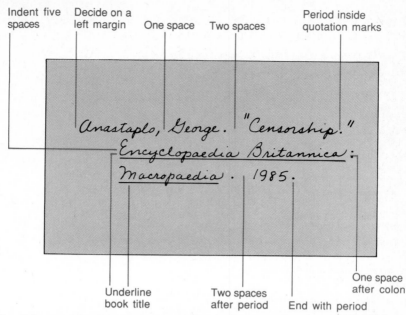

Indent five spaces · Decide on a left margin · One space · Two spaces · Period inside quotation marks

Underline book title · Two spaces after period · End with period · One space after colon

Fig. 10. Sample preliminary Works Cited card for an encyclopedia article.

all sorts of reference books by field, so if you check his book, you will be lead to other sources quickly. Figure 11 on page 72 shows you a portion of a page from this book as an example of the kind of sources it indicates.

- A **bibliography** will help you find additional source listings that you may consult in your search for information. Many are newly issued or updated so that recent publications on a specific subject or in a particular publication are readily available. For instance, the *Bibliographical Index: A Cumulative Bibliography of Bibliographies* lists, by subject, books and journal articles containing at least fifty bibliographic citations of works that have been published separately or that have appeared as parts of books, pamphlets, and periodicals. Figure 12 on page 73 shows how entries on cells have "see" listings (in addition to other entries) that can lead you to other pages in the index for further sources of information to include in your preliminary citations.

- A **directory,** despite its name, that may be helpful is the *Encyclopedia of Associations*. It tells which reference books identify organizations and institutions in a field. Its particular use for students' research papers is that from it you can find names and addresses to write to for special kinds of information.

- A **biographical reference book** will be helpful in finding out about persons mentioned in your research or the author of material on your

Buddhist

Akiyama, Aisaburo. Buddhist hand-symbol. Yokohama, Yoshikawa Book Store, 1939. 86p. il. **BE210**

Text in English and Japanese. An illustration is given for each symbol.

Bhattacharyya, Benoytosh. The Indian Buddhist iconography, mainly based on the Sādhanamālā and cognate Tāntric texts of rituals. [2d ed rev. and enl.] Calcutta, Mukhopadhyay, 1958. 478p. il. **BE211**

1st ed., Oxford Univ. Pr., 1924.
This comprehensive work is illustrated by more than 350 pictures and line drawings.

Chinese

Williams, Charles Alfred Speed. Encyclopedia of Chinese symbolism and art motives; an alphabetical compendium of legends and beliefs as reflected in the manners and customs of the Chinese throughout history. N.Y., Julian, 1960. 468p. **BE212**

"A re-issue of the . . . work originally titled *Outlines of Chinese symbolism and art motives* published 1931, rev. 1932." GR335.W53

Hindu

Banerjea, Jitendra Nath. The development of Hindu iconography. [2d ed. rev. and enl. Calcutta], Univ. of Calcutta, 1956. 653p. il. **BE213**

1st ed. 1941.
A comprehensive history dealing with the development and manifestations of Hindu iconography from ancient times.

Gopinātha Rāu, T. A. Elements of Hindu iconography. Madras, Law Printing House, 1914–16. 2v. in 4. il. **BE214**

In Sanskrit and English. BL1201.G7

Other signs and symbols

Dictionnaire des symboles: mythes, rêves, coutumes, gestes, formes, figures, couleurs, nombres. Sous la direction de Jean Chevalier. [Paris], Robert Laffont, [1982]. 842p. il. **BE215**

For full information *see* CF53.

Dreyfuss, Henry. Symbol sourcebook; an authoritative guide to international graphic symbols. N.Y., McGraw-Hill, [1972]. 292p. **BE216**

Symbols are grouped according to subject areas with an index by objects and ideas represented. AZ108.D74

Lehner, Ernst. Symbols, signs and signets. Cleveland, World, [1950]. 221p. il. **BE217**

No attempt at completeness is claimed. Clear reproductions of signs and symbols are given under such headings as "Symbolic gods and deities," "Astronomy and astrology," "Heraldry," "Monsters," etc.; each section is preceded by a brief introduction. Some sections are indexed, but there is no general index. Bibliography, p.217–21. AZ108.L4

Shepherd, Walter. Shepherd's Glossary of graphic signs and symbols. London, Dent, [1971], 597p.' **BE218**

An attempt at formal classification of "the written marks by which mankind records ideas."—*Pref.* Emphasis is on signs used in technical literature, but attention is given to signs encountered in inscriptions, manuscripts, maps, charts, and various alphabets. AZ108.S53

Fig. 11. **Portion of a page from Sheehy's *Guide to Reference Books*, 10th Edition.**
Edited by Eugene P. Sheehy. © 1986 by ALA. Reprinted by permission.

Céline, Louis-Ferdinand, 1894-1961
By and about
Carson, Jane. Céline's imaginative space. (American university studies, Series II, Romance languages and literature, v42) Lang, P. 1987 p193-8
Cell adhesion
Gorbsky, G. Desmosomal adhesion in development. *Am Zool* 26 no3:538-40 '86
Thomas, W. A. Dual adhesive recognition systems in chick embryonic cells. *Am Zool* 26 no3:563-5 '86
Cell biology *See* Cytology
Cell-cell interaction *See* Cell interaction
Cell communication *See* Cell interaction
Cell culture
Plant and animal cells; process possibilities; editors: C. Webb and F. Mavituna. Horwood, E. 1987 incl bibl
Cell cycle
Cell cycle effects of drugs; section editor, Lyle A. Dethlefsen. (International encyclopedia of pharmacology and therapeutics, section 121) Pergamon Press 1986 incl bibl
Cell differentiation
MacLean, Norman, and Hall, Brian Keith. Cell commitment and differentiation. Cambridge Univ. Press 1987 p221-36
Cell interaction
Hormones, receptors, and cellular interactions in plants; edited by C.M. Chadwick and D.R. Garrod. (Intercellular and intracellular communication, 1) Cambridge Univ. Press 1986 incl bibl
Cell junctions
Gorbsky, G. Desmosomal adhesion in development. *Am Zool* 26 no3:538-40 '86
Revel, J.-P. Gap junctions in development. *Am Zool* 26 no3:531-3 '86
Cellular biology *See* Cytology
Cellular interaction *See* Cell interaction
Cellulose
Biodegradation
Hoeniger, J. F. M. Decomposition studies in two central Ontario lakes having surficial pHs of 4.6 and 6.6. *Appl Environ Microbiol* 52:496-7 S '86

Fig. 12. **Portion of a page taken from *Bibliographical Index: A Cumulative Bibliography of Bibliographies*. Note the many entries related to "cells" as well as the cross-references to other parts of the bibliography.**
© 1988 by H. W. Wilson Company. Reprinted by permission of the publisher.

subject. *Who's Who in America, American Men and Women of Science, Contemporary Authors, Dictionary of National Biography* (usually referred to as DNB), and other volumes will give you dates of birth and death, nationality, and information about occupations. The *New York Times Bibliographical Service* is also helpful. The *Biography and Genealogy Master Index* lists 350 current and retrospective indexes and is much used for biographical research.

▪ A **subject heading guide** such as the *Cross-Reference Index* will suggest headings on a subject in several standard sources. Use it to help you find subject headings you might not otherwise think of looking under in your search for information. Figure 13 shows an entry from this index. Letters in the left column are abbreviations of the various sources cataloged in the index, each of which you might then consult under the appropriate headings listed.

FOOT WEAR. *See* Boots and Shoes

FOOTBALL COACHING, SOCCER COACHING, ETC.
   Use Athletics

FORAGE PLANTS. *Use* Crops; Pastures

FORCE AND ENERGY
LC   — —; s.a. Man (physics); Mechanics; Pressure;
          Vital force
SEARS   — —; s.a. Dynamics; Mechanics; Motion; Quan-
          tum theory
RG   — —; s.a. Dynamics; Pressure
NYT   PHYSICS; s.a. Atomic energy and weapons;
          Science and technology
PAIS   POWER RESOURCES; s.a. Atomic power;
          Hydroelectric power
BPI   PHYSICS; s.a. Mechanics

Fig. 13.   Portion of a page from the *Cross-Reference Index*.
Used by permission of R. R. Bowker Co.

■ **Indexes** in various subjects will also prove helpful sources for locating titles of works you may want to read for information. For example, if you are doing research in literature or the humanities, you can find information about essays and other writings within longer works by consulting the *Essay and General Literature Index*. It lists, by subject and author, the material you can't find in book titles alone. At the end of that index is a list of the publishers and dates of the books shown in the many entries, so you can have additional help in locating what you want to consult (see Figure 16 on page 79).

People writing about literature often use *Poetry Explication* as a resource. It is an index containing explications of individual poems and criticism of them which appeared in books and periodicals. A similar volume but on a different subject is *20th Century Short Story Explication*. The *Short Story Index* and *Granger's Index to Poetry and Recitations* are still other sources to consult.

Many other indexes are helpful in yielding information; some of them in libraries are listed in Appendix A. Such standards as *Business Periodicals Index, Social Sciences Index, Biological Abstracts (Biosis)*, and *Applied Science and Technology* are now available on computer-assisted retrieval systems (computer databases) as well as in print volumes. InfoTrac is an on-line system many libraries now subscribe to; it accesses many kinds of indexes selected by the library in which it is installed, so from it you can locate sources of information in periodicals.

- The **Public Affairs Information Service Bulletin** (PAIS) gives a brief summary of articles it lists. Since PAIS works from 1,400 periodicals as well as from government documents, it's obviously a good source to search for preliminary citations.

- The **vertical file** maintained by many libraries contains pamphlets, booklets, and other informational items that can't be classified as either books or periodicals. *The Vertical File Index: A Subject and Title Index to Selected Pamphlet Material* tells where and how to order additional materials. You may make preliminary citation cards on the basis of the *Index* and send for material listed if you have enough time and wish to do so. Otherwise, check the current file in your library to see if the material you want is already in its collection.

- **Government publications** are a rich source of information because the government is the country's leading publisher. The *Congressional Record* is the official daily report of proceedings of open sessions of Congress— a source you may be able to use for your research. The *Congressional Quarterly,* issued weekly and as an almanac, is a reliable news source which provides a summary of congressional developments. The *U.S. Government Organization Manual* is the official organizational handbook of the federal government and shows activities of departments, bureaus, and so on.

  If your subject has anything at all to do with the U.S. Government, the National Archives and Records Administration may have something useful for you. You may inquire by mail to Washington, DC, or if you live in or near Boston, New York, Philadelphia, Atlanta, Chicago, Kansas City, Fort Worth, Denver, Los Angeles, San Francisco, or Seattle, visit one of the National Archives Field Branches. The presidential libraries of Hoover, Roosevelt, Truman, Eisenhower, Kennedy, Johnson, and Ford also hold documents. Lists of available publications and ordering information are readily available, and many public libraries hold microfilmed copies of records from the National Archives.

  If you have access to one of the 1390 + libraries designated as a "depository library," you have an added bonus in quick access—through microforms and computer as well as in print volumes—to seemingly limitless information and publications generated by the United States government. (Figure 14 is an example.) Congressional Information Ser-

```
SUDOCS NBR.:  Y 1.1/5:99-5/v.1-2
ENTRY NBR.:       85022006
TITLE:        Developments in aging, 1984 : a report of the
              Special Committee on Aging, United States
              Senate, pursuant to S. Res. 354, March 2,
              1984, resolution authorizing a study of the
              problems of the aged and aging.
PUBLISHER:    Washington : U.S. G.P.O.,
DATE:         1985.
DESCRIPTION:  2 v. : ill. ; 24 cm.
SERIES TITLE:Rept. / 99th Congress, 1st session, Senate ;
NOTES:        Distributed to some depository libraries in
              microfiche.
NOTES:        "February 28 ... 1985."
NOTES:        Includes index.
NOTES:        vol. 1. [No distinctive title] -- vol. 2.
              Appendixes.
SUBJECT:      Aged--United States.
CO-AUTHOR:    United States. Congress. Senate. Special
              Committee on Aging.
SERIES:       United States. Congress (99th, 1st session :
              1985). Senate. Report ;
ITEM NBR.:    1008-C, 1008-D (microfiche)
FORMAT:       book
```

Fig. 14. **Example of a printout from a CD-ROM search of
          government documents.**

vices publishes indexes of bills, reports, documents, treaties, executive reports, publications, and public laws. There are so many items available, that documenting them can be difficult; in fact, there is even a book titled *The Complete Guide to Citing Government Documents* by Diane L. Garner and Diane H. Smith (Bethesda: Congressional Information Service, 1984).

In the *Monthly Catalog of United States Government Publications* you will find the titles and prices of all publications that come from government agencies. Even more important at this stage, it has subject, title, and author information or indexes to help you find potentially useful materials. Many items listed in the catalog may already be in the library you are using for your research (see Figure 15).

The library you are using may receive the Congressional Quarterly's weekly *Editorial Research Reports*—very helpful if you are searching for information on an issue of current national significance.

Preliminary citations from an index.   The form of citing an item from an index, bibliography, handbook, or other reference source depends on what you are recording—a book or periodical or nonprint material. Figure 16 is a sample section from *Essay and General Literature Index* and a preliminary citation card. See how the information recorded on it follows the conventions stated earlier in this chapter.

National Park Service — Interior Dept.

NATIONAL PARK SERVICE
Interior Dept.
Washington, DC 20240

88-9781

I 29.2:G 48/2

Information brochure for planning issues : Glen Canyon National Recreation Area : Orange Cliffs/Maze. ⌐ [Denver, Colo. : U.S. Dept. of the Interior, National Park Service], 1987.

    1 sheet : 1 map ; 43 x 28 folded to 15 x 28 cm. Shipping list no.: 87-541-P.

    1. National parks and reserves — Utah — Planning. 2. National parks and reserves — Arizona — Planning. 3. Glen Canyon National Recreation Area (Utah and Ariz.) I. United States. National Park Service. II. Title: Glen Canyon National Recreation Area, Orange Cliffs/Maze. III. Title: Orange Cliffs/Maze. OCLC 17424589

88-9782

I 29.2:G 76/7

Environmental assessment, modify wastewater treatment plant, South Rim : Grand Canyon National Park, Arizona. — [Denver, Colo.] : U.S. Dept. of the Interior, National Park Service, Denver Service Center, [1985]

    30 p. : ill., maps ; 28 cm. Distributed to depository libraries in microfiche. "September 1985." Bibliography: p. 29. "NPS D-92"—P. 30. ●Item 648 (microfiche)

    1. Sewage disposal plants — Arizona — Grand Canyon National Park. 2. Grand Canyon National Park (Ariz.) I. United States. National Park Service. Denver Service Center. II. Title: Grand Canyon National Park. III. Title: Modify wastewater treatment plant, South Rim. OCLC 17631481

88-9783

I 29.2:In 2/4

Action plan : America's Industrial Heritage Project. — Cresson, Pa. : Heritage Preservation Commission, America's Industrial Heritage Project, 1987.

    iii, 60 p. : ill., 2 maps, 1 form ; 22 X 28 cm. "Prepared by the Heritage Preservation Commission with the assistance of the National Park Service"—P. [3] of cover. Shipping list no.: 87-541-P. "August 1987." "NPS D-17A"—P. [3] of cover. ●Item 648

    1. America's Industrial Heritage Project. 2. Historic sites — Pennsylvania. I. America's Industrial Heritage Project. II. Heritage Preservation Commission (Pa.) III. United States. National Park Service. IV. Title: America's Industrial Heritage Project. OCLC 16859627

88-9784

Fig. 15. Portion of a page from the *Monthly Catalog of United States Government Publications*.

Use the examples of other kinds of works cited in Chapter 9, pages 220–39, as models to record the sources you find for your own research paper.

Chaplin, Charlie, 1889-1977
About
Sinyard, N. Kindred spirits: analogies be-
tween the film and literary artist. (*In* Sinyard,
N. Filming literature p99-116)
Chapman, George, 1559?-1634, tr.
About individual works
The Odyssey
Lord, G. de F. Chapman's Renaissance
Homer. (*In* Lord, G. de F. Classical presences
in seventeenth-century English poetry p5-36)

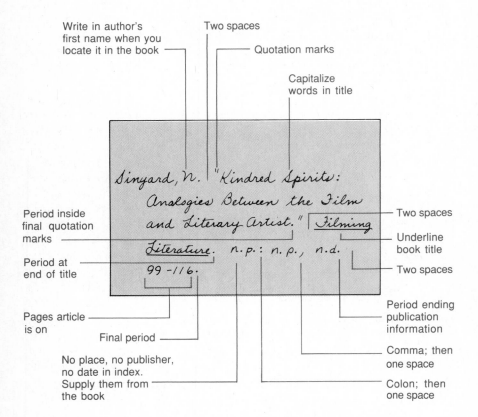

Write in author's
first name when you
locate it in the book

Two spaces

Quotation marks

Capitalize
words in title

Period inside
final quotation
marks

Period at
end of title

Two spaces

Underline
book title

Two spaces

Pages article
is on

Final period

No place, no publisher,
no date in index.
Supply them from
the book

Period ending
publication
information

Comma; then
one space

Colon; then
one space

*Sinyard, N. "Kindred Spirits:
Analogies Between the Film
and Literary Artist." Filming
Literature. n.p.: n.p., n.d.
99-116.*

Fig. 16. **Portion of a page from *Essay and General Literature Index***
and a sample preliminary citation card for the information
listed under the Charlie Chaplin entry.

Abstracting Services

Abstracts are summaries of what has been written, both published and unpublished, on a subject. Look for your research subject in an abstracting service publication to see what sort of material is available. Then, decide if you want to make a citation card for the work. Many abstracts are also available on computer databases or on microforms, that is, on microfilm, microfiche, or microcards. (Microforms can be read, and often photocopied, on machines made for the purpose.)

If your research has anything to do with education, ERIC (Educational Resources Information Center) is a good place to look. Through this federally funded program, unpublished materials are summarized and cataloged in such special collections as Reading and Communication Skills, Higher Education, Counseling and Personnel Services, Urban Education, and others. ERIC documents are available in libraries on microfiche or on microfilm; some documents can also be ordered on regular page copies, and many are available on computer through DIALOG, a computer database service described on pages 86–89.

Psychological Abstracts, Science Abstracts, Abstracts in Anthropology, Historical Abstracts, Biological Abstracts, and many others will lead you to journal articles or book titles that might be useful as preliminary citations, depending on the field you are working in. Other such indexes in special areas are listed in Appendix A, "Selected List of Reference Works Available in Libraries."

Dissertation Abstracts International (called *Dissertation Abstracts* before 1969) has recorded the dissertations of everyone awarded a doctoral degree. *DAI* is divided by subjects: Series A for humanities and social sciences, Series B for the sciences, and Series C for European dissertations. Most of these dissertations remain unpublished, but sometimes copies may be borrowed from the library at the institution which awarded the degree. Doctoral dissertations are an interesting source of information, for they represent both research of past work and original contributions by the author. You get the benefits of both—and sources of information listed by the writer.

A note of warning: *never* substitute an abstract for your own complete reading of the original source! If you can't locate the original article, discard that preliminary citation card, no matter how promising the abstract seemed.

As you locate material you think you can use, check "Standard Forms for Works Cited," pages 220–39, for the correct method of recording each type of citation.

The Card Catalog

Although many libraries still catalog their holdings on cards (hence, the card catalog), increasingly libraries have on-line (that is, computer) catalogs or microform catalogs. Printed catalogs are also in use; they are bound volumes in which pages show reproductions of the same cards that would otherwise be in the traditional library drawers. (*Card catalog* is the term used in this book, but substitute for it the kind of catalog you will be using in your library.) If you have ever looked for any information in a library, you have probably used the card catalog and are probably already familiar with much of the following information.

Every book in a library's collection is listed in its card catalog, so it is a prime source to get preliminary citations from.

- **Fiction** books each have two cards in the catalog: one by title and one by author's name.

- **Nonfiction** books each have at least three cards in the catalog: one by subject, one by title, and one by author's name. They may also have **additional cards** headed (and filed) by an alternate subject, by a story title within a book of collected stories, by a translator, or by a writer's pseudonym. Since catalog cards are made to help locate information, they are headed in as many ways as possible to aid you.

Audiovisual or government document holdings are also sometimes represented by cards in the catalog.

Libraries organize their holdings in one of two systems:

- A **dictionary catalog** lists all holdings in alphabetical order according to card headings. Thus, the author card [Miller, Arthur] would be close to [Misfits, The], a novel he wrote.

- A **divided catalog** has separate sections for author, title, and subject cards. A fiction book will appear in only the author and title sections. But there is no limit to how many times a nonfiction book may appear within the subject section of the catalog. For instance, a book about trees might be listed under "trees" and "forestry" and "ecology."

Each 3 × 5-inch card in a catalog drawer or shown on a computer screen represents a book (or other material) in the library. Therefore, each contains the "call number" of the classification system of that library—either a letter or a letter-number combination of the Library of Congress system or a number combination of the Dewey Decimal system (explained in Chapter 2 on pages 29–30). The call number tells you where the book is located among the library's holdings. Since cards are filed alphabetically according to heading, a notation on the outside of each drawer shows its contents.

What's on a catalog card.   **The author card** is basic to the catalog and is the prime entry card for each book in a library. When a book is published in the United States, copies of it are sent to the Library of Congress in Washington, D.C. The author card is printed there or by other library-supply sources; your library purchases the card from one of them. Libraries use that basic card to make their own title, subject, and other heading cards by typing the appropriate information above the author's name. Each library also adds a classification system number at the top left corner of the card, following guidelines of the system it uses.

Figure 17 shows author, title, and subject Dewey Decimal cards for the same book. Note the differences in the top line. In addition, you can also see the Library of Congress number on the second author card for the same book.

The many elements on a catalog card are identified in color for your information. You will only need a few of these to write a preliminary citation card for the book: author, title, location and name of publisher, copyright date, and call number.

The title card for both fiction and nonfiction books is the basic author card with the book title typed in black ink at the top of the card, above the author's name (see Figure 17 on page 81).

The subject card for each nonfiction book is made by having the subject heading typed, usually in red ink, above the author's name (see Figure 17). A book will have as many subject cards as it conveniently can, since the object of a subject card is to make it easy to locate the book for a variety of purposes.

"See also" cards are the helpful reference cards you read about earlier (see Figure 5, page 23). They are in the card catalog at the end of a subject section. They may lead to important sources of information, so don't overlook them when you are preparing preliminary citations. Check the listings on them that seem related to your subject and the approach you have already determined.

Cataloging customs. As a rule, catalog cards are filed alphabetically. Here are some other uniform practices of library cataloging that will help you find materials easily.

1.1 **If the same word is applicable to a person, place, subject or book title in a dictionary catalog filing, the cards follow that same order.**

EXAMPLES:

Washington, George (the person)

Washington, D.C. (the place)

Washington Square (a book title)

(Obviously, this practice could not be applicable to a divided catalog because authors, titles, and subjects are in separate groups.)

1.2 **Abbreviations such as "St.," "Dr.," "U.S.," and "19th cent." are filed as if they were spelled out: "Saint," "Doctor," "United States," "Nineteenth century," and so on.** If you were looking for the book *St. Thomas and the Future of Metaphysics* and didn't

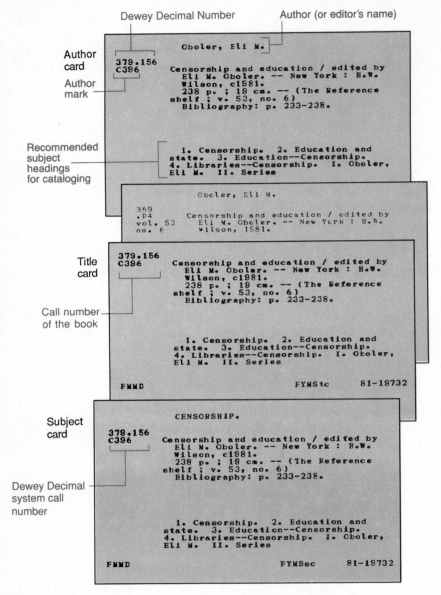

Fig. 17. **Sample of author, title, and subject cards for the same book.
The Library of Congress numbering system is represented on
the second author card.**

know the author, you would look for "Saint Thomas . . ." in the card catalog.

1.3 Filing is alphabetical word by word and letter by letter to the end of each word. It is *not* simply a letter-by-letter listing.

EXAMPLES:

Actual Catalog Order	*Not*
North Carolina	North Carolina
North Dakota	Northcote
Northcote	North Dakota
The Northwest	Northwestern
Wind	The Northwest Wind
Northwestern	

(Note that the article "the" is overlooked in alphabetizing, although it is written in the normal place.)

2. Customs About Author Cards

2.1 Names beginning with *Mac* or variations—such as *Mc,* or *M'*—are all filed as though they began with *Mac*.

EXAMPLE:

Proper cataloging order is: Mach
 McHale
 MacHenry
 Machiavelli

2.2 Foreign prefixes with names (such as "de," "van," or "von") are not used in the catalog filing. Instead, filing is by last name with the prefix following.

EXAMPLE: Beethoven, Ludwig van.

English names beginning with "De" or "Van" are filed by that prefix.

EXAMPLE: DeWitt, John

Spanish names are filed by the patronym (father's family name) rather than by the mother's maiden name or the place name, either of which, according to Spanish custom, is often added to an individual's given name.

EXAMPLE: Cervantes, Saavedra, Miguel de

2.3 Works by and about an individual in a dictionary catalog, and in your Works Cited, will appear in this order:
a. Books authored.

```
Dewey, John.  Art as Experience.  New York:
     Minton, 1934.
```

b. Books coauthored, if the name appears first on the title page.

```
Dewey, John, and Arthur F. Bentley.  Knowing
     and the Known.  Boston: Beacon, 1949.
```

c. Books cited.

```
Dewey, John, ed.  New York and the Seabury
     Investigators.  New York: City Affairs
     Committee, 1933.
```

d. Books about the person.

```
Hook, Sidney.  John Dewey: An Intellectual
     Portrait.  New York: Day, 1939.
```

e. Books about a person's works.

```
Blewett, John.  John Dewey: His Thoughts and
     Influence.  New York: Fordham UP, 1960.
```

3. Customs About Title Cards

3.1 Titles that begin with "a," "an," or "the" are alphabetized by the second word. Articles are either ignored for alphabetical purposes or shown following a comma at the end of the title.

EXAMPLE: Adventures of Huckleberry Finn, The

4. Customs About Subject Cards

4.1 Acronyms appear before words that are spelled out. Thus, cards about "OPEC" will be placed in the catalog before those on "oil."

4.2 Subjects—except history—are subdivided in alphabetical order.

EXAMPLE:

Songs	[subject]
Ballads	
Carols	
Children's Songs	[subdivisions]
Drinking Songs	
Folk Songs	
Madrigals	
Popular Songs	

4.3 History is subdivided according to historical eras or time.

EXAMPLE:

Gt. Brit.—History (By Period)   [header card]
     Roman Period, 55 B.C.–A.D. 449
     Anglo-Saxon Period, 449–1066   [subdivisions]
     14th Century
     War of the Roses, 1455–1584

Preliminary citations from catalog cards. If you write each preliminary citation card properly, you will only have to reproduce it (a real time saver!) on the typewriter or computer for the Works Cited listing at the end of your research paper.

When you write the preliminary citation card from a catalog card, be sure to copy accurately the author, full title, location and name of the publisher, and the copyright date. In the upper left corner of your card, write the call number exactly as it appears (so you will know where the book is located in the library).

Also, remember to follow the conventions for preliminary citations described on pages 62–67. Pay particular attention to the spacing after periods, commas, and colons; be sure to end the entry with a period. Figure 18 on page 86 is an example of how to do that.

Consult the examples of various kinds of citations—including such particulars as books with multiple authors, translations, books edited by one or more persons, books in a series, and other special situations—in Chapter 9, pages 220–27, and use them as models for the preliminary citation cards.

If you are getting information from more than one library, write the name of the library on the top right corner of the preliminary citation card.

Computer Databases

The most recent and innovative research aids are on-line computer databases. Using them early in your search strategy will save hours of looking through traditional library sources. Instead, a computer transmits messages that activate a search for the most specific kinds of information. Within minutes, you have the information you seek.

With the right combination of equipment—an ASCII-coded personal computer or word processor, a modem with interface, a telephone line, and some terminal software—you can have instantaneous access to millions of pieces of information that are searched for the specifics you request. The response is typed back to you on an ordinary printer used with the computer. ("On-line" means that there is a telecommunication connection through the lines of such networks as TELENET, TYMNET, UNINET, or WATS.)

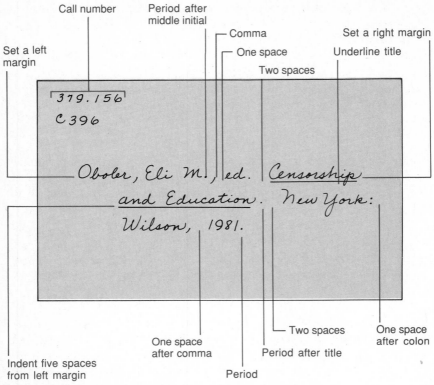

Fig. 18. Preliminary citation card for a book.

What a database is. A database is a collection of records about a particular subject that has been brought together for easy access. People accustomed to working with computers at home or in business often uses databases to store files and other information. You may even take notes for your research paper on a database so that you can call them up in an organized way.

DIALOG Information Retrieval Service is the largest database of its kind and is on-line with many libraries; it subscribes to more than 300 databases, all available to you. Among other popular computer databases are ORBIT, BRS [Bibliographic Retrieval Service] Information Technologies, and Mead Data Central, which has LEXIS (perhaps the best-known legal database) and NEXIS (which is news and public affairs). THE SOURCE has regularly updated business and general news, including abstracts of business magazines articles, and *NewsNet* has information from 200 specialized newsletters as well as wire services on line. NTIS [National Technical Information Service] is an agency of the Department of Commerce and holds more than 2,500 databases, data files, and computer programs. Its Bibliographic Database is available through BRS, DIALOG, Mead, and System Development Corporation.

A database subscribed to by the library where you do your research will most likely be the one you use to obtain resources for your preliminary citation cards. But businesses and professional people subscribe to many of these, as do some student clubs and dormitory groups. So do some individuals, who access the databases directly from home. For example, KNOWLEDGE INDEX is a service of DIALOG that offers low-cost access to more than 17 million summaries during evenings and weekends, when most DIALOG subscribers are not calling upon its facilities. (If you have access to such subscribers—or are already one—you can bypass the library and make your computer search from another terminal.)

How a database operates.   Database services are available by subscription, and the costs are generally passed along to the user. However, some college libraries now include a limited subscription to a database (such as DIALOG) as part of their operating expenses and do not require students to pay separately. Each database has a separate per/hour charge that may be assessed in addition to other monthly or connecting fees. If you use an on-line computer database service, the fee may be anywhere from just a few dollars to a considerable amount of money. You pay for time you use the telephone lines for transmission of both request and response information, as well as for the time it takes for the database computers to make their search. Be sure you understand the charges in advance of requesting any on-line service!

A librarian (or other specialist) who is trained in using the system will usually be the person to help you fulfill your request for information through a database. In a typical search, you give the librarian the subject about which you are looking for information. That person will probably ask you questions to help make your search as specific as possible, selecting concepts and synonyms used in the particular database. This step helps narrow the search so that the words actually typed into the computer are those that will be most likely to elicit the kind of information useful to you.

In DIALOG, for this narrowing, a series of "logical connectors" is usually used to fit together the key words for your search: this *or* this, this *and* this, this *but not* this. One, two, or all three of these logical connectors may be needed in order to focus on the most helpful information for you.

The many databases available through DIALOG are supplied to it by producers who collect, report, and organize the information (which may also be supplied to other users in print, but not in electronic form). DIALOG puts the data into a form for electronic storage and retrieval, then builds indexes to aid rapid searching.

DIALOG has four different kinds of databases: bibliographic (which is a record of descriptive information from books, journal and newspaper articles, and similar sources), directory (which provides information about companies, associations, and audiovisual materials), numeric (statistic tables, sometimes with text), and full text (complete texts of newspaper articles, encyclopedia entries, and other sources). An alphabetical listing of the databases you can request from DIALOG includes newspapers, magazines, journals, and government publications and ranges from ABI/INFORM® (which "stresses general decision sciences information which is applicable to many types of businesses and industries") to ZOOLOGICAL RECORD (the contents for which come from approximately 6,000 journals).

You do not need to know which kind of text or database to search; the librarian who helps you map the search will do that.

Once the key words and logical connectors have been determined by you and the librarian, the information is typed into the computer in specific form. Immediately, computers in California containing the more than 200 databases in the DIALOG system set to work searching for exactly what you need. The information is transmitted back to you and printed out as it enters the computer you are using. The average search takes just two to twelve minutes of on-line time!

The search session ends when you review the results of the information you have requested—or when you ask that some parts of it (such as a full text) be printed later and sent in the mail.

In doing the research for the sample research paper in this book (pages 257–78), eight likely-seeming databases in DIALOG were searched from Florida. Titles of articles that seemed to fit the requested parameters came back within seconds. The titles were scanned and requests for annotations were made from likely-looking ones. In a few cases, entire texts were requested, though it is usually less expensive to have full texts mailed (called "off-line" because the information doesn't travel on the computer phone lines). The entire printout received for the preliminary citations and research for the sample paper measured eight feet long and took only 13½ minutes of on-line time! Figure 19 shows part of a DIALOG search printout for the sample research paper in Chapter 10.

As computer use grows and more commercial databases are established, more kinds and numbers of materials are available. There are many abstracts, lots of statistics and directories, and now more full-text databases, thus making it possible for you to consult materials you want but that aren't in your library.

Preliminary citations from a database.   When you write a preliminary citation card from a computer information service, treat the author, title, and publication units as you would any other printed material. However, if the complete text comes from a computer service, you must add a *fourth unit* acknowledging where you obtained this information. Allow two spaces after the period that ends the publication unit. Then record the name of the database service where you found the citation and the file number you con-

```
 4/3/8
ED233732   IR050375
 A  Report  of a Survey on Censorship in Public Elementary and High School
Libraries and Public Libraries in Minnesota.
  McDonald, Fran; Stark, Matthew
  Minnesota Civil Liberties Union, Minneapolis.
  Feb 1983
  37p.
  EDRS Price - MF01/PC02 Plus Postage.

 4/3/9
ED232709   IR060007
  Libraries and the Censorship Issue. A Selected ERIC Bibliography.
  ERIC Clearinghouse on Information Resources, Syracuse, N.Y.
  Apr 1983
  3p.
  EDRS Price - MF01/PC01 Plus Postage.

 4/3/10
ED232307#   EA016011
  Conservative Pressures on Curriculum.
  Bryson, Joseph E.
  National Organization on Legal Problems of Education, Topeka, Kans.
  1983
  11p.; In its: School Law Update--1982, p137-47, 1983.
  Document Not Available from EDRS.
?T 4/7/1

 4/7/1
EJ288997   SP513405
  Legal Update--The Censorship of Library Books: Board v. Pico.
  Thomas, Stephen B.; Weisbaum, Renee E.
  Texas Tech Journal of Education, v10 n3 p189-93 Fall  1983
  Available from: UMI
  Language: English
  Document Type: LEGAL MATERIAL (090); PROJECT DESCRIPTION (141)
  Journal Announcement: CIJFEB84
  Supreme  Court  opinion  is  reviewed  on a case that involved the Island
Trees  Union  Free School District (New York) board of education's decision
to  remove  10  books  from  school  libraries.   The  court did not reach a
majority decision. Various justices' views on students' rights, censorship,
and school board authority are discussed. (PP)
?4/7/4

>>>Unrecognizable Command
?T 4/7/4

 4/7/4
EJ281390   IR511297
  Censorship Today and Probably Tomorrow.
  Donelson, Ken
  Canadian Library Journal, v40 n2 p83-89 Apr  1983
  Language: English
  Document Type: JOURNAL ARTICLE (080); POSITION PAPER (120)
  Journal Announcement: CIJSEP83
  Examines  preconceptions  of  censorship, citing problems posed to
librarians  and  teachers.  Highlights  include  censored books; individual
censors  (including  the  Gablers);  organized  groups  (including Save Our
Schools  (SOS),  Phyllis  Schlafly's  Eagle Forum, and the Moral Majority);
teacher  and  librarian  censors (moral, literary, sociological); and those
who aid and abet censors. (EJS)
?LOGOFF
```

Fig. 19. **Portion of a DIALOG search printout used for researching the sample research paper reproduced in Chapter 10.**
Reprinted by permission of Information Access Co.

sulted. Put a comma, a space, and then the number of the item; end with a period. Figure 20 shows how information from the database printout (but not the complete text) is recorded on a preliminary citation card.

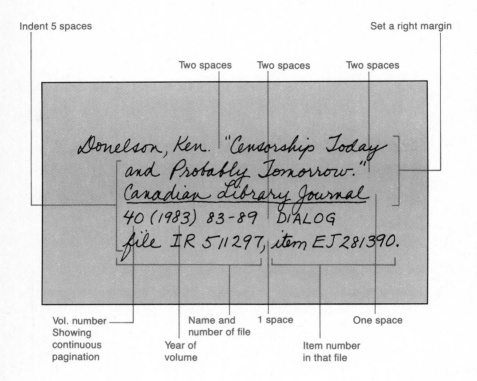

Indent 5 spaces   Set a right margin

Two spaces   Two spaces   Two spaces

Donelson, Ken. "Censorship Today and Probably Tomorrow." Canadian Library Journal 40 (1983) 83-89 DIALOG file IR 511297, item EJ281390.

Vol. number ——┘   Name and   1 space   One space
Showing   number of file
continuous   Year of   Item number
pagination   volume   in that file

Fig. 20. Preliminary citation card based on information (but not a complete text) taken from a database printout.

Periodical Indexes

Any publication that appears at regular intervals (daily, weekly, monthly, semiannually) is called a periodical, though certainly not every topic appears in every issue of a periodical. Even the journals, trade papers, or special interest magazines (such as *College English, Advertising Age,* or *American Indian Art Magazine*) do not always carry articles on the same subjects. So if you want to know in which magazine, newspaper, or journal you can find information about your research subject, you must search one or more periodical indexes.

In magazines and journals, which come out several times a year, you will find more current information than you will in books (which are often years in the writing and which usually take at least a year from manuscript completion to publication). Also, you will find a wider variety of information in periodicals than you will in books because the articles in each issue are short, precisely focused, and represent the thinking of several authors.

Conventions of entries in indexes.   In the front of each issue of a periodical index you will find a list of the periodicals represented in that publication, a key to the abbreviations used for their titles, and other information about the entries. Be sure to look at that list in each index you use, for there are variations among different indexes. Here are some conventions of entries in most periodical indexes and **what they mean to you** in preparing your preliminary citation cards.

1. **Subjects are divided and titled in as many categories as the compilers of that index believe will be necessary for you to locate information easily.**
   You may want to look under several headings to find all the material you can use on your chosen subject.

2. **The names of authors are usually recorded by surname and initials.**
   Although you will have to record them that way on your preliminary citation card, be sure that when you look at the actual article you get the full name (including first and middle names, unless the author uses initials) and record that additional information on the card. You will need *complete names* when you compile the Works Cited list.

3. **Titles are not enclosed within quotation marks and only the first word is capitalized.**
   Remember, however, that when *you* write the title of an article on your preliminary citation card (and on the Works Cited page of your research paper), it must be enclosed *within quotation marks* and the first letter of each principal word (that is, all words except articles, prepositions, and conjunctions) is *capitalized*.

4. **The index entry may contain abbreviations indicating that the piece is abridged, condensed, illustrated, or that it includes maps or diagrams.**
   Since such information is *not* entered in the Works Cited listing, there is *no need* to put it on the preliminary citation card.

5. **The title of the periodical in which a piece appears is usually abbreviated and isn't underlined though it may be italicized.**

Remember to *underline the complete title* of the periodical on your preliminary Works Cited card. Check the abbreviation listing at the beginning of the index if you're not sure of the full name of the publication.

6.   The volume number of a periodical precedes a colon and the page numbers on which the article appears.

Record the volume number *only* if the publication has continuous pagination, as explained on page 68. (However, you may want to note the volume number in the lower right corner of your preliminary citation card because in some microfilm collections the drawers holding the film rolls are labeled by volume number.)

7.   Page numbers on which an article appears will be shown in the index entry.

Record them as they appear, because they are part of all periodical Works Cited entries. Use two sets of numbers joined by a hyphen to show consecutive pages an article covers; use a plus sign (+) after the initial page number to show the article is continued on other, but not successive, pages.

8.   Publication dates are often shown in one- or two-letter abbreviations that are unacceptable for the Works Cited in the research paper.

Use the *conventional three-letter abbreviations,* followed by a period, for all months except May, June, and July (which are spelled out) when you write your preliminary Works Cited card.

Figure 21 shows a portion of the entries in a periodical index; this one is from the *Readers' Guide to Periodical Literature,* probably the best-known of the magazine indexes, and is characteristic of most periodical indexes. On page 93, features of an entry are labeled.

Magazine and journal indexes.   Periodical publications aimed at a mass audience are called **magazines.** *Newsweek, Psychology Today, Tropical Fish Hobbyist, Ebony,* or *Metropolitan Home* are examples of magazines. They may be directed toward either a general audience (as *Newsweek* is) or a specific audience (as *Metropolitan Home* is), but they usually have wide circulations through subscription and newsstand sales.

Probably the most familiar of all periodical indexes is the *Readers' Guide to Periodical Literature,* published since 1900. It indexes, by subject and author, articles appearing in more than one hundred general magazines, some of them on scientific subjects, and has a separate author listing for book reviews. Twenty-one issues of the *Readers' Guide* are published every year, monthly in February, July, and August, but semimonthly the rest of the year. These issues are put into cumulative form quarterly and annually. By all means consult the *Readers' Guide* if you think information on your selected subject is available in it. But beware that many academicians consider it inappropriate for any but the most superficial and general research material. Consider the *Readers'*

School libraries

Arkansas Library Association. Response to Concord book review committee report. *Arkansas Libr* 42:11-12 Mr '85

Authors protest Peoria ban on Blume books. *Publ Wkly* 226:21 D 7 '84

Blume books restricted in Peoria, Ill; five titles banned in Hanover, Pa. *SLJ* 31:7 Ja '85

Cole, T. W. Legal issues in library censorship cases. *Sch Libr Media Q* 13:115-22 Spr '85

Deenie is banned; ACLU appeals decision. *SLJ* 32:11-12 N '85

Defendorf, J. Censorship in the 80's and the school librarian (*In* Festschrift in honor of Dr. Arnulfo D. Trejo. University of Ariz. Graduate Lib. School 1984 p99-106) bibl

Douglas, L. An ounce of prevention: before the censor knocks. il *Ohio Media Spectrum* 37:41-2 Spr '85

Hopkins, D. M. The school library media specialist: dealing with complaints about materials. *Cathol Libr World* 56:172-4 N '84

Johnston, K. M. Working for intellectual freedom [Findlay, Ohio high school librarian] *Ohio Media Spectrum* 36:45-6 Wint '84-'85

McCracken, A. Concord: chronology of a crisis. *Arkansas Libr* 42:6-10 Mr '85

Peoria school board restores Blume books. *Publ Wkly* 226:26 D 21 '84

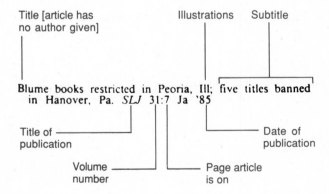

Fig. 21. Portion of a page from the *Readers' Guide to Periodical Literature* with the elements of a specific entry identified.
Reprinted by permission of H. M. Wilson Co.

Guide just *one of many* indexes in which you can find the titles and sources of articles for your preliminary citations.

Many computer databases in libraries now catalog what previously was available only in print form and required much time to work with. INFO-TRAC and Wilsonline BIP Plus are two such systems now widely used in libraries. Innovations such as laser-read computer disks, similar to the CDs that hold music (called CD-ROMs), are making more information available more quickly to library users.

Journals, generally published less frequently than most mass audience magazines, are directed toward narrow interests, often in particular professions or academic disciplines. Their circulations are usually smaller than those of magazines, but people read them for more specific information and often for reports of research in that discipline. *Personnel Journal, The Negro Educational Review, Foreign Affairs,* and *Signs (The Journal of Women in Culture and Society)* are examples of journals. Many journals are the publications of organizations in special subject areas, as are *College Composition and Communication* (the journal of the Conference on College Composition and Communication) or *The Journal of Southern History* (the publication of the Southern Historical Association).

The contents of specialized and technical periodicals (including scholarly journals) are distilled into many indexes, such as *Education Index, Art Index, Business Periodicals Index, Cumulative Index to Nursing and Allied Health Literature, Applied Science and Technology Index,* or *Book Review Digest.* Examine those indexes that seem relevant to your research subject to find possible sources of information you can record on your preliminary citation cards.

The *Social Sciences Index* and the *Humanities Index* (formerly together and at one time called the *International Index to Periodicals* and later by the cumbersome title of *A Guide to Periodical Literature in the Social Sciences and the Humanities*) are good sources of information about articles in foreign magazines and in a variety of specific and scholarly publications.

The *General Sciences Index,* one of the newest to begin publication, does not contain anything published before 1978. However, since it indexes about one hundred journals in the basic sciences (physics, biology, paleontolgy, and more), you should consult it if your research subject is scientific.

If you are curious about periodicals related to your research subject, you will be interested in looking at *Magazines for Libraries* (3rd ed., by Bill Katz and Barry G. Richards). There, labeled by subject, you will find an annotated list of 6,500 periodicals selected from 65,000 titles. Should you have occasion to write to a periodical, you could find the address, name of editor, and subscription information in *Ulrich's International Periodicals Directory.* More to your needs, however, Ulrich's tells where each periodical is listed.

You will find the titles of other periodical indexes listed under the subject headings in Appendix A, pages 279–93.

Preliminary citations from magazines and journals. Although the index entries for magazines and for journals are similar, you already know (from reading pages 67 and 68) that what you need to record on a preliminary citation card for each may vary, depending on the page numbering system each uses. Figure 22 shows a section from a magazine index with its parts identified. Then there is a model of a preliminary Works Cited card taken from one entry with *its* parts identified.

Newspaper indexes. Newspaper indexes are particularly helpful sources of information about current events or other newsworthy materials that may never appear in other kinds of periodicals. Chief among newspaper indexes is *The New York Times Index*. So many libraries have copies of *The New York Times* on microfilm that if you get some information for preliminary citation cards from this index, chances are you will be able to find the precise reference when you're ready to read it and take notes.

Many other well-known newspapers in this country are indexed (mostly since the 1970s) and copies of the papers are often available on microfilm in libraries. Among them are the *Index to the Chicago Tribune, Index to the Los Angeles Times, Index to the San Francisco Chronicle, Index to the Washington Post,* and (since 1949) *Index to the Christian Science Monitor.* Indexes to foreign papers are also available; the library you use may have *The Times* [of London] *Official Index,* and you may have occasion to consult it. And if your research subject has anything to do with business, you ought to look at the *Index to the Wall Street Journal.*

Facts on File, published weekly, is a world news digest that will give more information. It also has a cumulative index.

The Gale Directory of Publications (formerly *Ayer's*) is geographically organized and gives information about daily and weekly newspapers, such as editorship, circulation, days of publication, and advertising rates, as well as about consumer, business, technical, trade, professional, and farm magazines. One use for *Gale's* is to lead you to a way of finding out about local coverage of a news event by giving you a way to locate newspapers you might not otherwise know exist.

Preliminary citations for newspapers. *The New York Times Index* seems to be accessible to many students all over the country, so the sample of a newspaper index in Figure 23 on page 97 is taken from it. The parts identified will probably look familiar, since they are similar to those found in other periodical indexes. You can readily see in the preliminary Works Cited card taken from one entry how the relevant parts are incorporated.

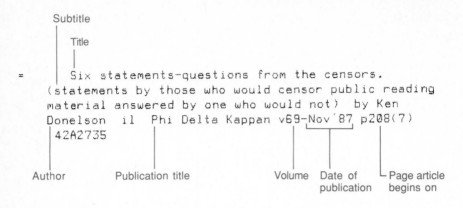

Subtitle

Title

=   Six statements-questions from the censors.
    (statements by those who would censor public reading
    material answered by one who would not) by Ken
    Donelson   il Phi Delta Kappan v69-Nov'87 p208(7)
    42A2735

Author   Publication title   Volume Date of   Page article
                                                       publication begins on

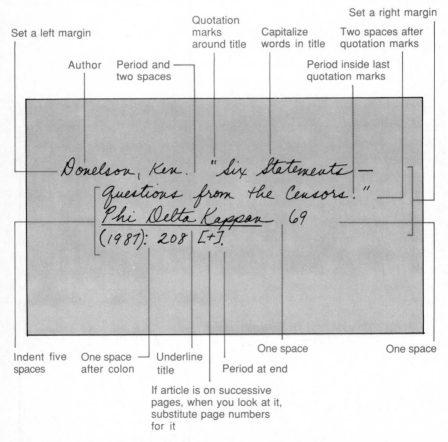

Set a right margin

Set a left margin

                                  Quotation
                                  marks   Capitalize   Two spaces after
                                  around title words in title quotation marks

        Author   Period and   Period inside last
                  two spaces   quotation marks

Donelson, Ken. "Six Statements —
questions from the Censors."
Phi Delta Kappan 69
(1987): 208 [+]

Indent five   One space — Underline   One space   One space
spaces   after colon title
                                      Period at end

If article is on successive
pages, when you look at it,
substitute page numbers
for it

Fig. 22. **Portion of a printout from a magazine index computer
          printout with the elements of a specific entry identified. The
          information taken from one of the entries is reproduced in
          this sample Works Cited card.**

Article
contains graph

Headline —— **Ministers of oil-producing nations call for emergency meetings in wake of recent sharp decline in crude oil prices**; graph; Egyptian Min Abdelhadi Kandil asks other non-OPEC nations to review situation at London meeting; 20% decline has brought average price of OPEC oil to between $13 and $14 a barrel, with Texas crude declining at slower rate; downward pressure is caused by record production rise by non-OPEC nations amid only moderate demand and widespread OPEC discounting (M), Mr 9,I,1:2

Summary of article

Designates length of —— article (M = medium)

Page and column article is on

Date of publication

Set a left margin

Section article is in

If article in paper shows author, revise card to include name first

Put headline in quotation marks

Capitalize words in title

Set a right margin

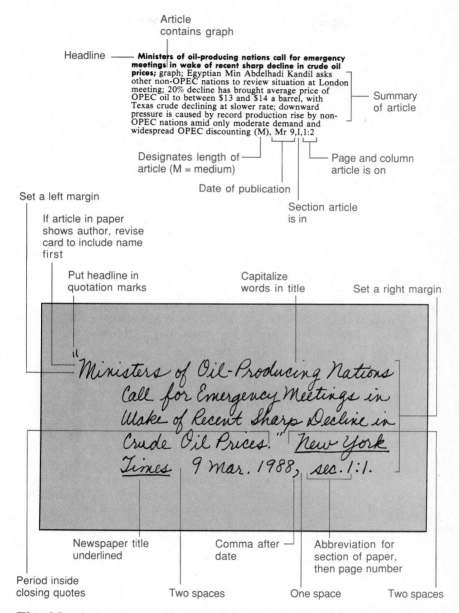

Newspaper title underlined

Comma after date

Abbreviation for section of paper, then page number

Period inside closing quotes

Two spaces

One space

Two spaces

Fig. 23. **A single entry from the *New York Times Index* (with parts identified). The important information from this entry is reproduced in a preliminary Works Cited card.**

Because the edition and section of a newspaper are often crucial in helping you locate the information you're looking for—articles sometimes appear in one edition of a paper but not in another, or locations may change depending on the urgency of news—make every effort to include edition and section details on the preliminary Works Cited card. (If you cannot find that information until you examine the actual article, add the details to your card when you *do* get them.)

More Sources of Print Information

1. **Corporations, agencies, and professional organizations** publish reports, pamphlets, booklets, charts, maps, and more materials that libraries don't know about and couldn't catalog and store if they did. Consider making arrangements to gather material you think may be relevant.

   EXAMPLES:

   Write to an auto manufacturer if you are researching auto safety.
   Contact the local airport manager about the role of the airport in the county's economy.

   If you read or hear about free offers of information, send for what seems relevant. The *Vertical File Index* will lead you to some such material.
      You cannot make preliminary citation cards for any of these resources, because you don't know what you will have to work with. If you *do* receive what you ask for, make the citation card then. Follow the forms on page 231, depending on the kind of material for which you need a Works Cited entry.

2. **Specialized library collections in museums, historical societies, legal or medical or engineering groups, and others** are available in many cities; find out if they exist where you are and, if your subject is one that lends itself to those available, take advantage of them. Make your preliminary citation cards based on what you find when you visit the collection.

3. **Interlibrary loans** are sometimes a possibility. Increasingly, consortia of college or public libraries share their resources. Electronic mail systems facilitate such exchanges.
      Be encouraged, then, to record as many references as you can from the sources available in the library where you do your primary work. Even if the specific materials are not in that library, they may still be available to you.

4. **Computer and laser disks** are carrying an increasing information load and will be more useful to you in research as the trend continues.

Much bibliographic information formerly available only on the printed page is now available in computer-usable formats. Find out from a librarian, if you don't already know, what is on disk in the library you are using for your research. A sample of how to make a Works Cited card for material from this source is on page 90.

5. **Letters from an individual or an organization** can give you certain information you want for your research paper. You must, obviously, initiate any correspondence, and you should do so with a brief letter containing *specific* questions. You stand a better chance of a response if you address a specific person within an organization by name, or at least by title. A librarian can help you locate reference material to identify the person you should address. (Vague letters to generalized groups often go into the wastebasket.)

Allow enough time for an exchange of correspondence before you have to write your paper, for you won't always receive an instantaneous response. But you may be pleasantly surprised at how many busy or well-known people are willing to take time to write someone working on a well-defined school project, and the letters you receive may result in excellent help for your research. (They may also provide you with some primary source material!)

Again, you will have to wait until receiving a response to your letter before you can make a Works Cited card, but the form to use for one is on page 231.

Sources of Nonprint Information

The notion that all research sources are in a library is certainly outmoded! You do so much learning through what you hear or what you see (in addition to reading) that you should certainly include such sources of knowledge in your search strategy. Besides, if you ever have occasion to do research in your vocation, you may discover that print sources will not be enough: you have to interview people, watch a traffic flow, or otherwise rely on information that isn't written out and stored somewhere.

The extent to which nonprint information sources are useful to you depends on the subject you're researching. But you should certainly be familiar with the kinds of material available and how to use them to your advantage.

Audiovisual Materials

Most school, college, and university libraries have collections of tape and disk audio recordings, films, slides, filmstrips, and videotapes. Increasingly, they also have computer programs, videodiscs and interactive video programs available to help students learn in a variety of disciplines. These nonprint sources may be housed in a section of the library or in a separate media center. Sometimes the holdings are listed in the library's general card catalog, but they may be cataloged separately in the media center.

The media center or audiovisual department of a school can usually order special materials for you, either through a consortium arrangement with other schools or for rental or preview. The people in charge of such orders are likely to have shelves of catalogs and indexes, too. If you can, seek help from those who know what's available.

By all means explore these nonprint sources because they will give added dimension to your research. You could, for example, use a newsreel film, a videotape, a recorded lecture, or a set of reproductions of paintings as sources of information. If your research subject is a film or the work of a director or performer, the film would be a primary source of information.

Preliminary citations for audiovisual materials.   When you make a preliminary citation card for an audiovisual resource, the element you intend to emphasize comes first. Thus, if you were citing a feature-length film, the title would take precedence. But if your paper were about the director, screenwriter, or a particular performer in the film, *that* person's name would appear first in your citation. Figure 24 shows the catalog cards for a feature-length film in 16mm film and videocassette formats and two possible preliminary citation cards for it, depending on what is most important to the particular research paper.

Certain information that is analogous to the publication information in print sources is important to listeners or viewers of nonprint materials. The distributor of a film and whether it's in black and white or color are critical; for a videotape, the width of the tape is important; for an audiotape, the speed at which it runs must be stated.

Because there are so many kinds of audiovisual materials, you should look on pages 233–39 for samples of the forms for the preliminary citation cards of the ones you locate. Then, treat the materials just as you would a printed source, taking notes and incorporating the item in the Works Cited list of your research paper.

Radio and TV Programs

Using this source for information may be elusive—but rewarding. You may not have much advance warning that something will be broadcast, maybe only that morning's newspaper. Students often discover that a television program they see by chance turns out to be helpful for their research papers. And of course you can't make a preliminary citation card for a program unless you know it is going to be aired. Therefore, you may end up listening to or watching something before deciding if it will be useful in your research—and only then writing out a Works Cited card and some notes.

```
A-V
North      Citizen Kane. [Videorecording] / RKO
VC-1979-   Radio Pictures. -- [s.l.] : Nostalgia
VC-1980    Merchant, 1978?, made 1941.
           2 cassettes, 120 min. : sd., b&w. ; 3
           /4 in.
              CREDITS: Producer and director,
           Orson Welles; orginal screenplay,
           Herman J. Mankiewicz, Orson Wells;
           music, Bernard Herrmann; photography,
           Gregg Toland.
              CAST: Orson Welles, Joseph Cotten,
           Dorothy Comingore. Agnes Moorhead, Ruth
           Warrick.
              SUMMARY: A study of a powerful
           newspaper publisher as told by those
           who knew him best, or thought they did.
              1. Feature     films. I. Welles,
           Orson, 1915-

FMMD    26 JUN 80 CR           FYMSdv
```

```
F-F130
          CITIZEN KANE [Motion picture]  Mercury Produc-
             tions.  Released by RKO Radio Pictures, c1941.
             96min.  sd.  b&w.  16mm.
             Issued in three parts.
             Summary:  The classic Orson Welles film based
          on a fictional account of the life of publisher
          William Randolph Hearst.
             1. Citizen Kane  [Motion picture]  I. Mer-
          cury Productions, inc.  Hollywood, Calif.  II.
          RKO Radio Pictures, inc.  III. Citizen Kane
          [Motion picture]
```

Welles, Orson, prod. and dir. *Citizen Kane*. With Welles, Joseph Cotten, and others. RKO, 1941.

Hermann Bernard, music. *Citizen Kane*. Prod. and dir. Orson Welles. Screenplay by Herman J. Mankiewicz and Welles. With Welles, Joseph Cotten, Agnes Moorhead, and others. RKO, 1941. 2 videocassettes.

Fig. 24. Sample catalog cards for film and video of *Citizen Kane*. Preliminary citation cards, listed by director and by musical director, are also shown.

The prevalence of home audio and video recording equipment, especially that which you can set for automatic recording, makes it easier than ever to incorporate radio and television programs into your search strategy and into your research work itself.

Preliminary citations for radio or TV programs. If you *do* know a program of use to your research will be broadcast, by all means make a preliminary citation card for it. The problem for such cards is often getting the names you ignore on the radio or that fly by on the television credits: writers, the director, and so on. You have three recourses.

1. Transcripts of some programs are available for just a few dollars and you could send for appropriate ones.
2. Call the radio or television station (if it's a local one) and ask for the names of people involved or other information to help you complete the Works Cited card as custom dictates.
3. If you know of a program in advance and record it, you can repeat an audio tape until you get the needed information or you can freeze-frame a videotape to show the names you need.

Figure 25 illustrates a typical Works Cited card for a television program. Because this was a particular episode in a series, the title of the episode is put in quotation marks and the title of the series is underlined.

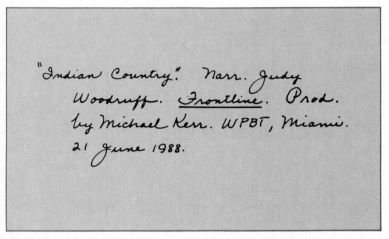

Fig. 25. Preliminary Works Cited card for a television program.

As with other audiovisual media, the order of information in your citation depends on the emphasis in your paper. Also, details of the broadcast serve as "publication information." See examples of some other forms by turning to Chapter 9, pages 235 and 236.

Interviews

Sometimes you can find published interviews with people of consequence in the subject you are researching. Occasionally you can find a recorded audio or video interview; or, you may listen to an interview on the radio or observe one on television. But the most useful kind of interview for your own research may be the one you set up yourself—either in person or over the telephone.

The person interviewed may be an expert in the field. Or, you may simply need some kind of personal response from individuals, and you can get that by setting up one or more interviews. Find people to interview by looking in the phone book for those in specific jobs or businesses and by asking people you know. At schools, on the faculty, there are bound to be specialists you can interview. For example, if you were researching the subject of airplane safety, an interview with an airline pilot or mechanic would give you insight into the subject that no reading can provide. Besides, interviews give you a primary source to work with!

The big advantage of an interview is that you can, to some degree, control the conversation. That is, you can ask the person you interview to repeat or clarify—or you can move the conversation in a different direction by the questions you ask and the responses you make during the conversation.

Make an interview worthwhile for your research by using the following guidelines:

1. Have good reasons for deciding upon the person or persons you want to interview. And know in at least a general way what kind of information you're seeking through the interview.
2. Call or write in advance for an appointment specifically for the interview.
3. Be prepared for the interview. Know the subject you will talk about (and, perhaps, the person you interview) sufficiently to ask intelligent and useful questions.
4. Prepare at least key questions in advance, and be sure you control the interview in such a way that you get responses to the questions most important to your needs.
5. Be sure to record both questions and answers accurately. A tape recording that is later transcribed is excellent, if the person you interview agrees to allow you to tape. (*Always* ask permission to tape-record a person.) Experienced interviewers use both notes *and* a tape recording for maximum accuracy—especially for any quotations you want to use.

6. After the interview, let the interviewee know what you decide to actually use in your paper, especially if you plan to use any quotations. Doing so is a courtesy to anyone who has permitted an interview.

Preliminary citations of interviews.   An interview you read or hear or observe is cited like any other material in that medium. You may or may not be able to make a preliminary citation card for such an interview, depending on whether or not you found a printed source listing it (as in a magazine article) or happened to tune in an interview on the radio.

However, an interview you conduct is cited in a slightly different way. And when you make the appointment for the interview, you can write the preliminary citation card for it. Figure 26 is an example of the format to use for a personal interview. See page 233 for the form to use for a telephone interview.

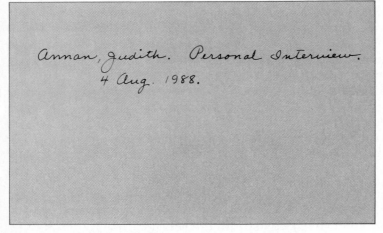

Annan, Judith. Personal Interview.
4 Aug. 1988.

Fig. 26. Preliminary Works Cited card for an interview.

If, for any reason, the day of an interview is changed, be sure to make the change on your preliminary citation card. And, of course, if the interview is canceled, discard the card.

Lectures and Speeches

You may have occasion to attend a lecture or speech (or hear one broadcast or listen to a recording) that relates to the subject you selected to research. Consider it part of your research. You may even have the opportunity to ask questions of the speaker either as part of an open forum or informally after the presentation.

Recording during a live presentation is usually prohibited, but you should plan on taking complete and careful notes. Listen particularly closely for points the speaker makes that are most relevant to your research concerns. If you are listening to or watching a recording, you have the option of a second or third hearing or viewing.

Preliminary citations of lectures and speeches. Make a preliminary citation card if you know in advance that you will be listening to a lecture or speech related to your research work. If you don't know beforehand, make the Works Cited card after you hear the presentation.

Obviously, there is no publication information on an oral presentation. However, the more information you can give, the more useful will be the citation to a subsequent reader of your research paper. For example, if the speech was a Keynote Presentation or a Closing Address, note it on your citation. Figure 27 illustrates a preliminary citation card that you may use as a model for your own work. Also, see page 235 in Chapter

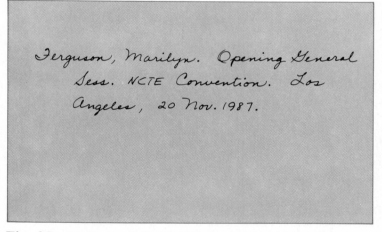

Ferguson, Marilyn. Opening General Sess. NCTE Convention. Los Angeles, 20 Nov. 1987.

Fig. 27. Preliminary Works Cited card for a speech or lecture.

Questionnaires, Surveys, and Polls

One kind of primary and original research you may wish to use is a questionnaire, survey, or poll that you prepare, administer, and evaluate. Rarely do you have time to develop extensive statistics or write a computer program to handle the data and produce usable results, though that may be your object or inclination. At any rate, you should consider using these methods of gathering information if you think one will be helpful to your research and to the paper you will write. Much of the value of a questionnaire, survey, or poll depends on carefully framed questions and on the people you select to answer those questions, so choose both carefully.

If you seek written responses to a questionnaire, technically you are probably using a written source. But for purposes of this book, you may consider a questionnaire among the more "exotic" sources of information. The category into which you put it is less important than the material for your research paper you can develop from it.

Preliminary citations for questionnaires.   Write a preliminary citation card when you decide to develop a questionnaire, survey, or poll. You may use slightly different forms, depending on whether it was answered anonymously or by people who signed their names. Of course, if many people answer your questions, you can't cite them all as sources. And, in fact, you yourself are the author if you use an original questionnaire. Figure 28 shows the form of a citation card for a questionnaire; use the same form for a survey or a poll. Also see page 234.

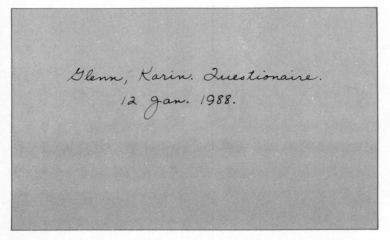

Glenn, Karin. Questionaire.
12 Jan. 1988.

Fig. 28. Preliminary Works Cited card for a questionnaire.

Videodiscs and Interactive Video

New technology makes new demands on the researcher, both in finding appropriate material and in citing its use. As the educational community embraces videodiscs and interactive video, more resources in those media will become available.

A videodisc looks like a phonograph record, but coded on it are motion pictures. Together with a computer, they comprise "interactive video" because controlling both the computer and the videodisc enables a person to move from one to the other. Increasingly, programs for this new medium are being developed, and before long you will be able to look for resources on them that will help you complete a successful research paper.

Citations for videodiscs and interactive video.   A preliminary Works Cited card can be made for a videodisc alone or for an interactive video program. Since these are similar to computer software and to video sources, the Works Cited card draws from both those sources. Figure 29 shows what such a card might look like.

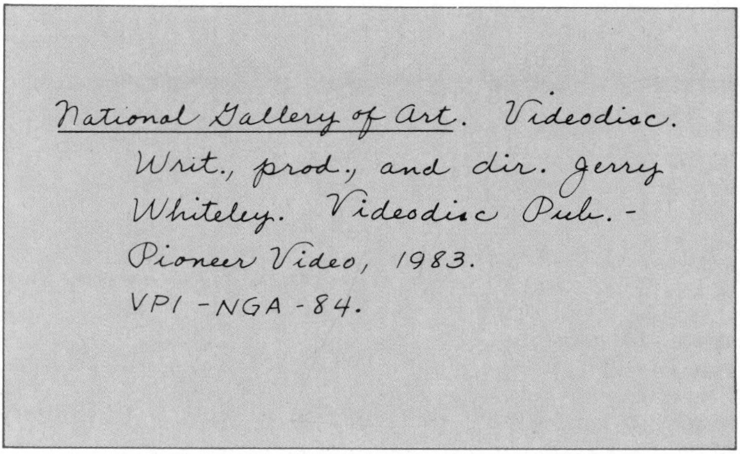

National Gallery of Art. Videodisc.
Writ., prod., and dir. Jerry
Whiteley. Videodisc Pub. -
Pioneer Video, 1983.
VPI - NGA - 84.

Fig. 29. **Preliminary Works Cited card for a videodisc.**

A Final Check and Search Strategy Record

Use the following "Search Strategy Record" to make visible a framework within which you can start looking for information for your research paper.

Given the wide array of resources, both print and nonprint, both inside a library and outside it, you will have much to choose from, so exercise your selectivity when it is time to read what appears to be the most promising sources for your research.

Also, use the Search Strategy Record sheet to check up on your readiness to move ahead in the next step of the research process. For instance, you can do one or more of the following:

- Make sure you have fulfilled the requirements of the assignment. For instance, if you were supposed to include both magazines and journals as resources and you didn't locate any journals, ascertain that now. If it was an oversight, you can immediately rectify it; if there were no relevant journal articles, you should confer with your instructor about the problem.
- Share your preliminary citation cards with someone who knows the contents of this book and your classroom assignment. That way, you can get an outside view of your research paper work thus far.

RESEARCH PAPER SEARCH STRATEGY RECORD

SUBJECT: _____

AUDIENCE: _____

	Date Checked	Anything Useful?	
General Reference Information			
Encyclopedias	_____	Yes _____	No _____
Reference Books & Indexes	_____	Yes _____	No _____
Bibliographies	_____	Yes _____	No _____
Abstracting Services	_____	Yes _____	No _____
Handbooks	_____	Yes _____	No _____
Other	_____	Yes _____	No _____
Card Catalog	_____	Yes _____	No _____
Periodical Indexes			
Magazines	_____	Yes _____	No _____
Journals	_____	Yes _____	No _____
Newspapers	_____	Yes _____	No _____
Computer Database Search	_____	Yes _____	No _____
(Which one(s)? _____)			
Nonprint Sources			
Audiovisual Materials	_____	Yes _____	No _____
(Which kind? _____)			

Radio or TV Programs   _____ Yes ____ No ____

Interviews: Appointments Made?   _____ Yes ____ No ____

Lectures and Speeches   _____ Yes ____ No ____

Questionnaires, Surveys, Polls: Plans Made?   _____ Yes ____ No ____

Videotapes/Videodiscs   _____ Yes ____ No ____

Audio Disks/Tapes   _____ Yes ____ No ____

Other Sources

Those Sought? _____ on _____

_____ on _____

_____ on _____

POSSIBLE PRIMARY SOURCES (list below)

Chapter 5

Recording Information

At last you're ready to take down some information from all the potential sources you identified by searching out materials. Again, you will be able to use time more effectively if you record information in an organized rather than a haphazard way.

A good method is to record information from materials in the same order that you pursued your Search Strategy. Therefore, begin by reading one or more relevant entries in encyclopedias and other general reference works. Then, assemble some of the books and articles you listed on the preliminary citation cards. Most people find it easier to take notes from print rather than from nonprint sources, so if you follow this order, by the time you get to films, interviews, and other nonprint sources, you will be a more adept notetaker.

Reading to Take Notes

Effective readers use different methods for different purposes of reading. You might read a light fiction book very quickly, but you probably read new material for a class quite slowly in order to learn it. You also need to acquire the habit of reading resources in different ways, depending on your purpose.

Previewing

Previewing means to get an overview, a feel for your subject. Don't try to take notes as soon as you open a book or turn to a newspaper article. Instead, begin by getting familiar with the subject you are going to read about. You do so by previewing a selection of materials you will be reading.

- **Read the tables of contents of several books** to see what this subject you are researching is all about.
- **Look through the indexes of several books** to discover the specifics that might be included in your subject.

When you are ready to start detailed reading, use previewing techniques to find out what to focus on so you can take notes most effectively.

- **Read over the table of contents of each book before you start to work with it.**
- **Look at prefaces, forewords, glossaries, indexes, and appendices** before examining the content of a book. In short, know the structure of the work you are going to read.
- **Pay attention to chapter titles, headings, and subheadings before reading selections so you will know what is coming.**
- **Discover the organization of what you are about to read.** You can follow a train of thought or a line of reasoning if you are able to anticipate by understanding the structure an author has used in a work.
- **Look at beginnings and endings, at introductions and conclusions of whole works and units within them.**

Take the time to preview your resource materials and you will not only begin to define your subject field, but you will also be able to read more effectively. Then, later, you won't spend time on what isn't essential to your needs.

Skimming

Skimming means to look through a work quickly in order to get an *overall impression* of it. Skimming serves two purposes:

1. to get at the main idea of a selection and see it as a whole without undue attention to its details, which may distract;
2. to tell if there is enough relevant information in the source to read more closely. If there isn't, you've saved yourself time.

Skimming is particularly important when you have an entire book to go through and need to find the specific information from it that will be useful.

Use the table of contents or index to locate the information by pages; then skim them to decide whether or not the contents warrant additional reading.

Scanning

In scanning, you look for *specific information* quickly, without reading word by word or, in better reading technique, phrase by phrase. When you scan, look for *key words,* names, dates, or other specifics that indicate you have found information to take notes on. Rather than stop to read everything on a page slowly and carefully, scan until you come to information that indicates you should pay close attention.

You have to know in advance what you're looking for in order to scan effectively; you will know by skimming first if what you're looking for is in a particular source.

Evaluating Source Materials

The materials in a library have already been evaluated on several scores. First of all, they wouldn't have been published without being scrutinized and deemed worthy of being printed. Second, they have been evaluated by librarians before purchase, usually on the basis of reviews. Third, if you are working at a school library, recommendations for acquisition have been made additionally by faculty or other qualified persons.

You will need to make evaluations at two stages of recording information for your research paper: before you read something and while you are reading it. Also, the more closely you evaluate material, the more refined you make your judgment and thus the more you hone your independent thinking abilities.

The following are some questions you can use as guides to evaluating materials. (You can also use them to help you make annotations on your citation cards; see pages 253–54 for an explanation.)

Before You Read

1. Which authors seem outstanding in the field?
If some names recur as you gather information, it's a safe assumption that those people are probably experts in the field and thus reliable sources of information.

EXAMPLE:

> Carol Matz, author of the sample research paper that begins on page 257, discovered that only the name of Ken [Kenneth] Donelson appeared

twice in her sources (though it did appear in articles on book, but not specifically library, censorship). She also saw his name on articles in indexes but not available in the library where she did research. She therefore inferred that he was someone who studies censorship enough to write about it often; he must be outstanding in the field.

An author's credentials may be a useful guide to his or her standing in a field. For instance, an article on merchandising by a department store executive or one on Mars soil experiments by a NASA geologist is likely to be authoritative.

Where can you find out about an author? Many journals identify authors briefly by stating an academic affiliation and previous publications. You can also learn something about an author's work by checking a biographical reference book such as *Who's Who in America, Contemporary Authors, Biography and Genealogy Master Index,* or similar sources. (Donelson, a professor at Arizona State University, is, at this writing, a member of the Standing Committee Against Censorship of the National Council of Teachers of English.)

2.   *What is the date of publication?*

While all that is new is not necessarily better, more recent materials are likely to summarize or be based on earlier works. Some will also lead you to works previously published. Read materials in the order of their publication to help see a development of ideas.

EXAMPLE:

Issues of censorship have been with us since the founding of the United States (and prompted some parts of the Constitution), but not until after the push of students' rights movements in the 1960s did writing about censorship take on its present complexion. As more citizens' groups demanded increasing control of curricula, censorship issues extended to the public schools, and therefore more articles about that aspect of censorship appeared with the 1960s and early 1970s.

Some scientific and technical fields (such as computer technology) change so quickly that finding recent materials may be a prime consideration for your research study. Or, a research subject may depend on reaction to a book at the time it was published or to an event when it took place.

Remember, too, the time lag between writing and publication is often a matter of years, especially for books and journal articles.

3.   *How credible does a source seem? Does the publisher have a good reputation?*

If a resource or a publisher is unfamiliar to you, ask your instructor or a librarian about the company. Authors sometimes contract with book publishers to bring out their own works. (Teachers and librarians can usually tell you the names of some of these "vanity presses.") But you can assume that a work published by someone other than the author has enough quality and credibility for a company to have put out money to publish the work. Although some privately published works are of high quality, there is a difference between paying to have your own work put into print and somebody else thinking enough of it to lay out the money.

Also, some publishers have known biases that might be reflected in the work they put out, so it's helpful to be aware of bias.

EXAMPLE:

>An article in a magazine published by a particular religious denomination will probably reflect the theological attitudes of that denomination.

Magazines for Libraries and the *Classified List of Periodicals for the College Library* are two reference sources that librarians use to determine the bias, authority, and credibility for specific periodicals; you could consult them for the same information.

How a book was received by the critics is another guide to credibility. You can find publication reviews in *Book Review Digest*. Be aware, though, that the responses you read may influence your own.

The **documentation an author provides** to support statements is another measure of a source's credibility. If at least some of that documentation is from primary sources, it is likely to be more credible than if most of it had passed through many hands (or sources).

The completeness of material in the introduction, preface, index, and bibliography of a book is further evidence of scholarship and, therefore, of credibility of a source.

If your resource for information is a person, make sure it is someone qualified to give what you're looking for. You may get opinions about the need for a piece of state legislation from interviewing shoppers on a downtown street, but if you interview legislators who voted for *and* against the legislation, you are more likely to get informed opinions—and, therefore, credibility.

When You Read

1. What does the language of a source tell you?

Language reveals something of the beliefs and attitudes of the writer, and if you are properly attuned you may be able to learn more from your source than is immediately apparent.

The audience addressed by a source, whether specialized or lay, is also a clue to the kind of material you encounter.

Language that is obviously slanted might affect your use of the material—
or the use you want to make of it. Discovering bias in a work doesn't mean
that you must distrust the source or not use it; it simply means that you
should be aware of the bias when using the source or making judgments
about it.

2.   *Which sources seem to give you the most information?*
Some reference materials will tell you more than others about the subject
you're researching. Also, some are especially provocative and lead you to think
about issues or ideas you might otherwise not have considered. Others are
valuable because they suggest additional sources you might decide to consult.

3.   *What facts keep reappearing in your reading?*
If information is repeated in several sources, it is probably particularly
important. (It may also be "common knowledge" and thus doesn't need
specific documentation, as explained on pages 129–130 of this chapter.) Once
you have a sense of recurring facts from your preview reading of several
sources, you can also tell if something that seems standard is omitted. If it is,
perhaps the source that doesn't include it is less reliable than others.

Qualities of Good Notes

The quality of a research paper can only be as good as the notes on which it
is based. Several weeks or even months may elapse between the time you
write notes and the time you use them to write your research paper. Social
events, other studies, all sorts of distractions will intervene. Therefore, you
should be especially careful to take notes you can read and work from with
ease. Unreadable or garbled notes are worse than useless, and redoing them
will waste your time and effort. But if your notes are legible, accurate, and
complete, they will serve you well.

Legibility

Here are suggestions to help you prepare legible and useful notes.

1.   *Take notes on 4 × 6-inch cards*   unless you are going to do so on a
computer database or your instructor specifies otherwise. Cards are easy to
arrange and rearrange as you work; this size has enough room to accommodate most notes. Even if you've never taken notes on cards, do so now; it will
pay off.

2.   *Take notes in ink,*   unless you are typing or using a computer. Pencil
writing may smudge or become difficult to read after much handling.

3. ***Write on only one side of a card;*** it facilitates arranging them later. Use the reverse side only to finish a statement or complete a quotation. Should you need additional cards for an especially long note, identify each card in the series by number and author and staple them together in order.

4. ***Put only*** **one** idea ***on a card.*** The less complicated the wording on a card, the easier it is to work with when you need to arrange ideas for your outline and writing.

5. ***Use whatever abbreviations you find convenient for notes,*** as long as they make sense to you all the time. Many people have developed symbols and abbreviations they use in taking class or lecture notes; use what you're comfortable with. Just be sure to be consistent. If you use the letter G as a private abbreviation for "Goethe" one day, be sure you don't use it as an abbreviation for "God" on another day.

Accuracy

When you're ready to write your research paper, you will have only your notes to work from. Therefore, they must reflect precisely the information you obtained from your research sources. Here are some suggestions to help you prepare accurate notes.

1. ***Read your research material carefully.*** That may sound like elementary advice, but distortions and misrepresentations result when material is misread. One word mistakenly substituted for another in reading can change the whole meaning of a passage—and possibly of an entire portion of your paper.

2. ***Record precisely.*** Emphasize only what the source of information emphasized; don't second-guess or misrepresent an author's words. Be especially careful to *check wording and spelling* when you work with materials that are unfamiliar or highly technical.

EXAMPLES:

      Differentiate between *entomology* and *etymology.* The words may look and sound similar, but there's a world of difference between them.

or

      Affect and *effect* are words people often confuse. Be sure you write down the correct one, especially if your note card is a quotation.

3. ***Distinguish among fact, inference, and opinion.***

- *A fact* is a statement that can be verified by evidence from the senses: something a person can see, hear, taste, touch, or smell.

- *An inference* is an educated guess based on at least one, but usually on several, facts.

- *An opinion* expresses a belief held by an individual, but is not observable or verifiable.

You should be able to distinguish among these three when you take notes in case you need to call upon that information when you write your paper. Either use the letters *F* or *I* or *O* enclosed in a small circle or write out the whole words at the lower left corner of the note card.

Be sure to indicate if statements on note cards are *your own* opinion or belief rather than those of a source you consulted. You wouldn't want to mislead your readers and let them think an inference or an opinion comes from published writing or from the words of another person when, in fact, it comes from you. Writing "personal comment" at the bottom of a note card (as explained on pages 127–28) is one way of doing this.

4. Use conventional mechanics of spelling, capitalization, and punctuation when you write your note cards so that you can easily transfer what you need to the draft of your research paper.

Completeness

If your notes are legible and accurate, they will probably also be as complete as they ought to be. It is frustrating to discover, while you are writing a paper late at night, that important information is missing because you failed to write it down. And you've wasted time if you have to look at a source again to clarify some point you didn't bother with initially.

Write down everything you think you need (and later discard any excess note cards) rather than find you must make another trip to the library. (The call letter or number of a book or the location notation on each preliminary citation card will help you locate materials quickly if you *should* have to recheck them.)

1. Identify the source of what appears on each card.
The top right-hand corner is a convenient place to note that information because it can be seen easily. Write the **author's last name** alone if you have only one work by that person to consult; otherwise, use both the name and a title. Identify other materials by **title or a shortened form of it. Dates of periodicals** will be helpful for quick identification.

2. Note the page numbers from which you obtained information by putting them in the top right-hand corner.
Then you can easily write documentation in the text of your research paper. Be sure to record all page numbers from which you got specific information, even if you are summarizing a long passage.

If you use a *quotation that goes from one page to another,* note on your card where one page ends and another begins so you can be accurate in documenting the passage. A virgule or diagonal line (/) is conventional for the purpose. (See an example of this in Figure 32 on page 127.)

3. *Identify the subject of each card in the top left-hand corner.*
The sample note cards in this chapter will serve as illustrations. Using these key words or "slugs" (after the printing term) will simplify the later work of organizing your notes. Then, instead of having to read through each note card for contents, you will be able to tell at a glance what each contains and easily arrange the cards in any desired order.

Conventions of Writing Notes

Readers expect to see certain customs followed when they read quotations, punctuation, italics, and spelling in a research paper. The easiest way to be sure your audience is not disappointed or surprised is to follow those customs or conventions from the start of your writing—the notes you take for your research paper.

Spelling, of course, is easy enough. If you encounter unfamiliar words in the sources you consult, write the accurate spelling in your notes and it will always be before you. You can rely on your dictionary for help with other words.

Punctuation should also pose no special problems. If in doubt, consult a handbook or a composition text. Some dictionaries also contain a section on general punctuation conventions.

The following list gives you the conventions that apply to some special problems you may encounter in taking notes. If you follow them in writing note cards, you will find that writing your research paper goes more smoothly.

1. *Quotations.*
All wording taken completely from a written or spoken source *must be acknowledged in two ways:*

   a. by enclosing the words in quotation marks

   and

   b. by crediting the source.

(Figure 32 on page 127 is an example of a note card containing a quotation and showing the proper form to use.) Making the proper acknowledgment on your note card is one way of preventing inadvertent plagiarism, a matter discussed more fully on pages 130–32.

Quoted phrases may appear anywhere within a sentence, as long as the sentence makes sense.

When you write the text of your paper, *quotations of four or fewer typed lines* will be incorporated within the text. Longer quotations *are indented in the text of your paper.* See examples on pages 179 and 181.

2. *Quotations at page breaks.*

If the passage you want to quote continues from one page to another, *indicate the page change with a virgule* (slash mark) after the last word on the page. Also, *write both page numbers* at the top right corner where you record the source. (Figure 32 on page 127 shows how to do that.)

3. *Quotations within quotations.*

You will, of course, use the usual double marks that show a quotation. If the source you are quoting contains a quotation you want to include, signal that fact by using single quote marks within the double ones. Use the same system in your notes and in your research paper.

EXAMPLE: Justice Abe Fortas wrote, for the Supreme Court,
             "Students in school as well as out of school are
             'persons' under our Constitution."
                  (Snyder 132)

To see how this passage was incorporated into the final text of the sample research paper, see page 271.

4. *Punctuation for quotations.*

Use conventional punctuation for both your notes and the written text of your paper. That is, quotations within a sentence are separated by a comma from your own words unless the quotation is part of the main portion of the sentence.

EXAMPLE: "What's 'good for us,'" according to P.E.N.
             reports, "differs greatly from community to
             community."
                  (Kakutani)

5. *Poetry quotations.*

For short passages, use virgules with a space on each side to indicate the end of each poetic line; retain the capitalization and punctuation of the original poem. Quotation marks must, of course, also be used.

EXAMPLE: "Busy old fool, unruly sun, / Why dost thou
             thus, / Through windows, and through curtains,
             call on us?"

If a line you are quoting begins at a point other than the left margin of the poem, imitate the spacing or use ellipses.

If the poetry you want to quote will take *more than three lines* when you write it in the final text of your research paper, you must *follow the typography of the poem* you are quoting. Therefore, copy the poetry onto your note card exactly as it appears on the printed page that is your source. (Long lines across a page may require you to make such accommodations as recording on paper rather than on a card.) Do not use quotation marks unless they are in the original; then, change those to single quote marks.

6. *Words omitted from a quotation.*

If you decide to omit a word, phrase, sentence, or paragraph from a passage you are quoting, such omission cannot violate the sense of the original wording or idea. You must indicate that something is left out. Do so by replacing the omitted words with an **ellipsis:** three periods with a space before and after each one.

EXAMPLE: "The main counterforce to book banning must
             . . . rest upon political action, particularly
             at the local level" (Dorsen 191).

If the words you want to omit in a quotation come at the end of a sentence you write, put the period that marks the end of the sentence and then the three spaced periods of the ellipses.

EXAMPLE: Dorsen points out (191) that citizens must begin
             to act in their own communities because "The
             main counterforce to book banning must . . .
             rest upon political action. . . ."

             or

             Dorsen points out that citizens must begin to
             act in their own communities because "The main
             counterforce to book banning must . . . rest
             upon political action . . ." (191).

7. *Titles within sources.*

The source materials you use may show book, story, or film titles in italics, in quotation marks, or in boldface type. However, you should write all titles in your notes the same way you will write them in the final text of your paper rather than try to emulate the original source.

That is, if you write in your notes the names of books, plays, pamphlets, long poems, periodicals, films, computer software, record albums, radio or television programs, paintings or sculptures, or even spacecraft—underline them. If such titles are within a passage you are quoting, retain the underlining. Exceptions are the titles of sacred writing, such as the Bible, the Koran, or the Talmud, which are not underlined.

Put in quotation marks the titles of short stories, poems, essays, chapters in books, newspaper or magazine articles, songs, lectures or speeches, and individual episodes of radio and television series. Retain that convention when you write your paper. However, sections of sacred writing, such as the names of books in the Bible, are excepted from this custom.

8. *Italicized or foreign words.*

If a word within a quotation is in italics, underline it in your notes and in the text of your research paper. If you write or quote a foreign word or phrase, underline it in your notes and in your paper, even though it does not appear that way in your source.

9. *Interpolations.*

An interpolation is an interrupter you supply to the text of a quotation or to your own wording as you write. **Enclose an interpolation in square brackets** both in your notes and in the text of your research paper. Most computer keyboards and some typewriter keyboards have the square brackets on them. If yours does not, draw the brackets in by hand.

The following three examples show some of the reasons you may want to make an interpolation.

    a. **To relate a pronoun to its antecedent noun** when the noun doesn't appear in the quoted passage.

EXAMPLE: "They [students] may have to go to court to prove that the action was not disruptive."

            (Snyder 133)

    b. **To show that something is copied accurately, even though it's wrong.** The word *sic,* meaning "so" or "thus," is evidence that you are aware something in your paper is wrong (such as spelling or punctuation), but that you have copied it accurately. Sometimes printing errors do occur, but you must not correct them; just copy what you see and indicate to your own audience that you recognize the error.

EXAMPLE: "Many resent [sic] right to know cases come to
             mind."

c. **To express a personal comment.** Your comment can clarify an idea
   or wording drawn from some other source, or it can merely be a
   remark that comes to mind when you are writing the note. Include
   your comment by putting it in square brackets in your notes. You
   may, however, choose to omit that comment in writing the paper.

EXAMPLE: "I will read this most vile of all pieces of so-
             called literature aloud [Vonnegut's irony was in
             full force by then—he was talking about the
             Constitution] so that those who dare can feel
             the full force of it."
                          (<u>Publisher's Weekly</u>)

Taking Notes

Once you have previewed some materials to get an overview of your research subject and have skimmed some specific materials gathered from your preliminary citation cards to judge their usefulness, you are ready to begin another task. Now is the time to read and take notes on those sources that seem to be worthwhile. Concurrently, you will probably also want to begin interviews or use other nonprint resources for which you have preliminary citation cards. Take notes in the same ways from any of these sources.

You can take any of the four basic kinds of notes: **summary, paraphrase, direct quotation,** or **personal comment.** A **combination** of two or more is another possibility.

Remember that each single note card will be limited to just one idea. You have already read about two kinds of identification to put on each note card. Now it's time to add a third:

- top left corner: slug line identifying subject of card
- top right corner: author and/or title and page number(s) of material on the card
- bottom right corner: the kind of note on that card

Putting these identifications on each card will save you from trying to decide later if the note is a summary or a paraphrase, and so on—and where you got the information from.

Summary Notes

A summary is *a statement in your own words of the main idea of a passage.* It tells *only what the author has said* and may *not include your own interpretation or comment* on the meaning. (Save those for personal comment note cards or clearly mark your additional comment on a summary note card.) Follow the organization or order of the original source in a summary.

Use summary notes to record

- a general idea, or
- a large amount of information succinctly.

When you write a summary, a page in the original may become a paragraph in your notes, and a paragraph may become a sentence or a few words on your note card. Therefore, summary notes are particularly useful—and widely used—because they pack a lot of content into a little space.

In order to write a successful summary note, you must separate what is most important from what is less important in a passage. Making that distinction is partly a reading skill. (If you've ever had a reading course or studied reading in an English course, you will have learned how to distinguish main ideas from their supporting statements.) Making the distinction is also closely related to writing skill, for every time you compose a main idea (or thesis) and develop it, you are using the same skills.

Here is an example of a paragraph from a book found in research for the sample research paper on pages 257–78. Figure 30 illustrates how the student writing the paper made a summary note.

EXAMPLE:

Original Passage

The difficulties in seeking relief through the courts should not be underestimated. School library facilities are limited and hence a selection has to be made. Legitimate reasons for excluding or removing books are manifold. Decisions by the school authorities necessarily involve judgments on the contents of the book, the merit of the ideas expounded, and the establishment of priorities in subject matter and form. And the individual decisions made day by day are almost without number.

(Norman Dorsen, ed. *Our Endangered Rights,*
New York: Pantheon, 1984, 191.)

Summary

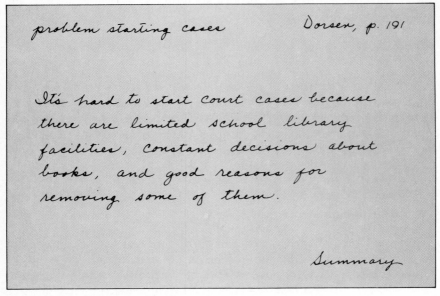

problem starting cases   Dorsen, p. 191

It's hard to start court cases because
there are limited school library
facilities, constant decisions about
books, and good reasons for
removing some of them.

                                                    Summary

Fig. 30. Summary note card

Comment.   The paragraph states several reasons that schools don't usually start court cases about removal of materials from their libraries. The essence of the paragraph is caught in one sentence for the note card. The student can expand on this idea if she wishes in writing the research paper, but she is sure the words (expanded or not) will be her own.

Writing summaries in complete sentences is a good idea because of the practice that doing so affords. However, a summary note is a reminder of material you will probably—but not definitely—include in the text of your research paper. Don't feel that you are held in any way to the wording you put on a note card (unless it's a quotation). When you begin to draft your paper, you may want to change the wording on a summary note card; feel free to do so.

Paraphrase Notes

A paraphrase is *a statement in your own words, phrase by phrase, of the original passage.* Because it follows the original so closely, it has the same organization and is also approximately the same length. *Do not interpret* material in paraphrasing; just restate it.

Paraphrasing is particularly useful in

- translating technical passages or other specialized information into lay language (or other language that is appropriate to your audience and helpful to your own understanding), or

- exploring the meaning of poetry by "expanding" poetic expression into prose, or

- making sure you understand exactly what an author said.

If you select a passage for paraphrasing, examine each phrase and thought carefully; then write each in your own words. Remember that a paraphrase is *a complete rewriting,* not just a game of rearranging words.

Figure 31 shows a paraphrase on a note card; it was written by the student whose sample research paper appears on pages 257–78.

Paraphrase

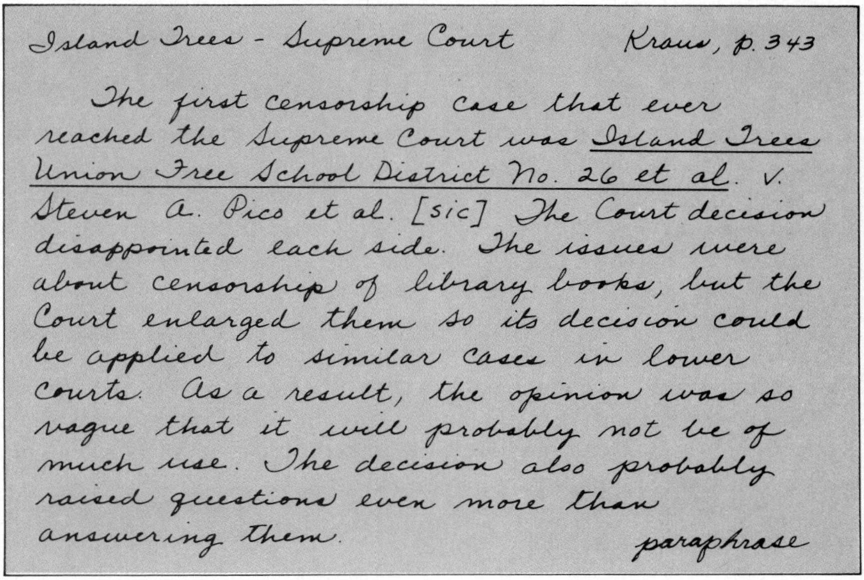

Island Trees – Supreme Court   Kraus, p. 343

The first censorship case that ever reached the Supreme Court was <u>Island Trees Union Free School District No. 26 et al.</u> v. <u>Steven A. Pico et al.</u> [sic] The Court decision disappointed each side. The issues were about censorship of library books, but the Court enlarged them so its decision could be applied to similar cases in lower courts. As a result, the opinion was so vague that it will probably not be of much use. The decision also probably raised questions even more than answering them.

                                          paraphrase

Fig. 31. Paraphrase note card

EXAMPLE:

Original Passage

Island Trees Union Free School District No. 26 et al. v. Steven A. Pico et al. was the first case dealing with censorship issues to reach the Supreme Court. The results of the Court's deliberation were generally disappointing to each side. As usual, the specific issues in the case were very narrow in scope, revolving around the question of censorship of library books. However, Supreme Court decisions are generally broadened in the application to related cases in lower courts. The vague opinion in *Island Trees v. Pico* will, in all probability, be of little use in this regard. Furthermore, the decision raised as many, if not more, questions than it answered. This paper will examine the questions the case did answer and those raised, but not answered, by the decision.

(Larry L. Kraus, "Censorship: What *Island Trees v. Pico* Means to Schools," *Clearing House* 57 (Apr. 1984) 343.)

Comment.   This is a tightly worded paragraph and thus not easy to state in your own words. (Well-written material is *usually* harder to paraphrase than weak writing in which the wording is less specific and the sentence structure looser.) The paraphrase does follow the original sentence by sentence. However, the last sentence of the original is omitted because in it the author tells what he will do in the remainder of the article; that information isn't needed in your notes because you will use the main idea of the paragraph in other ways within your research paper.

Paraphrased notes are often preferable to summaries because they are more detailed and specific. They are often preferable to quotations because the text is in your own words rather than in someone else's, thus ensuring that the wording of your paper will be original and in your own style.

Because a paraphrased note is so close to the original, you should give it proper documentation (explained in Chapter 8) in the text of your paper; the people whose ideas and opinions you refer to deserve credit.

There isn't much to gain by paraphrasing some passages rather than summarizing them. The choice of which kind of note to take is based on personal preference and what you think you might use in your research paper. However, the paraphrase can always be turned into a summary when you write your paper, although the opposite isn't true.

Direct Quotation Notes

A direct quotation *copies exactly what your source said or wrote* and is therefore the easiest kind of note card to write. Taking direct quotation notes requires absolute fidelity to the written word (down to every comma or misspelling in the print) or to the spoken word.

Take direct quotation notes if

- the style of your source is so perfect, so suitable, or so vivid it seems beyond changing, or
- the material is so significant or controversial that wording must be exact, or

- the source is so authoritative you want to be sure not to violate the precision of the wording, or

- the wording of the source needs to be transmitted with absolute accuracy.

Follow carefully the customs regarding quotations as described on pages 118–22 of this chapter in the section headed "Conventions of Writing Notes." Figure 32 is an example of a note card of a quotation.

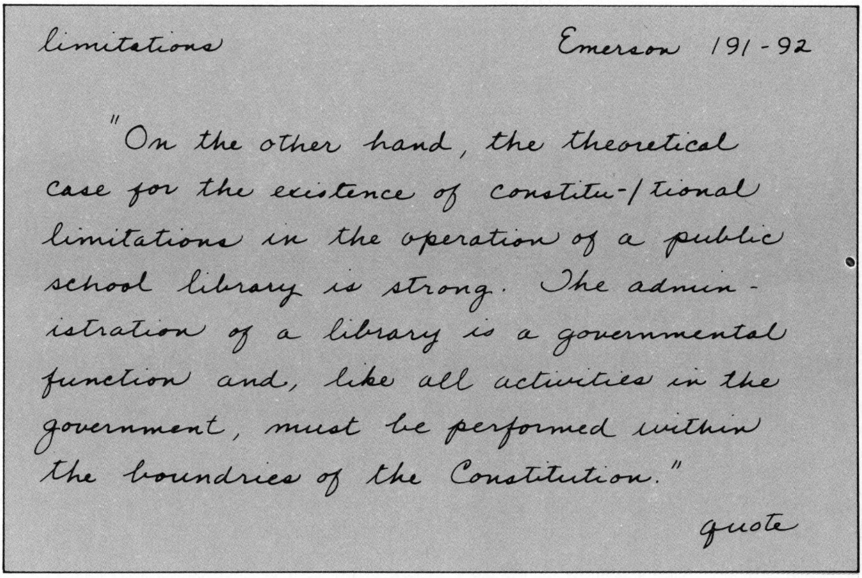

> *limitations*   *Emerson 191 - 92*
>
> "On the other hand, the theoretical case for the existence of constitu-/tional limitations in the operation of a public school library is strong. The admin-istration of a library is a governmental function and, like all activities in the government, must be performed within the boundries of the Constitution."
>
> *quote*

Fig. 32. Quotation on a note card (showing quote on two pages)

Resist using direct quotation notes unless there is good reason because the more note cards with quotations you have, the more tempting it is to overuse quotations in your research paper. Then, instead of being an original piece of writing, the paper easily becomes a cut-and-paste collection of other people's words. Furthermore, in a paper overloaded with other people's words (and their styles of writing) your own sense of person can't come through.

Personal Comment Notes

Your own thoughts on your research subject are particularly important while you are taking notes because

- they catch your own insights quickly and preserve them in writing for your future use, and

■ they help you make the synthesis between what you discover about your subject and your own ideas—the basis of a research paper.

Record all these thoughts, opinions, and fleeting notions on note cards rather than leaving them to memory or to random scraps of paper. Use essentially the same form for your own comments that you do for other note cards, except that you can't have a title source in the upper right corner. However, write *"personal"* in the lower right corner as a reminder that the contents of that card are original. Figure 33 shows a personal comment note for the sample research paper on page 257–78.

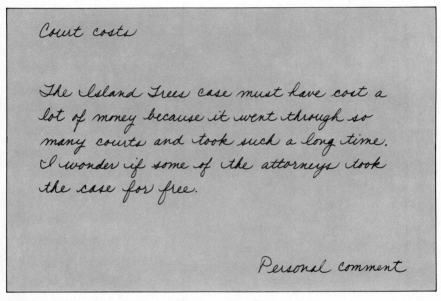

Court costs

The Island Trees case must have cost a lot of money because it went through so many courts and took such a long time. I wonder if some of the attorneys took the case for free.

Personal comment

Fig. 33. **Personal comment note card**

Combination Notes

You can combine summary, paraphrase, quotation, or personal comment notes in any way that is workable for you. Just be sure to note the source at the top right, so you can give accurate attribution, and record at the lower right what form of note the card is. The next passage is followed, in Figure 34, by a combination note card written from it.

EXAMPLE:

Original Passage

   The problem for the school librarian is complicated because the librarian shares responsibility with the teachers, and both are responsible to higher authorities, the school principal, the school district supervisors and superintendent, and, ultimately, to the board of education. This division of responsibility probably makes it easier for the would-be censor to attack school library materials with the hope of success.

(Richard Darling, "School Libraries and Intellectual Freedom,"
Intellectual Freedom Manual, 2nd ed., Chicago: ALA, 1983,
120–21)

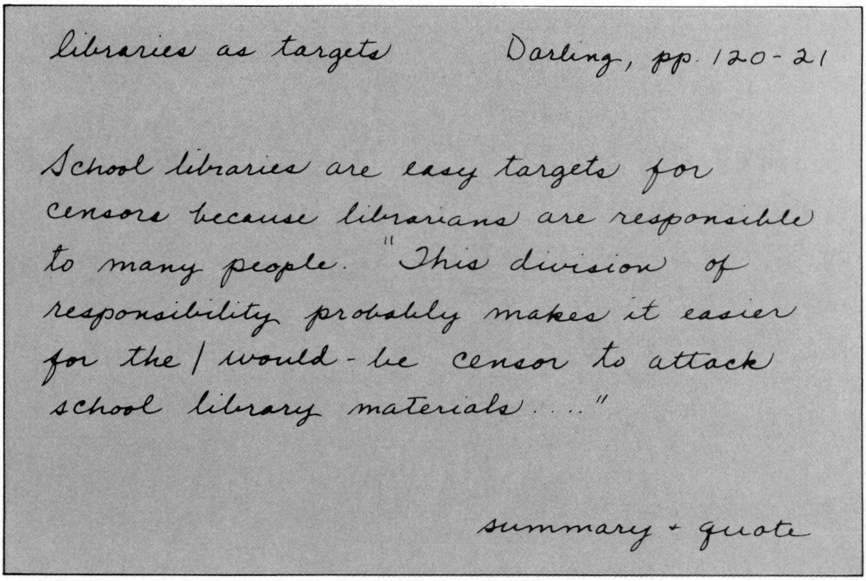

libraries as targets   *Darling, pp. 120-21*

School libraries are easy targets for censors because librarians are responsible to many people. "This division of responsibility probably makes it easier for the / would-be censor to attack school library materials. ..."

summary + quote

Fig. 34. Combination summary and quotation note card

Common Knowledge

Much information is *so basic to a study or so well-known* that it is called "common knowledge." Such information *does not require documentation.* Information you read in a number of sources as you gather material for your paper is common knowledge—and *does not require documentation*. You may want to write a note card about this information, but you do not need to cite the sources from which it came.

EXAMPLES:

- dates of a well-known person's life
- chemical formula of a familiar substance
- location of a famous battle

Even if the information is new to you, finding it in several sources means it's common knowledge.

Certain *value judgments* may also be considered common knowledge and not require documentation. For instance, so many critics have said that Shakespeare's *Henry IV, Part I* is a better play than his *Henry VI, Part II* that you may consider this judgment a matter of common knowledge.

Of course, if you want to quote a particular person's rendering of common knowledge, you must give credit to that individual.

If you are not sure whether or not particular information is common knowledge, a safe rule to follow is, "When in doubt, give credit."

Number of Note Cards

Nobody can tell you how many note cards you will need for a particular research paper. If you take effective notes, you will need fewer cards. If you already know something about the subject, you will need fewer cards than if everything is brand-new to you. Some students find that thirty note cards suffice for a 2,500-word research paper; others need three times that many. The *quality* of notes counts, not the quantity.

If you are in doubt about whether to record information, better write it down. Should you discover later that you have more information than you need, set aside some of your note cards and don't use them. No rule says you have to use every card you write on! But it's better to have too many note cards than not enough; discarding some is easier than having to track down more resources.

Plagiarism—and How Not to Commit It

Often the source you work from has stated an idea so well you can't imagine saying the same thing any other way. It's tempting to record those words on a note card; but if you do, don't forget the quotation marks and an accurate record of the source and page number on which it appeared so you can give proper credit in your research paper. Otherwise you will be guilty of plagiarism.

Or you may get so involved in writing note cards that you forget to indicate whether your card is a paraphrase or a combination of a paraphrase and a quotation. Again, if you forget to credit the source on your note card, you probably won't be able to give proper credit when you write the paper— and you will have committed plagiarism. These may be slipups, but they're still plagiarism.

Plagiarism is using someone else's words or ideas without giving proper credit to the person who devised them. It is wrong to plagiarize, whether you do it deliberately or thoughtlessly. Both print (including maps, charts, and graphs) and nonprint materials (including films and still photos) are protected by copyright, and to present such materials as your own is to break the law as well as to act unethically.

The most blatant kind of plagiarism is submitting another person's paper as your own. Whether a friend lets you borrow a paper or you buy one from a term paper or research service, letting a reader think you did work that you really didn't do is cheating yourself and others.

A more subtle kind of plagiarism is to let your reader think that certain words, phrases, or ideas are your own when they are, in fact, the property of other people you failed to acknowledge. Paraphrases and summaries, as well as individual groups of words—facts, opinions, ideas—may be plagiarized. Changing a word here and there or changing singulars to plurals won't protect you from the label of "plagiarist." Even presenting common knowledge in somebody else's words, without credit, is plagiarism.

At two stages in the research paper process you must be careful not to plagiarize:

1. when you take notes, be sure to credit your source fully and carefully on each note card, and
2. when you write the paper, be sure to observe the conventions of documentation in acknowledging the sources of words, ideas, or illustrations. (Chapter 8, pages 192–201 will show you how to acknowledge sources in the text.)

An example of properly acknowledged content on a note card is Figure 34 on page 129. It is a combination card, but the quotation is clearly marked and the source is written on the card.

You will *not* commit plagiarism if you do the following:

1. Use quotation marks around all words and phrases from any research source and cite the source both on note cards and in the text of your paper. Quotations require both kinds of acknowledgment; one alone won't do.

2. Credit the source of any ideas, including summaries and paraphrases, by documenting them when you write your paper. The style shown in this book, which is recommended by the MLA [Modern Language Association], suggests that you dispense with superscripts and footnotes in favor of parenthetical documentation in the text. Thus, you credit each source immediately, and you can't overlook one because you were busy writing out a thought. (Two other widely used sources of information about style, those by the University of Chicago Press and by the American Psychological Association, also recommend parenthetical documentation.)

3. Be sure every source in your documentation is also in the Works Cited. That is, acknowledging something that is not original must appear *both* in the text of your own research paper and in the Works Cited at the end of the paper.

4. Give an adequate introduction or otherwise clearly delineate borrowed words and ideas. Always give enough information for your audience to tell clearly what is your original work and what isn't. (Examples of how to do this when you write your research paper are on pages 174–78.)

See the documentation forms by which you credit materials that you don't originate in Chapter 8, "Documenting Your Paper," pages 192–216. Examples of how to give adquate introductions to quotations, paraphrases, and borrowed ideas as you are writing your paper are in Chapter 7, "Writing Your Paper," pages 174–78, and in the Sample Research Paper in Chapter 10, pages 257–78.

Notes That Don't Plagiarize

Note taking is the first crucial step in avoiding plagiarism. Therefore, be particularly careful that your summary or paraphrase notes are just what you intended—your own notes—and not inadvertent plagiarism.

A Note About Photocopying

Most libraries now have readily accessible photocopying machines, and thus a new way of recording information is open to you. Instead of spending hours in a library taking notes, it's now possible to make quick, inexpensive copies of needed research materials and work with them in other places or at other times.

But you can't write a paper from photocopies! No matter how much you underline or otherwise mark up your photocopies, they are no substitute for actually taking notes on cards!

Only notes on cards can give you information readily at hand, in flexible or movable form, and often in summary or paraphrase. A photocopy is a convenience. But you will still need to take from it legible, accurate, and complete notes. So photocopy if you must, but use the material with discretion and work *from* it, rather than with the copy itself.

If You Use a Computer . . .

If you are familiar with microcomputers, if you have one readily available, or if you are accustomed to working on one, you may want to use it in preparing your research paper. Although most students who use computers seem to use them for word processing—that is, for writing and revising papers—some software is available for other parts of the research paper process. And if you are someone who is very good with computers, you may even write your own programs to help yourself over hurdles.

A database program is one way to take notes with a computer. Using such a program, you can store information you choose in a format you devise. Later, you can call up and print out those units of information you want.

If you set up a database program to take notes, use the same categories of information you would put on a note card:

Slug line or key word
Author (with title, if needed)
Title (if no author is given)
Call number of book or location of periodical
Page number(s)
Text of note
Type of note (that is, paraphrase, summary, and so on)

The difference between where you put this basic information on a database program entry and on a note card is dictated by the difference in the way you write in each of these media.

Leave plenty of room for your text. And remember to limit yourself to just *one idea to a screen or item,* just as you would if you were taking notes on 4 × 6-inch file cards.

If you do not know how to set up a database—or prefer not to—you can achieve the same effect by setting up what is called a "template" on the computer through a word processing program. That is, use the categories shown for the database suggested, but write them out on a word processing program and repeat them a number of times. Save them all to the data disk and then simply fill in the spaces when you take notes. A complete printout will give you these notes, and you can cut them apart to organize your information.

In all other aspects, adhere to the same customs and recommendations about writing note cards that you have been reading about in this chapter, including the conventions of writing notes, being complete and accurate, taking various kinds of notes, and avoiding plagiarism.

Chapter 6

Organizing Ideas

A research paper is very much like an iceberg because what you can see isn't the whole story. Ordinarily, 90 percent of an iceberg is under water and remains unseen; only people who know something about icebergs can fully comprehend and appreciate their immense size just by seeing the part above water.

Similarly, an enormous part of the work of a research paper isn't immediately evident to someone unfamiliar with the entire process of selecting a topic, locating and assembling and recording information, selecting what is most useful, and organizing the whole into a coherent work. What takes only fifteen minutes to read in its final form is the result of many hours of painstaking work. But you, and others who have the experience of writing a research paper, understand and appreciate the process!

The part of the process you are about to start is probably one of the most challenging:

- looking long and hard at what you've gathered,
- evaluating the notes, and
- organizing those you select.

At this stage you show your critical judgment when you are willing to discard anything you decide is irrelevant or repetitive. No matter how difficult it is to omit material you've spent time finding and recording, it's better to keep the flow and focus of your paper than to try fitting in every single note card.

134

When you organize ideas, think again about *the audience* for this research paper you're writing:

- What background or basic information does the audience probably have about this subject? (There is no need to repeat it.)
- What will the reader(s) be likely to want to know about this subject? (This serves as a guide to what the content should be.)

In order to organize ideas effectively, consider again some *decisions you made:*

- Are you satisfied with the approach you selected? (If not, can you vary it and still fulfill the assignment?)
- Will the materials you gathered and your thinking support the approach you selected (or were assigned)?
- Do you need/want to consult any other resources? (Do so now.)

Transition Time—From Parts to the Whole

Until now, you have been working with parts of your research paper—with the individual sources and separate note cards. As you begin organizing the ideas you've collected, you make a transition from working with the separate parts to seeing them as elements in the whole unit: the research paper.

Help yourself make the transition by reviewing what you've done so far and using that review as a focus for what comes next.

1. Study the cards for the Works Cited list.

Put them in alphabetical order according to the author's last name or the first word in titles of anonymous works. Be sure you've consulted all the sources you can. If you were instructed to use both primary and secondary sources, both books and periodicals, some nonprint media, and articles from scholarly journals as well as from the popular press, make sure you have fulfilled all those qualifications.

2. Consider each note card on its own merits.

Read through them and begin thinking about the main point you want to make in your paper. Will what you've written on a particular card relate directly to what you think you want to put into the paper? If not, put the card aside rather than try to cram in extraneous material. (Keep all note cards; you may decide you want some of that information as you begin writing.)

3. *Arrange the note cards according to slug lines or key words in the top left corner.*

If you've done a good job on these identifying words, you have a ready-made way of grouping ideas, and one step of organization is done. If you have too many with the same key words or find that some don't really express the idea of the note as well as you thought when you wrote them, try "renaming" the note card. Look again at cards you can't match or pair up with others and consider renaming them in order to make groups.

If you've taken notes on a computer database, now is the time to sort them by key words. You should also make a printout, or hard copy, of this information so you can see exactly what you have to work with.

4. *Add personal comment note cards.*

In learning about your subject, and in thinking about it now, you surely must have encountered ideas you want to question or comment on. If you haven't already noted them, do so now.

As an informed source on your subject—which you are now—your comments are worth considering, and writing them on note cards now will ensure that you don't overlook them in the haste of writing. Besides, incorporating your own views is an important part of the synthesis that separates a research paper from a simple report.

5. *Look for a central idea in all that you've learned through the research.*

As you go through the note cards, remember that you now know enough to be able to take a stand about your subject and to be able to support it. Decide what you want to emphasize about your subject, what you want to build your work around. That central idea will become the thesis statement for your paper.

What a Thesis Statement Is

A *thesis statement* **is a specific declaration that summarizes the point of view you will take in your paper.** It may be one sentence or several, depending on the length of the paper you plan to write and the complexity of your subject. Usually, the more succinct and specific you make your thesis statement, the easier it is to make an outline on the basis of it. (The outline, explained on pages 147–58, is the next step in organizing ideas and should be completed before you actually begin writing your paper.)

People arrive at thesis statements in different ways. For some, the statement comes first—an immediate, overall, global view of the work and a sense of what the paper will be about. For others, the statement evolves only after grouping individual ideas into units (according to the slug lines on note cards), then looking at the units in order to see how they fit together in a general way. Whichever method you use, the goal is to develop a thesis statement that you can work from in organizing the ideas within your paper.

Here are the characteristics of a successful (that is, a workable) thesis statement:

1. The thesis statement is limited so it can give direction to the paper.

Earlier you decided to examine or analyze your subject, evaluate it, compare and contrast it to something, establish a relationship, or argue a subject. If your research and study leads you to change some earlier ideas or choose a different approach (provided it will still meet an assignment), now is the time to make that change. The thesis statement sets limits on the scope of what you will cover in the paper, and it should be an accurate statement.

UNLIMITED: `Barriers hinder the handicapped.`

LIMITED: `Architects are now aware that people with phys-`
    `ical, hearing, and sight limitations need easy`
    `access to and within public buildings.`

2. The thesis statement is specific.

Anyone reading the thesis statement should know what the paper is about. Vague words won't do.

VAGUE: `Some TV programs are bad for children.`

SPECIFIC: `Television programs depicting violence numb`
    `children's tolerance for and sensitivity to`
    `real-life acts of violence against people.`

3. The thesis statement is a way to unify the ideas in the paper.

That's why it is *written first*, before you begin an outline, and certainly before you begin writing the paper itself. If you stick to the thesis statement when you compose the outline (and when you write the paper), you will keep yourself from straying to extraneous ideas, no matter how individually interesting they may be to you.

4. The thesis statement is an aid to coherence for your paper.

A good thesis statement holds together diverse aspects of the paper. When you write the outline, check everything you plan to put in it against the thesis statement and omit anything that doesn't relate directly to it.

In short, a thesis statement is the touchstone of your paper—the starting place. It is a statement of the scope of what you want to include in the research paper and the viewpoint or stand you take in relation to it. In Chapter 1 you read that a research paper shows your originality in synthesizing your discoveries about a subject and your evaluation of them. In the thesis statement you make that synthesis.

What a Thesis Statement Is Not

Sometimes it is easier to understand an idea when you can see what it isn't, rather than only what it is. Accordingly, the four following statements tell what a thesis statement *is not*.

1. ***A promise or statement of purpose cannot serve as a thesis statement.***   If you propose to do something in your paper, go ahead and do it. But phrase the thesis statement to show that you have fulfilled your expectation, not simply that you are going to do so.

PROMISE (Not a Thesis Statement):

In this paper I am going to show how the ancient Egyptians were able to build so many huge temples and tombs.

THESIS STATEMENT:

The ancient Egyptians were able to build so many temples and tombs because their dependence on agriculture left seasons when farmers had time to do other kinds of work, their religion encouraged people to do work that glorified their gods and pharoahs, and busy masses were necessary for political and economic stability.

2. ***A topic or subject by itself cannot serve as a thesis statement.***   That information tells what the paper is about, but not what you have to say about the matter.

SUBJECT (Not a Thesis Statement):

Fitness craze

Capitalizing the first letter of each word, or even adding a few words, won't make a thesis statement, although it might make an acceptable *title* for a paper.

TITLE (Not a Thesis Statement):

The Fitness Craze in the United States

Adding a predicate to a subject, however, might yield a thesis statement.

THESIS STATEMENT:

The fitness craze in the United States has resulted in a population more aware of the role of exercise and good eating habits in lengthening people's lives and making them more productive.

3. *A few words added to a title, but __not__ forming a complete sentence, cannot be a thesis statement.*

NOT A THESIS STATEMENT:

Money and Lives in the Space Program

That's unsatisfactory wording because although it "suggests" the contents of the paper, it doesn't express an attitude toward the subject (the space program) or tell what the content of the paper will actually be. Moreover, it isn't a sentence and is therefore not a complete thought.

THESIS STATEMENT:

The money spent and the human lives lost in the space program do not justify its continuance.

Now you can see clearly what the paper is about and the approach (argumentive) it will exemplify. The paper will be easier to write because the thesis statement is a framework that only requires development to express what you have discovered through research and what you believe about it.

4. *A question cannot serve as a thesis statement* because it is not a statement at all! A question can only mean that an answer will follow.

QUESTION (Not a Thesis Statement):

What will Maya Angelou's place in literature be?

Obviously, the question neither tells anything about the content of the paper nor suggests any framework for the presentation of information. However, an answer to that question might suggest some framework for the thesis statements.

WEAK THESIS STATEMENT:

```
Maya Angelou will have a secure place in several genres of
literature.
```

The statement is weak because it is vague. A reader would want to know what is meant by "secure place" and what the "several genres" are. It isn't a statement that would help a writer organize information to include in the paper; therefore, it's not a useful thesis statement.

IMPROVED THESIS STATEMENT:

```
Maya Angelou is an accessible writer whose prose, poetry,
and filmscripts will long be read because they deal with
human conditions, not just with "black problems."
```

Such specific wording for a thesis statement gives the paper direction and provides for unity and coherence. You could easily develop from such a thesis statement an outline that presents substantial information in a logical order.

How a Thesis Statement Evolves

Think about the central idea for your paper while you gather note cards together, sort through them, and look at the contents carefully. If you haven't already decided on a main emphasis, now is the time to make that decision.

Write out a statement you think will serve as a controlling idea or thesis for your paper. A thesis statement in your head won't serve the same purpose as one on paper; it's too fleeting, too elusive. You need to put it in writing so you can see in front of you what you're working with—so you can tinker with it, rephrase it, or further limit or enlarge its scope.

However, don't try to keep stretching a prospective thesis statement to make it accommodate every phrase or idea that comes to you. Trying to cram every single thing you've learned about your subject into one research paper will surely weaken the work. You have to be willing to discard ideas just as you must discard note cards when they don't fit a structure.

Carol Matz, the student whose research paper is the sample in Chapter 10 (pages 257–78), was assigned to write a persuasive research paper, so she knew that her thesis statement had to express a position she could defend—and convince her audience (classmates) to accept. After recording information from her research sources, she decided that she was against library censorship. Here is the evolution of the thesis statement for the paper; it shows Ms. Matz's various tries at the thesis statement and her evaluation of each.

FIRST TRY: `Books should not be banned from school`
`libraries.`

COMMENT: Yes, that's what I mean.   And it is persuasive, so it will fulfill the assignment.   But that statement sounds too general for a research paper.   It doesn't tell anything about the content of the paper, either.

SECOND TRY: `The First Amendment rights of students are vio-`
`lated when books are banned from school`
`libraries.`

COMMENT: That's more specific.   But emphasizing constitutional rights this way in the thesis makes it seem that I'm arguing a case of law and obviously I'm not qualified to do that.   Also, it doesn't express the idea of intellectual freedom that interests me.

THIRD TRY: `Removing books from school libraries limits`
`students' free access to ideas and information.`

COMMENT: That sounds better.   I like the wording that emphasizes ideas and information because I think that's what students ought to get from schools. If you can't get to ideas, you can never learn to think for yourself and you can't think clearly about issues that affect everybody.
I'll go with this one!

How an Outline Evolves

A thesis statement leads the way to an outline, a pattern to follow when you write the paper. If you've already grouped note cards according to similar ideas by checking the key words or slug lines at the top left corner of each card before composing the thesis statement, you have completed the first step toward writing an outline. If the note cards are not yet grouped, you must do that now.

A good way to work is to put the written thesis statement in front of you, where you can keep looking back at it. Then arrange the *groups of note cards,* according to the slug lines, in an order you think will help you guide your audience to the same understanding and belief about your material that you have already reached. (Some kinds of order are suggested in the next section.) Only after deciding on an order will you be ready to start committing that structure to paper in a form you can develop into an outline.

The groupings you choose for the note cards in your collection are a preliminary step to an outline from which to write your research paper. Well-organized information at this stage will make your task easier as you continue.

The content of some subjects dictates the best way to organize the content of the research paper, such as chronology (if you are tracing the sources of an author's later works stemming from the earlier ones) or problem to solution (if you are proposing a better way to handle rush-hour traffic in your city).

Often a thesis statement points the way toward organizing the content of your paper. Here are some possibilities based on sample thesis statements shown earlier in this chapter.

THESIS STATEMENT:

```
Architects are now aware that people with physical, hear-
ing, and sight limitations need easy access to and within
public buildings.
```

Because the word "now" appears in this thesis statement, a paper based on it could be organized through *comparison and contrast.* That is, the author could point out characteristics that have been incorporated into recently designed structures (however the word "recently" is interpreted) that were not considered earlier.

Earlier	*Now*
1. Steps	1. Ramps
2. Narrow doorways	2. Wide doorways
3. Revolving doors	3. Automatic-opening doors
and so on	and so on

Certainly, specific buildings would need to be cited as examples throughout such a paper to keep it from being too general.

Here is another kind of thesis statement and another kind of organization:

THESIS STATEMENT:

```
The ancient Egyptians were able to build so many temples
and tombs because their dependence on agriculture left
```

```
seasons when farmers had time to do other kinds of work,
their religion encouraged people to do work that glorified
their gods and pharoahs, and busy masses were necessary
for political and economic stability.
```

This thesis calls for an *effect-to-cause organization* to explain the huge building program for thousands of years in ancient Egypt.

EFFECT:

Building many huge temples and tombs

CAUSES:

1. Agricultural seasons (thus, periodic work)
2. Religious teachings and observances
3. Political stability
4. Economic stability

Alternately, someone working with this thesis might decide to turn the organization around and lead from the *causes to the effect* in structuring an outline.

Ways of Organizing Content

The limited examples above show how a well-stated thesis statement may lead to ideas about organization, though not to the outline itself. If you don't feel a "necessity" for organizational form stemming from your thesis statement, consider the following six possible ways of organizing information: time, known to unknown or simple to complex, comparison and contrast, general to particular or particular to general, problem to solution or question to answer, and cause to effect or effect to cause.

If you have ever taken a composition course, the information that follows will look familiar. These are ways of organizing material for *any* kind of nonfiction writing, from answering an essay exam question to writing a magazine article. You should choose the method that will most easily and clearly help you convey to the audience your approach to your subject and the content of your thesis statement.

Time

Many subjects clearly lend themselves to presentation in chronological order. Some examples are a paper that examines various critical receptions of a novel over a period of time, one that shows background leading to an historical event, or a research paper meant to persuade a plant supervisor to install a new manufacturing process.

Known to Unknown or Simple to Complex

These two methods of organizing ideas are similar, but one leads readers from what is familiar to what might not already be known or understood. The other begins with what is simple or easy to comprehend and takes readers to more difficult content. For example, a paper on the effects of prolonged space trips might begin by discussing the more familiar (and easier to understand) concepts of time we know, rather than time as perceived on space trips. Or a research paper on the theater of the absurd might be developed by briefly reviewing the more traditional and familiar theatrical types before going on to explain the absurd.

Comparison and Contrast

Both comparison and contrast show relationships among things, ideas, or people. But comparison dwells on similarity, while contrast concentrates on dissimilarity—often, however, after first establishing shared characteristics. Although the methods may be used separately, they are usually combined when material for a research paper is organized.

One effective method of organizing a paper for comparison and contrast is *point by point*. That is, you deal with one aspect of the topic at a time, showing comparison and contrast before moving on to another element of similarity or difference. This method is often used because the reader can readily see the relationships you point out.

EXAMPLE:

You are comparing and contrasting Idea A to Idea B and have four elements of relationship.

Present the information in this *point by point order:*
Compare Point 1 of Idea A to Point 1 of Idea B
Contrast Point 1 of Idea A to Point 1 of Idea B
Compare Point 2 of Idea A to point 2 of Idea B
Contrast Point 2 of Idea A to Point 2 of Idea B
and so on.

Another way of organizing a comparison and contrast paper is by presenting all the material about one subject before moving on to all the material about another subject. This is the *item by item order.*

EXAMPLE:

You are comparing and contrasting Idea A to Idea B in four respects.

Present the information in this *item by item order:*
Explain Points 1,2,3,4 of Idea A
Show how Points 1,2,3,4 are the same in Idea B
Show how Points 1,2,3,4 are different in Idea B

One drawback some readers find in coping with this organization is that by the time they finish reading extensive information about one element, they forget what came at the beginning and therefore have some difficulty following the comparison and contrast the author is trying to establish.

You might use comparison and contrast to organize information if you were presenting the platforms of candidates for elective office, the relative merits of three different sites for a new sports stadium, or an analysis of two different publications addressed to members of the same profession.

General to Particular or Particular to General

If you begin with some fairly broad ideas or statements and then arrange the remaining information as a series of specific supporting points, you are following the general to particular arrangement of the content of your research paper. Or, you might organize your paper on the opposite basis: by presenting a series of specific pieces of information which you then show how to organize into a general conclusion or statement. Of course, there will be specific and supporting points within any good piece of writing, but they aren't the same as the structural or organizational framework now being discussed.

For example, a research paper on the short stories of James Agee (or any other writer) might begin with the broad issues he examined and then move to the instances of those issues in particular short stories. Or, the entire organization of the paper could be reversed, with the examination of the stories first.

Problem to Solution or Question to Answer

If your research has been about how a problem was solved—or how to go about finding a solution to something—you might use the problem-to-solution organization for your paper. That is, you would begin by stating the problem that exists (or existed) and then make suggestions for its solution (or show how it was solved).

Many business and technical papers are written to seek solutions, so this kind of organization is often used on material written outside of school situations. A familiar scientific-paper format that proceeds from formulating a hypothesis, to evaluating proposals, and then to solving a problem is also a variation of the problem-to-solution organization.

Sometimes a question is posed (although not as the thesis statement!) and a paper is developed around an answer to it. The question is, in effect, the problem to be solved. For example, a paper might begin by posing the question of how the federal government has coped with illegal aliens and be organized by showing various answers that have been proposed as well as tried.

Cause to Effect or Effect to Cause

Both these methods of organization are built around the notion of causality, so you have to establish and maintain that idea throughout the paper. You could begin by writing about an event and then show its result. Or you could specify a situation and then trace its causes. Some topics that lend themselves to either of these two forms of organization are how plastics have influenced industrial design or how reorganizing the administration in a county office would bring about more effective service to people and more efficient use of employees' time.

Relating Organization to Overall Approach

In Chapter 3 (pages 50–53) you read about five possible approaches to the subject you decide to research: examine or analyze, evaluate or criticize, compare and contrast, establish relationships, and argue or persuade. You were also urged to select one of these approaches before you began searching for information and recording it. That global approach is not the same as the organization with which you will present the content, and though it may suggest the organizing principle, consider a variety of possibilities.

EXAMPLES:

> *Approach: Examine or Analyze*
>
> | Possible Subjects | Possible Organizing Methods |
> |---|---|
> | national park system | time |
> | black holes in space | known to unknown |
> | learned dependence of elderly | problem to solution or effect to cause |

Approach: Establish Relationships

Possible Subjects	Possible Organizing Methods
diet and health	cause to effect
TV violence and children	general to particular

Approach: Argue or Persuade

Possible Subjects	Possible Organizing Methods
hazardous waste disposal	problem to solution
school library censorship	particular to general

Courses or books about composition will show how to go about presenting the content within each of the organizing methods. In general, the emphasis is on supporting statements or contentions with details—and in a research paper, many of the details will come from the notes you have already taken and the sources you consulted (and which will be documented according to the techniques you will read about in Chapter 8).

Outlines

An outline is **an orderly plan, in writing, showing the division and arrangement of ideas.** Its principal function is to indicate the relationship of ideas to each other, to show which are important and which are subordinate.

The outline is put together *after you have decided on the thesis statement* because its purpose is to amplify the many ideas inherent in the thesis statement and to show their relationships, each to the others. It is *usually developed after you decide on a way of organizing* your material, because then you have a guide to how you proceed. (You may, however, find one organization doesn't work well and need to try another.) And an outline is *always written before the text of the paper.* Making an outline after a paper is written just to fulfill an assignment is foolish and useless!

Even though you have an order of presentation in mind when you write the thesis statement, the outline is important because it

- keeps ideas firmly in mind, even if writing the paper takes a long time,
- lets you rearrange ideas without difficulty,
- shows you how parts and transitions fit together, and
- exposes strengths and weaknesses in time to make adjustments before writing.

When you write the paper, you need only follow the plan—the outline—you've made. (And you still have the option of making minor alterations as you write.)

Don't be surprised if your outline isn't "perfect" the first time you put it down on paper. Few processes in writing are! The whole point of an outline is to work out the structure of your paper.

An outline is to a completed research paper what a blueprint is to a completed house. Obviously, nobody would build without a blueprint! The architect envisions a completed house but makes several sketches of its floor plan and elevation before being satisfied. When the blueprint is finally drawn, it shows exactly where the walls, plumbing, and electric wiring will appear in the finished house.

So, too, although you may make several outlines—or change parts around within one—the final outline helps you bring the many ideas of your research paper into focus and proportion.

Keep the thesis statement before you when you start working on the outline. Many people begin with a preliminary outline that is just a listing of the main topics they want to cover. There must be at least two such main ideas, though there may be several more than that. The number of main ideas depends on the extent of information you want to cover, but research papers under 3,000 words probably need fewer than ten.

If you don't find the main ideas readily, prompt yourself with a bit of role-playing: pretend to be your audience and ask questions based on the thesis statement. Jot down the questions and then consider that the responses may well be the main ideas that ought to be developed in your paper. (If your actual audience, such as classmates, is available, let them ask the questions based on the thesis statement.)

The outline that finally emerges becomes the sketch for your research paper. As with a painting, the subsequent details of the work emerge from that sketch. The outline shows key ideas and emphases and where various levels of development fit. Then, when you write from the outline, you fill in the details.

There is no way of telling how long an outline should be in relation to the finished paper. Since it is only a guide, it shouldn't be so minutely detailed that it becomes a paper in itself. On the other hand, it shouldn't be so brief or vague that you need to guess about what is meant in order to get a general picture of a paper from reading its outline. Just as anyone who can read a blueprint will have a pretty good idea of how the finished house will look, so anyone who reads an outline should be able to get an overall sense of what the finished paper will contain.

Forms of Outlines

Outlines follow very specific forms. The two principal ones are **topic outlines** and **sentence outlines.**

The **topic outline** is widely used because the wording is succinct. After each of the traditional outline symbols, you write your ideas in *a word, a* *phrase, or a dependent clause.* Thus, the wording of a topic outline will look something like this:

```
I.   Issues of censorship
     A.   Intellectual freedom
     B.   Values taught
II.  Censorship in past
```

Notice that there is no punctuation after the words because there are no complete sentences. However, do try to use a parallel and consistent grammatical structure throughout a topic outline.

The **sentence outline** presents *statements as grammatically complete sentences.* It is widely used because you have to think through ideas completely in order to write them in full sentences. Whereas a topic outline allows much leeway and flexibility—a few words are expected to serve as a reminder for whole ideas—a sentence outline, like any sentence, forces you to commit yourself to a complete thought. Many students find that requirement helpful. The wording of a sentence outline (using the same ideas as the example above) will resemble this:

```
I.   The issues of school library censorship stem from two
     principal sources.
     A.   Some people feel that schools must foster the
          intellectual freedom of students.
     B.   Some people feel schools have the obligation to
          impart values to students.
```

Note that because the wording after each symbol is a complete sentence, a period ends each one.

You should also know that there are two other outline forms, though they are not as widely used as topic or sentence outlines.

A **paragraph outline** has the same symbols as topic and sentence outlines (as shown in the next section on conventions), but each symbol is followed by several sentences that make a paragraph. Such outlines are generally used for extended (certainly more than 3,000 words) and complex material. Because of the amount of writing involved, paragraph outlines are not as quick to make as topic or sentence outlines. Nor do they encourage experimenting with the order of ideas, as do the shorter forms. Also, there is a danger that students who aren't careful constructing the paragraph outline end up writing their whole papers, merely putting outline symbols in front of each paragraph. Then, the work ceases to be an outline (because it's no longer a *plan* but an executed work), but it is not really a paper, either.

A **decimal outline** has a different symbol system from those just explained. Each main item in this kind of outline is assigned an arabic numeral, and the support for it carries the same numeral followed by a decimal point and numerals to indicate further subdivisions. Thus, a decimal outline looks like this:

```
1.
    1.1
        1.1.1
        1.1.2
        1.1.3
    1.2
        1.2.1
        1.2.2
2.
```

Phrases usually follow each numerical designation, although sometimes sentences are used throughout. This kind of outline is used more frequently in business and scientific writing than in other academic or professional work.

Conventions of Outlines

The most general convention of outlining is to use a **consistent form.** Decide in advance which one you will use and *stick to it throughout.* If you start with a topic outline, you may not write sentences within it. If you start with a sentence outline, you must write sentences all the way through.

The customary symbols, punctuation, and indentation most people associate with outlines are not ends in themselves. Rather, they are aids to show the relationships among ideas recorded in the outline. You should follow these conventions for the sake of clarity and for the help they afford you in arranging ideas thoughtfully before you begin writing your research paper.

1. Numbers and letters are used alternately in an outline (except, as already explained, in a decimal outline). Therefore, ideas of equal importance in the overall concept of the paper will have the same kind of symbol.

- Roman numerals show the major divisions of the paper, so each major idea you propose to write about will be noted next to this symbol.
- Capital letters indicate the first subdivision.
- Arabic numerals show divisions of the content given by the capital letters.
- Lowercase letters are used to further subdivide information.

Even finer subdivision is possible but seldom necessary for school research papers. However, should you want to use it, follow the numeral-letter sequence, first using arabic numerals within parentheses, then small letters within parentheses.

2. ***Symbols in an outline must always appear at least in pairs.*** That is, if you have an *A*, you must also have a *B;* if you have a *1,* you must also have a *2,* and so on. The reason for this convention is obvious: an outline shows the *division of ideas* you will include in your paper, and since *you can't divide anything into just one part, you must have at least two parts of every idea you divide.* If you can't find two subdivisions for a unit, try combining the ideas of that single symbol with the one above it.

   Two other notes about divisions:

■ You may have *more* than two subdivisions.

■ There is no need to make an equal number of subdivisions, even under similar symbols. Your material and what you have to say about it should be the only guides.

EXAMPLE:

I.

  A.

    1.
    2.
    3.

      a.
      b.

  B.
  C.

II.

  A.
  B.

    1.
    2.

      a.
      b.
      c.

3. ***Every symbol in an outline is followed by a period***   (except those in a decimal outline). Notice how this convention is followed in the example of outline symbols above. The period acts as a separation between the symbols that establish the relationships and the wording itself. Allow two typewriter spaces after a period following a symbol and before the words begin.

4. ***Capitalize the first letter of the first word after every symbol.***   You would normally do that at the beginning of a sentence (and thus in a sentence outline), but an outline convention is to capitalize even in a topic outline. Thereafter, capital letters are used for words only in the normal fashion: titles, names, places, and so on.

5. ***Grammatically complete sentences require normal sentence punctuation,***   so there may be commas, colons, and semicolons, as well as periods, in sentence and paragraph outlines. However, the one punctuation mark you *should not use* is a question mark because an outline makes statements; it answers questions rather than asks them.

6. ***All symbols of the same kind should be in a vertical line***   to emphasize the relationships among ideas and to make reading an outline easy. That will take a little juggling because the roman numerals will take one, two, or three spaces, but you can compensate and set up an easy-to-read outline.

   Type the first roman numeral two spaces (three columns) in from the left side margin (which should be one inch from the edge of the paper). Roman numerals of two digits can then be indented one space and those with three digits begun at the left margin. To keep successive columns of symbols even, indent each five spaces, or a multiple of five spaces, from the left margin. Thus, all capital letters will occur in the same column, all arabic numbers in the same column, and so on. (The outline on page 153 is an example.)

7. ***Begin succeeding lines of writing under the start of the first word after a symbol***   if a statement requires more than one line. This format prevents interference with the vertical alignment of the symbols of the outline that make relationships among ideas visible, so adhere to this custom whether you type or write in longhand. Thus, the format of your outline should look like this:

```
A.  This is an especially long statement and requires
    three lines, so the subsequent lines begin under
    the first word after the symbol.
```

8. ***Type an outline in double spacing,*** just as you do the rest of your research paper. The following format, used for the outline of the sample research paper on pages 257–78, is a convenient one:

```
The Problem of Censorship in Public School Libraries
```

THESIS: Removing books from school libraries limits
                students' free access to ideas and information.

```
  I.   Principles of free access
       A.   Meaning of intellectual freedom
       B.   Impediment of censorship
 II.   Censorship in past
       A.   Banned books
       B.   Who attempts censoring
       C.   Reasons for book removal
       D.   Frequency of censorship attempts
```

The entire outline is on pages 257–58.

Content of Outlines

The *most important part of an outline is what you put into it*—the words that carry your ideas and help you organize what you plan to say in your research paper. Even after you choose an outline form and adhere to the conventions of symbols, punctuation, and spacing you have just been reading about, *what you have to say* is by far the most important element in developing an outline. Here are some guides for making the content of your outline meaningful and therefore helpful to your writing.

1. ***Every word in the outline should say something about the content of your paper.***
   Only then will it really be the guide to write from that an outline is meant to be. For that reason, "Introduction," "Body," and "Conclusion" are words that *don't* belong in an outline. They only describe the parts of *any* piece of writing—which has to have a beginning, a middle, and an end—but give no information about the subject or what you plan to say about it. Instead of such "empty words," always use content-giving words in an outline.

Similarly, "who" or "why" phrases (as in "Who responds to the ads" or "Why magazines are used") are useless in an outline. Anybody looking at such wording would certainly ask, "Well, who *does* respond?" or "Why *are* magazines used?" Instead of this vague phrasing, use language and information so specific that anybody looking at the outline can tell exactly what your final paper will contain.

THESIS: Environmental damage from inadequate disposal of hazardous waste materials continues in many states.

"EMPTY" WORDING:

I.   Introduction
II. Problems about hazardous waste
    A.   Where it is
    B.   Who does it

CONTENT-GIVING WORDING:

I.   Sources of hazardous wastes
II. Current disposal methods
    A.   Landfills
    B.   Incinerators
    C.   Storage
        1.   Deep-well injection
        2.   Containers

2. *The information for each subheading must be directly related to, and subordinate to, the heading under which it appears.*

The outline shows relationships among ideas, so the entire content is a matter of showing visually how each thought relates to every other one. That is, although some content will be of equal importance to other content, what is supportive and subordinate must be so designated.

Note also that because the entire content of the outline (and of the research paper) is related to and subordinate to both the title and the thesis statement, *neither one can appear as an individual item* within the outline itself.

If you find you have only one thing to say about any part of the outline (and you know you can't divide something into just one part), instead of trying to make artificial subdivisions, revise the wording or rethink the idea.

THESIS: Arthur Miller used elements of a sophisticated
              mistress in one story and a childlike wife in
              another to develop the character of Roslyn Taber
              in his cinema—novel <u>The Misfits</u>.

WRONG OUTLINE:

I. "The Misfits" was published in 1957.
    A. The story concerned three cowboys on a mustang
        hunt.
        1. Roslyn meets them.
    B. Roslyn is an eastern sophisticate.

IMPROVED OUTLINE:

I. Roslyn appears in "The Misfits" published in 1957.
    A. She meets three cowboys going on a mustang
        hunt.
    B. She is an eastern sophisticate.

The second outline is improved because the single item was combined with
another.

However, since the thesis statement indicates that this research paper is
going to focus on Roslyn, a character in the novel, the focus of the outline
ought to be on her.

BEST OUTLINE:

I. Roslyn is an eastern sophisticate in "The Misfits"
    (1957)
    A. She enjoys new sights and experiences.
    B. She feels sorry for hurt animals.
II. Roslyn is a charming . . .

Reference to the three cowboys and their mustang hunt is omitted because
the paper is about Roslyn, not them. Whatever needs to be said of the men
will be worked into the content when the author writes from the outline.

3. *Make relationships clear by using the same symbol (that is, roman numer-
    als, capital letters, and so on) for ideas of equal importance.*
    Because the outline divides ideas, the symbols must show how the content
of the paper will be divided or subdivided into groups of thoughts related to
one another.

THESIS: Ernest Hemingway's writing evolved from his own
               life.

WRONG OUTLINE CONTENT:

  I.   Early journalistic career
 II.   Participation in WW I
III.   <u>The Sun Also Rises</u>
    A.   Other successful early novels
    B.   <u>A Farewell to Arms</u>
 IV.   Sympathy with Loyalists
    A.   <u>For Whom the Bell Tolls</u>
    B.   Participation in Spanish Civil War

The phrases after each roman numeral in this example give three different kinds of information: periods in Hemingway's life, a book he wrote, and an attitude he had. Sections III and IV not only differ from the others but they also are not of equal importance in the outline. In light of the thesis of the paper, Hemingway's beliefs should be emphasized, not a particular book. Here is an improved version because the content shows that the paper will follow from the thesis statement:

PROPER OUTLINE CONTENT:

  I.   Early journalistic career
 II.   Participation in WW I
III.   Expatriate novelist years
    A.   <u>The Sun Also Rises</u>
    B.   <u>A Farewell to Arms</u>
 IV.   Participation in Spanish Civil War

In the revised outline, each symbol represents ideas of equal importance. The roman numerals show key periods in Hemingway's life, and the capital letters show books written during one period. The third book title in the original outline is omitted because it would have had to stand alone. However, the author could easily say something about *For Whom the Bell Tolls* in section IV, even without noting it in the outline.

4.   *Only principal points appear in an outline.*
    Illustrations, amplifications, and development of the main points are added in the actual writing. You will be reminded of these matters when you

rearrange your note cards to coincide with the structure of the content you have decided upon. Thus, you should concentrate on putting principal ideas, rather than their support, in your outline.

Revising Outlines

Don't be satisfied with your first outline, even if you think it's pretty good. The next version will be even better. Test it constantly as you work by thinking through each idea in relation to the others you want to express. Move ideas around and try them out in different relationships until you feel comfortable with the structure and content of what you will be writing. It's easy enough to make adjustments from one outline draft to another. When you think you've finally formulated a satisfactory outline, put it away and forget about it for a few days.

When you take the outline out again, test it by putting yourself in the position of the audience. Could that person (or persons) follow your ideas and understand your viewpoint on the basis of the outline? If the audience will be someone from whom you expect no familiarity with the subject, try out your outline on a friend or relative for whom the subject is new; if your "stand-in" audience can get a sense of what the final paper will be like, you may have completed the outline.

Here is an example of two drafts of a topic outline developed by a student. On the left is an early (though not the very first) version; on the right is her final version.

THESIS: Animals can fulfill the social, physical, and emotional needs of elderly people whom society has neglected.

Early Version	*Final Version*
I. Early man–animal relations	I. Precedents
II. Current statistics	II. Benefits
A. Elderly population	A. Companionship
1. Nursing home costs	1. Physical
	2. Communication
B. Animals as pets	B. Decreased isolation
III. Benefits of animal relationships	C. Medical
A. Mental	1. Blood pressure
B. Social	2. Heart disease
C. Physical	

IV. Research studies   D. Reduced depression
 V. Support   E. Better self-perception
     A. Organizations   1. Esteem
     B. Government   2. Autonomy
         legislation   III. Arguments for use
                                      A. Individual
                                      B. Professional
                                      C. Governmental

Comment.   Notice that the student cleared up some of the difficulties evident in the early verion: problems of division of ideas (as in IIA-1), of focus (statistics and research studies ought to support ideas, not be considered principal points by themselves), and of emphasis (the three elements cited in the thesis are buried within the outline as divisions of III). You can see from the proportions of the final outline that section II will be the emphasis of the paper. Also, note that although the thesis statement cites three benefits, the student has not limited herself to just three subdivisions but has augmented them according to what she wanted to include in her final writing.

When you feel you have revised the outline so that it seems a good plan for your writing, **put your note cards into working order** by keying each card at the top left corner with the outline symbol to which it corresponds. That is, you might write *I. A. 2.* on one card, indicating that it contains information about the second item listed under roman numeral I and capital letter *A*. If you write these symbols in a color of ink different from what you wrote the note with (for instance, in green or red), you'll be able to locate them quickly. Also, if the cards should become scrambled, having these outline symbols on them will let you put them back into working order quickly.

Visual Ordering—Mapping and Clustering

Outlines are linear creations—they require you to start at one place and proceed in order to another. And while they are still the preferred way of organizing ideas in this final stage before writing the research paper, not everyone takes easily to the concepts of outlining.

Some people, either through habit or because of the way they think, find that working with something more visual—with diagrams rather than only with words—is easier, more agreeable, or preferable for them. The result is an ordering of ideas, but one arrived at in a slightly different way from the linearity of an outline.

Called **mapping** or **clustering** (although slightly different, the terms are often used interchangeably), these visual ways of ordering ideas depend on using key words in some way that shows their relationships to each other. Although clustering is generally begun with one word in the center of a circle from which lines are drawn and more circles added to show relationships, mapping and clustering have no conventions and no formulas to follow. Rather, they are completely idiosyncratic, with one person's visualization (and, therefore, the map) being in the form of, say, a tree trunk with branches, another's perhaps in the form of a drawing with recognizable things or people in it.

Since there are no rules or conventions to follow when you are engaged in mapping and clustering, it's a more freewheeling way of organizing information than is making an outline. However, it has the same purpose: to serve as an organizational plan for writing your paper. In fact, most people who approach organizing through such visual ordering find that they use it as a transitional device between completing the note cards and writing an outline on the basis of this visual ordering.

Clustering begins with the subject of your research in the center of a circle on the page. Mapping begins with any idea you wish, though usually it, too, starts with the subject that becomes part of a picture. From then on, the map or cluster may resemble a series of doodles that only you can make sense of; indeed, you may choose a different visual respresentation for a later version than you do for an earlier one. Here are two versions of such visual organizations for the sample research paper on pages 257–78.

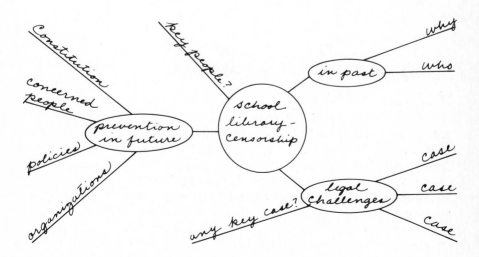

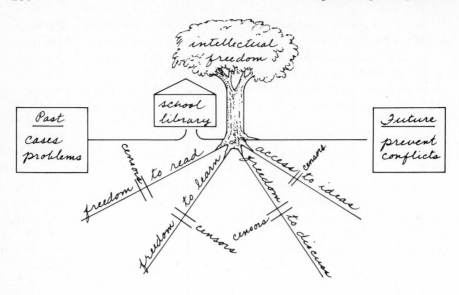

You can see from the cluster how the author of the sample research paper progressed with her ideas. The map, above, seeks to make visual the abstractions that will be dealt with: a journey from past to future with a stop at a school library shaded by a tree representing "intellectual freedom." The roots, which are the various freedoms, are in danger of being cut by censors, and that would kill the tree.

The complete outline for the sample research paper in this book is on pages 257–58. Compare it to the visuals above and you will see how an outline can evolve from these alternate ways of organizing ideas.

Computer Aids to Outlining

If you are comfortable enough to do word processing on a microcomputer, you may also want to make an outline on the computer. One possibility is to use the computer as you would pen and paper in making an outline, though you would have the advantage the computer gives of making changes and of moving words around easily. On the other hand, the computer screen displays only a few lines of text at one time. If you work best by having everything visible simultaneously on sheets of paper, you may be comfortable using the computer for your outline only if you can print a hard copy after working out ideas on-screen.

Another possibility is to use one of the commercially available "idea processor" programs designed to format your "loose" ideas into an outline or an approximation of one. Such programs may be individual or, increasingly, part of word processing packages that help you through the writing process from generating ideas to a completed composition.

The most popular of the idea processing programs shows relationships among ideas by indentation but doesn't have any of the conventional symbol systems built in. You have to supply those, perhaps by overriding the program to add them in the computer, perhaps by typing them on a hard copy.

As software developers have become aware of the importance of organizing ideas before writing, more such programs have been developed. Variations will probably continue to come onto the market.

Before Moving Ahead . . .

When you have a satisfactory thesis statement, an outline that sketches the order and proportion of what you want in your research paper, and your note cards in order, you are ready to begin writing a draft. But stop a minute before moving ahead. A good outline should let *anybody* see exactly what your research paper will contain. So unless your instructor objects, show your outline to at least one other person. That "other" may be your instructor, especially if she or he is following along the research paper process with you, or one of your classmates.

Ask whoever reads your outline to really give it a critical—which means evaluative—reading. The least helpful remark you can get is, "Yes, it's good." Have your helper make sure that

- the outline shows a progression of ideas that supports your thesis statement,
- major and subordinate ideas are so designated by units and symbols, and
- subordinate units are somewhat balanced throughout the outline (rather than eight units under one heading and only two under its parallel heading).

Ask your helper to tell you what he or she expects to find in your research paper. If the response doesn't coincide with what you plan to write, ascertain areas of disagreement and either adjust the outline or your proposed writing. Because your research paper is being written for an audience, let your helper serve as an audience for you at this stage of the process.

Chapter 7

Writing Your Paper

If you've completely and carefully done all the work described in this book so far, you are now ready to begin writing your paper. Writing doesn't come easily for most people, and you may be one for whom words don't flow readily onto paper. Don't expect your writing habits to change suddenly and dramatically, even if you've done your preparatory work well. And don't expect that just because you've done the necessary preparatory work you can quickly write out a paper, then merely "fix up" spelling and punctuation before turning it in. Writing just doesn't work in those ways.

But *do* expect all your serious and concentrated preparation to make this research writing easier once you take pen to paper (or sit before the typewriter or computer keyboard). And *do* be prepared to produce a good piece of writing because you have a plan to work from and the material with which to fill it in and see your research paper take shape.

Writing is a complex activity that involves constant thinking through of ideas and searching for the best wording and phrasing—all the while putting words on paper. New thoughts will occur as you write, and you should certainly fill in as you go with common knowledge and with your own thinking rather than relying solely on what you took down as notes from various sources. You may even find yourself half a page beyond a certain point when you think of a better way to phrase what you've written. If so, take time to make the changes. If you write in this forward and backward way, sometimes rushing ahead with ideas, sometimes proceeding very slowly, you are writing in the way that research has shown most competent writers perform!

People write in all sorts of ways. Some say they can only work on notebook paper when they sit in the library; some swear by late-night sessions at the computer. Some prefer to write slowly and carefully from the beginning, making corrections and changes as they go along. Others find the best way to write a first draft—what you will be doing at this stage—is to put everything down on paper as quickly as possible and then later make extensive revisions. For most good writers, taking care of the mechanics of spelling and punctuation comes near the *end* of the writing process.

Since time is always a problem for busy students, and since last-minute writing is seldom good, a useful method is to set aside chunks of time during which to write out a draft of your research paper. Work at it as much as you feel you can in sessions as long as you can manage without interruption. If you don't have time to revise certain passages as you go, write yourself a note or use some symbol to indicate you will pay special attention to that part when you next work at writing your paper.

Many people find that writing on a computer is less inhibiting than writing in longhand or on a typewriter. It's also easier to revise as you compose, and to make subsequent changes when you write. You will probably also want to follow the lead of many authors who compose on the computer but need to see a hard copy of the work to make final revisions and be completely satisfied with what they've produced.

If you are going to use word processing to write your paper, be completely familiar with the program *before* you begin writing. Trying to figure out how a computer program operates at the same time you're figuring out how best to present the material you've found just doesn't work.

Writing Style

Writing has few hard and fast rules. But writing a research paper does have some stylistic customs you will probably want to observe.

1. ***Usually, write in the third person.*** That is, the words "I," "we," and "you" will not normally appear in your text (though of course they may appear in quoted materials). A sense of distance between you and your material is customary in a research paper. Besides, the focus has to remain on *what you have to say* (rather than on you, the person who is saying it). Writing in the first person (I) focuses attention on the author, and writing in the second person (you) draws the attention of the audience to itself. Therefore, by using the third person you direct the reader's entire attention to what you have to say.

2. **Write straightforwardly.** The style should be neither artificially formal nor as loose and relaxed as a personal letter. Many teachers feel that contractions are out of place in this style of writing. For example, the preferred phrasing is usually "Writers do not usually. . ." rather than "Writers don't usually. . . ." Check with your instructor if in doubt about her or his preferences.

3. **Always refer to individuals by their full name (given and surnames) or by surname alone** —*never* by their first (or given) names. Thus, "Steinem says . . ." or "Gloria Steinem says . . ." is the form to use—*not* "Gloria says. . . ." Follow this custom in writing even if you've interviewed a person with whom you are on a first-name basis or if you've read enough of (or about) a person's work to feel you know the individual well. You may, however, use a title with a person's name as identification (Dr. Jane Smith, President Truman, Dame Sutherland, and so on).

4. **Write as specifically as possible.** Avoid sweeping statements. Stay away from unsubstantiated generalizations; beware of catchall words, too. "Young" may mean any age from six months to twenty years, depending on the age and orientation of the audience, but "five years old" is specific. Strive to say *exactly* what you mean and never let an audience guess at your intention.

5. **Change or eliminate wording that shows bias toward a person's age, sex, race, political attitude, religious beliefs, sexual orientation, or national origin** unless such information is necessary to what you are writing (or appears in a passage you quote). Changes in job designations have helped eliminate some biases: police officers and flight attendants may be either men or women. But usually the way you phrase your writing makes a difference. "He" and "his" are masculine pronouns, so rather than use them as pronouns that refer to groups that include both sexes, recast your wording.

    Unless an individual's religion is an issue or has some bearing on what you are writing, you may safely omit the reference *even though* a source you worked from might have mentioned the matter. The same is true for biases about national origin and the other common biases listed above.

    In sum, fairness should be evident your own writing. But you cannot change what other people have written or said. You must quote accurately, even if your source exhibits an obvious bias that *you* would not want to use.

6. **Refer to a composition textbook or handbook for particulars about writing style and conventions,** as well as for information about being accu-

rate and specific when you write. Remember that your prime objective in writing this paper is to communicate clearly to your audience. You want the reader or readers to understand exactly what you have to say in this important piece of work!

Starting Your Paper

People write in different ways: slowly, stop and start, straight through. Some are ready to begin a paper as soon as they sit down; they may already have thought out much of the wording and have only to commit it to paper as they begin a first draft. Some simply can't get those first words started, even though they are thoroughly familiar with their subject matter. For many, the actual writing doesn't come as easily. An outline helps, but the actual act of writing may be difficult.

You will probably find the opening of your research paper fairly easy to write because of the preliminary work you've done. But if you have trouble getting started or if writing the opening of a paper intimidates you, don't waste time worrying over it. Instead, begin with another part of your outline and *return* to the opening. No rule says you have to write material in the same order your audience is going to read it!

Good Openings

Some research papers open with an expansion of the thesis statement, with the main ideas of the paper developed into a first paragraph. But that is not necessarily the way you should begin *your* paper. Here are nine different kinds of starts you might use to begin your research paper, each illustrated by a sample beginning for a paper.

As with many other suggestions for writing, consider these as idea starters, rather than as anything you should imitate slavishly. The best opening for your *own* research paper is the one that comes most naturally to you on the basis of what you've decided to write about your chosen subject.

1. Clarify the subject   you are going to write about.

```
The language used in cigarette advertisements in maga-
zines and newspapers has long been governed by the guide-
lines of various organizations. Now the declaration by the
Surgeon General that cigarettes are addictive may make
still other changes. Despite such restrictions, differ-
ences in word emphasis and other elements of slanting make
```

it possible to trace changes in cigarette ads over the
last twenty-five years.

(*from* "Changes in the Language of Cigarette Advertisements"
by Yamily Gueli)

This paragraph sets a time limit and a subject limit ("word emphasis and
other elements of slanting") for the research paper that follows. Such clarification prepares readers for concentration on language, as promised by the
title.

2. *State your position*   on the subject you have chosen.

The 1980s are being called the "Information Age" and we
often hear of our culture being called a "Computer Society" because of the rapid growth of computer technology.
As population in this country grows and the government's
responsibilities to its citizens increase, fulfilling
those responsibilities requires federal agencies to accu-
mulate more and more information about individuals.
Because computers make gathering, storing, and disseminat-
ing that information easier and more extensive, individuals should be sure that their long-cherished right to
personal privacy is not violated by either the government
or its technology.

(*from* "Computers, Government Files, and Personal Privacy"
by Jason Roberts)

This example shows how it is possible to state a line of reasoning that
will lead the reader through a research paper that proves a point. In this one
paragraph the author's position is made clear: he is going to show that
government storage of information about individuals may be a threat to
personal privacy.

3. *Relate your topic to something current or well known.*

Twenty-seven states now have lotteries. The latest one
to begin a state lottery [at the time the student wrote this research
paper] is Florida, and during its first <u>day</u> of operation,
people bet more than $13,500,000! Consider the amount of
money bet daily in the state lotteries, at race tracks
around the country, in Nevada and in Atlantic City as well

as other legal places to gamble--and add the money spent
on gambling that isn't regulated by states. No wonder that
the compulsion to gamble has often been the topic of psychological and sociological studies. The psychology of
the gambler has also spurred the imaginations of creative
writers. In "The Queen of Spades" by Pushkin and in The
Gambler by Dostoevsky we have portraits of two gamblers by
master writers. The works are similar in the development
of the major characters and in the approaches both authors
take to the workings of gamblers' minds.

> (*from* "The Compulsion to Gamble as Shown by Pushkin and
> Dostoevsky" by Mirischa B. Cooke)

The author of this research paper began with comments about gambling
that her readers would certainly recognize and relate to, yet indicated why
she was making those statements: to prepare the audience to read about
gambling in two literary works.

4. Challenge some generally held assumption about your topic.

Joseph Stalin ruled Russia for 56 years. He was constantly in the news, both in his own country and abroad.
One might think that a person so much in the spotlight
would be well known. Yet that is not the case. Not even
the name "Stalin" was his own; he first used it in 1910
and adopted it permanently seven years later. He himself
undoubtedly destroyed most of the records which might have
shed some light on his true personality and character.
During his rule of the Soviet Union, the history of his
life underwent repeated revisions as inconsistencies were
eliminated and his place in the revolution and in the
development of Communism was changed and distorted. The
real Stalin "died" many years before his death.

> (*from* "Stalin Since His Death" by Mike Perez)

This student challenges the assumption that Stalin was well known because
he was a very public figure. Since the paper was about evaluations of Stalin's
impact on history, it was begun by suggesting that Stalin was not really known
at all—contentions supported later in the paper.

5. ***Show something paradoxical***   about your subject or about the material you will present.

```
Television is certainly one of the most influential
forces on society in this last half of the twentieth cen-
tury.  Yet though it is called "educational," it teaches
little.  Though it is called "real," it is fakery of the
worst sort.  Though it is said to be a disseminator of
American values, it has worked to destroy them. It encour-
ages violence, passivity, complacency, and illiteracy
simultaneously--characteristics illustrated in the novel
Being There.
```

(*from* "*Being There* May Be the 'Great American Novel'") by Michael Davidson)

The paradoxes of television are introduced here as a way of developing the paradoxes the reader will enounter in reading about this novel in the research paper.

6. ***Use a brief quotation***   (if you can find one applicable) that is provocative or that makes a general statement about your subject.

```
As Arbuthnot wrote:
          Children's freedom is in their world of play,
     where the avenues they pursue are those of their own
     invention and are limited only by individual crea-
     tivity and imagination.  But children are highly
     prone to suggestion, and this suggestion begins in
     the nursery.  As images [in children's rhymes and
     poems] grow more complex and more subtle, they
     quicken the child's perceptions, stimulate his
     imagination, and presently begin to suggest fuller
     and deeper meanings. (246)
```

(*from* "Some Effects of Violence in Nursery Rhymes" by Bernice Miller)

This quotation sets the tone and content for the research paper that follows. The author of the quotation is an authority on children's literature, so the student who wrote the research paper decided Ms. Arbuthnot's words would carry weight in setting the stage for her own thesis.

7. ***State some striking facts or statistics***   you discovered about your topic.

```
Children today seem to be glued to the silver tube
called television.  By kindergarten age (five years old),
```

the average child who started watching television at age
three will have consumed 5,000 to 8,000 hours of television a year, and watched more than 30,000 commercials <u>per
year</u> (Fransecky) [underscore mine]. If this is the television viewing of a five year old, simple multiplication
will produce astonishing amounts of TV viewing for older
children. Since violence appears in both live-action and
cartoon programs, every child today has undoubtedly seen
many thousands of hours of violence and untold thousands
of violent acts while watching television.

(from "TV Violence and Children" by Marla Ledford)

Although readers may have seen statistics about television viewing, and
even about the amount of violence shown, repeating them at the beginning
of a research paper on this subject focuses the reader's attention on how much
violence young children view.

8. ***Place your topic in time*** by giving some historical or chronological
information.

For as long as there have been liars, there have been
attempts to find the truth. Those on trial in ancient
China were made to chew rice powder while testifying. If
the powder was dry when the suspect spat it out, he was
judged guilty because it was assumed that nervousness over
telling lies had dried the saliva in the suspect's mouth.
Other ordeals were set up for suspected liars in other
times, including being subjected to boiling water or red-
hot stones ("Lie Detectors in Business"). Finally, with
the invention of the modern polygraph (commonly called a
lie detector) in 1921, it seemed that there was at last a
foolproof way of finding out if people answering questions
were lying or being truthful.

(from "Polygraph Tests and Employment Practices"
by Ronnie B. Londner)

This opening paragraph of a research paper doesn't include the thesis
statement but, rather, leads to it in the next paragraph. Ms. Londner felt she
needed to sketch historical methods of lie detection as a way of opening the
door to her subject, the modern polygraph as used in employment practices.

9. *Give a brief description or background résumé of some person or event of significance to your topic.*

> Lady Murasaki Shikibu was born about A.D. 978 and died about 1030. She had the enviable position of being a member of the Fujiwara clan and a member of a family which produced mikados, statesmen, and at least one celebrated Japanese poet. Because she was of the nobility, she had the time and the education to write. Her book <u>Genji Mono-gatari</u>, known in English as <u>The Tale of Genji</u>, is now the West's chief source of information about court life in 11th century Japan.

(*from* "Amorality in 11th Century Japanese Life"
by Margaret Haag)

Since *The Tale of Genji* provides one of the chief sources of information for this research paper, the author opened by establishing the identity of the author of that book. Readers who may have been unfamiliar with Lady Murasaki are thus informed and will accept the veracity of the information in the research paper that comes from her writing.

Bad Openings

Just as there are good openings for your research paper—first paragraphs that draw the reader into your work—so there are also poor openings that detract from the quality of your paper. Six ways you *should not* begin a research paper follow.

1. *Don't repeat the title.*   It has already been read, usually right before beginning the text of the paper, so repeating it in the first paragraph is an obvious attempt to fill space and stall for time.

2. *Don't tell what you propose to do in the paper.*   Such a statement may be a desirable style in some business and technical reports, but not for research papers written for class. Simply *start doing* what you propose. Any writing that says "In this paper I am going to . . ." is not only juvenile, but it also puts off readers and makes them impatient. It also shows of lack of imagination and subtlety.

3. *Don't feel compelled to repeat the thesis statement completely in the opening of the paper.*   Although you may certainly use the wording of the thesis statement, remember that you wrote it mainly as a *guide to your*

own preparatory work and as a way focusing your paper. Besides, your thesis statement may disclose more information than you want the audience to know at the outset.

You could, however, begin by stating an idea inherent in the thesis statement. Or you could vary the wording of the thesis statement in order to use its ideas in the opening of your paper.

4. ***Don't ask a question.*** You might get an unexpected answer.

5. ***Don't give a dictionary definition.*** There is nothing wrong with referring to a dictionary as you would to any other source of information. But beginning with a definition—*especially* since most of them in dictionaries are not particularly well-written—suggests that what follows the opening will be just as dull and lifeless as the definition.

Instead, you can probably define any necessary terms more effectively in your own words. If you really think you must quote from a dictionary, try holding off until later in your research paper.

6. ***Don't write a cute or folksy opening.*** Such wording often falls flat and ruins the whole effect of your paper. Besides, many people feel that since a research paper is a serious work of scholarship, there is no room in it for cuteness or excessive informality.

Writing the Body of Your Paper

The body of your paper is that part in which you explain and support your thesis. Obviously, as your writing progresses you will acknowledge the sources you consulted. But remember that you are doing *original writing* about your subject, *not* just stringing together a series of quotations and paraphrases.

All the skills you have learned in writing courses through many years of school should be applied to this task! Take time to put into practice all you know about explaining and supporting ideas fully. Clarify information that may be new to your audience and give needed background or illustrations to your reader(s). Even terms or names that may now be familiar to you may have to be defined or identified for your audience.

A full explanation of all the qualities of good writing that should be part of your paper would take up a whole book. You will find that information in any book on composition or rhetoric. Take time to consult one or more such volumes—either those you use (or used) in classes or those available in any library.

The next four sections are reminders of some qualities of good writing that you should be particularly aware of in writing your research paper. If they sound familiar, it's because you have probably read the same information in your composition books.

Unity and Coherence

A **unified** paper is one that deals with a single subject and a single idea. If you have chosen a subject carefully and prepared a good outline—and stuck to it as you wrote—you may be certain that your paper is unified. Don't get carried away with ideas that strike you while you are working, for digressions detract from the unity of a research paper.

A **coherent** piece of writing is one that hangs together well, that not only holds the attention of readers but also helps them move from one point to another. A well-structured outline from which you write a carefully organized piece helps tie everything in your paper together.

The following are additional elements of writing that make for unity and coherence.

- **Transitional words** ("therefore," "however," "because," and others) **and phrases** ("in the second place," "at the same time," "as a result," and others) are flags to signal a reader that you are moving from one thought to another and that you are establishing a relationship between them. Use transitions between sentences, to move from one idea to another, and to tie paragraphs together.

- **Pronouns** (such as "he," "she," "they," "them," and "those") give variety to sentence structure, so you will undoubtedly find yourself writing with many of them. Remember, however, that the noun which each pronoun replaces (that is, its referent or antecedent) must appear just before the pronoun—not several lines before it and certainly not after it. Clear and unequivocal pronouns help writing attain coherence.

- **Repetition** of key words and phrases acts as an interlocking device. Repetition *doesn't* mean simply beginning a sentence with the words that ended the previous one; that's boring and is usually unnecessary. And repetition does not have to be precisely the *same* wording.

EXAMPLE: From the early 1970s to the present, this pressure has been felt strongly
                 enough to bring the issue of censorship in school libraries into the
REPETITION: courts. Most litigation efforts during this period . . .

"Litigation" says the same thing as bringing "the issue . . . into the courts."

- **Consistent point of view** means that the attitude or stance you take toward your subject remains the same throughout. To jump from being one who figuratively sits back and contemplates the overall view of a situation to one who vigorously supports a course of action in relation to that situation is to be inconsistent in point of view. The writing that results tends to be fragmented rather than coherent.

- **Integration of information,** so that quotations, summaries, and other information drawn from sources are joined within the text, makes the writing flow. If these elements are merely plopped down, one after the other on a page, the result is choppy and disjointed. But if they are carefully introduced and integrated, the entire research paper holds together and sounds as if one person—you—wrote it. Such careful integration of materials is special to the research paper and not, like the other suggestions in this section, qualities of all good writing. A separate section of this chapter, beginning on page 174, is about integrating resources.

Adequate Support

Writing that simply tosses out thoughts has little believability, no matter how worthwhile or intriguing the ideas may be. On the other hand, were those same thoughts supported adequately, they would demand credence and even acceptance by readers.

Support for various statements in your research paper can take many forms (details of which are in most composition books). You might offer *statistics*. Or you could give your reader *examples* to make a particular point.

The *documentation* you offer throughout your paper will be the major support for what you write. Using *authoritative sources* is part of such documentation.

Emphasis

When you speak to somebody, you can emphasize what you believe is important by repeating words, as well as by using your voice to stress particular ideas or by pausing before making an important statement. Not all of these avenues are open to you when you write. Therefore, you need to use other ways of emphasizing what you want to bring to the special attention of the audience for your research paper.

You achieve this emphasis by

- using proportion to give more space to more important ideas,
- repeating words and ideas that are important,
- positioning what you want to emphasize where it will be seen easily, such as at the beginnings or ends of paragraphs, or
- using visual devices such as underlinings, special layouts (as you see here), or subheads in units.

Concreteness and Specificity

Good writing tells the audience exactly what the writer wants to convey, leaving nothing to chance or to guesswork. Therefore, as you write your research paper, choose wording that is concrete rather than abstract, and specific rather than general.

Concrete words name what you can ascertain through the senses: what you see, hear, smell, touch, and taste. "A blue two-story house with red shutters" is concrete because the words tell what you can see. **Abstract words,** on the other hand, name feelings, beliefs, or ideas. "Beauty," "happiness," "honor," "intellectual freedom," and "the American way" are examples of abstractions because they may signify different concepts to those who read or hear such words. Because concrete words represent fairly definite concepts, they leave less to the imagination of the reader than do abstract words. Therefore, when you strive to use concrete words, you are helping to convey your own thoughts (even abstractions) directly to your audience.

Specific words limit meaning in another way; they narrow the concept expressed by a **general word.** "Animal" is a general word because it signifies a wide range of living creatures, from whales to amoebas. "Whale" is a more specific word, but even *it* can be made more specific: "baleen whales" describes a particular group, and "humpback whale" differentiates between that species and other kinds of baleen whales. In writing your research paper, the more specific wording you can use, the more accurately you convey your thoughts to readers.

Integrating Resource Information

The chief characteristic of research writing is that it must *document all sources used* in the paper. But those sources are the backup for what *you* have to say; they are meant to support and explain what you offer. Documentation isn't an end in itself. And don't let the resources become the dominant element in your research paper.

To keep the focus of your writing on your own ideas instead of on your source documentation, you must integrate the two *smoothly* so as not to disrupt the flow of writing in your paper or call attention to differences in style and tone between what you write and what your reference sources wrote.

Citing the sources you used is easy when you write **parenthetical documentation.** That is, you acknowledge sources right in the text at the point where you use them. (The specifics of doing so are explained in Chapter 8.) Such documentation is the standard for research work in the humanities and is recommended by the MLA [Modern Language Association]. (Other disciplines use slightly different styles, as shown on pages 211–16.)

Nobody can tell you how much documentation to include in your paper. Certainly you need to give the sources of everything you didn't already know or what isn't common knowledge—that is, anything that isn't your own thinking in the paper. Obviously, the more new information you discovered, the more you will have to document. Sources on your notes should be a guide. Your concern at this point, in writing the paper, is how to work all those quotations and summaries, paraphrases and personal comments into the body of your research paper—and how to do so smoothly.

The mark of a well-integrated resource item is that it doesn't call attention to itself! Here are six ways you can integrate documented information into the text of your research paper.

1. ***Lead into a quotation, paraphrase, or summary.*** One reason for providing such a lead is so the reader can differentiate between what is your own wording or ideas and what isn't—and thus prevent misunderstanding or confusion. A second reason for the lead is to keep your audience from suddenly coming upon any wording that may disrupt the flow of your text.

   Note especially, in the following examples, that because you are using parenthetical documentation (see pages 193–201 for details), information included in the introduction to a quotation, paraphrase, or summary does not need to be repeated.

   EXAMPLE: The Office for Intellectual Freedom's case summaries report that . . . isn't to be withdrawn by the whim of the school board (147).

   or

   Thomas Emerson writes that in the American Civil Liberties Union's 1982 survey . . . reported pressure from the censors (191).

2. ***Vary the wording of introductory phrases.*** Easy as it is to write that a person "says" or "writes" something you use in your research paper, good writing style demands that you be more imaginative (and less repetitive) in introducing such material. A dictionary or thesaurus may be helpful in solving this problem.

   POSSIBILITIES:

   Professor Jason Roberts *states*
   asserts
   believes
   thinks
   insists
   contends
   confirms

declares
emphasizes
adds
affirms
points out

This sort of varied wording may be used to introduce indirect, as well as direct, quotations and any other material you are documenting.

3. ***Use documented information anywhere in a paragraph, not just at the end.***   Looking at a paper with documenting parentheses at the ends of paragraph after paragraph gives most readers the impression that the author has done little more than just lay out pieces of information, one item after another, without much thought of the relationship of other peoples' ideas to the author's own. Your goal in writing should be to avoid such a cut-and-paste look!

EXAMPLES:

Documentation at beginning of sentence:

<u>Books Behind Bars</u> lists many award–winning novels that
have been banned, including . . . and Alice Walker's
<u>The Color Purple</u>.

Documentation in middle of sentence:

Drawing conclusions from his 1984 survey, Professor
Ken Donelson ("Almost Thirteen Years" 98) reports that
the most frequently banned authors are John Steinbeck
and Judy Blume, both award–winning novelists.

Documentation at end of sentence:

Or, they may have withdrawn books from shelves and
listed them as "lost" or "stolen" (106–08).

4. ***Make documented material fit grammatically into your own sentences.***
   Do this in three different ways:

   a) Delete words from a quotation and use ellipses to show you have
   done so.

EXAMPLE: A New York attorney who filed . . ."'means the
              doors to the courthouse are open . . . to

explore and ventilate school board decisions. . ..'" (qtd. in Wermiel).

b) Use **square brackets** to clarify information that appears to be out of context in your own writing.

EXAMPLE: Kraus notes that as our country moves away from being a "melting pot" [a term seldom heard these days] and becomes more diversified, demands are being made to the schools to impart values to students.

c) Use **only the most relevant part** of a passage you document; no rule says you must use every single word you take on a note card.

EXAMPLE:

Note card:

Am. Lib. Assoc's. OIF pub. newsletter, tracks cases, statistics, sets rules for librarians on handling probs., has Lib. Bill of Rights (see other notes)

In the research paper:

The Office for Intellectual Freedom of the American Library Association publishes a newsletter on the subject, tracks current cases, and provides statistics on censorship cases.

5. *Avoid writing paragraphs in which you document every single line.* Such writing suggests you have little to say for yourself, is unnecessary, and is certainly awkward. Rather, you may be able to combine ideas, either from a single source or from several sources, and use only one citation.

EXAMPLE: Several writers have explored some of the many "reasons" censors give for wanting books removed from school library shelves (Pell 118; <u>Books Behind Bars</u>; Darling 120).

6. *Use paraphrases and summaries, not just quotations* to support what you say. Certainly you will want to use quotations in your research paper. But as you come to a note card containing a quotation, consider whether you might convey the same idea by paraphrasing or summarizing it in the text of your research paper.

EXAMPLE:

Note card quotation:

```
"Forty of these were on the elementary level, 77 on the
junior high school level, and 386 on the high school
level. Sixty-four affected all levels, K-12." Nolte 213
```

In the research paper:

```
In the decade from 1965 to 1975, over 500 censorship
cases were reported to have occurred in public school
libraries (Nolte 213).
```

Punctuating Quotations

If someone else's words are especially good or clear, or they are from a primary source and so will carry weight, you will want to use them in the body of your paper, even though you are using quotations sparingly. Your note cards show the spelling, punctuation, and capitalization used in the original source. Now you need only copy that information into your text, following the usual rules of punctuation and a few conventions that are found in writing handbooks and textbooks.

Short Prose Passages

A "short" prose quotation of either fiction or nonfiction is one that occupies *three or fewer lines of text* in your research paper. Follow these usual writing customs for such quotations within your own sentences:

- If the end of a quotation is also the end of your own sentence, put the period inside the concluding quotation marks; otherwise, use a comma inside the end of the quoted sentence and a period at the end of the entire sentence.

- Question marks or exclamation marks that end a quotation (and that you use in your own writing) go inside the concluding quote marks, even though your own sentence continues to its conclusion and may have a period at its end.

- Quotations are either part of a sentence or are separated from introductory wording by a comma, depending on the construction of the sentence. Only occasionally does a colon introduce a short quotation.

- Quotations are separated from concluding wording by a comma inside the concluding quote marks (unless the quotation ends with a question mark or an exclamation mark).

- Use a capital letter to begin a fully quoted sentence even if it does not also begin your own sentence of text.

As in any sort of writing, quotation marks are used to acknowledge that familiar words are used in a special sense. And also as in all writing, a quotation within another quotation (that is, when the source you quote contains a quotation) is indicated by single, instead of double, quotation marks. Any comma ending the quotation appears before either of those quote marks.

Parenthetical documentation is put as close as possible to the passage and outside the quotation marks, usually after them but occasionally in the lead-in wording. The main guide is that documentation shouldn't interfere with the flow of the text.

EXAMPLE: The Board removed the books because, it stated, they were "anti-American, anti-Christian, anti-Semitic, and just plain filthy," and justified the removal on grounds of its "duty, or moral obligation, to protect the children in our schools from this moral danger . . .." (qtd. in North 134).

Longer Prose Passages

Quotations of *four or more lines of typewritten text* in your research paper are considered "longer" and are signaled to the audience in a different way. The introductory wording often (but not necessarily) ends with a colon. The entire quoted passage is then *indented ten spaces from the left margin*. Do not use quotation marks and do not change the double spacing of your typewriter or word processing program.

Donelson is quick to point out this problem:

    Once the door is open to anyone to censor, then it cannot be closed because one kind of censorship is said to be good and another is said to be bad. All censors would argue that they cen-

```
sor for good and moral reasons.  ("Enemies
Within" 109)
```

The parenthetical documentation occurs *two spaces after the concluding period* of the quoted passage.

Do not indent the first word of a single paragraph or part of a paragraph. However, if the longer quotation is two or more paragraphs, signal the subsequent paragraphs by indenting the beginning word of each by three spaces in addition to the ten spaces from the left margin.

Retain any special punctuation or other markings of the original passage when you reproduce it as a quotation in your paper.

Short Passages of Poetry

Incorporate a single line, or part of a line, of poetry as part of a sentence in your text by following the conventions noted above. Record up to three lines as you did on your note cards: that is, by using a slash mark (virgule) with one space before and after it to indicate the typography of separate lines of poetry.

```
EXAMPLE:    In Sonnet 116, Shakespeare announces "Let me not
            to the marriage of true minds / Admit impedi-
            ments. Love is not love / Which alters when it
            alteration finds."
```

Longer Passages of Poetry

Quotations of *four or more lines* should appear in the same way they do in the original poem and each line should begin ten spaces from the left margin of your typing. The text continues to be double-spaced. Show the source two spaces after the last period of the poetry, just as you do for prose.

However, if you cannot get a complete verse line on a single line of type that's indented ten spaces, or doing so would make the quoted poetry look unbalanced, you may begin each line closer to the left margin.

Since accurate quotation of poety requires you to reproduce the original typography, you may need to ignore customary research paper indentation when you quote a poem with unusual typography. Then, copy the poem exactly as it appears in the original source, as in this example of the poem "Easter Wings" by George Herbert.

```
EXAMPLE:    Lord, Who createdst man in wealth and store,
                Though foolishly he lost the same,
                    Decaying more and more,
```

```
                    Till he became
                      More poore:
                      With thee
                      O let me rise,
                  As larks harmoniously,
              And sing this day Thy victories:
          Then shall the fall further the flight in me.
```

Identify the author and title of poetry quotations as part of the text (as shown above) or at the beginning of the poem, this way:

```
                   Easter Wings
                by George Herbert
```

Drama

Since dramatic quotations will either be in prose or poetry, follow the form recommended for either of those genres. That is, up to three lines of dialogue or stage direction may be incorporated into the text, but longer passages (four or more lines) should be indented ten spaces from the left. Be sure to include the name of the character speaking, either in the introduction to the quotation or just as it appeared in the source you used.

EXAMPLE:

Run-in Quotation

```
Romeo begins the so-called balcony scene by saying, "He
jests at scars that never felt a wound."
```

Full Quotation

```
Here is the beginning of the so-called balcony scene:
"Rom. He jests at scars that never felt a wound."
```

If you quote a passage that includes several speakers, be particularly careful that each one is indicated.

Comment Notes

The parenthetical notes you use to document sources of information are generally all you need in the text of your research paper. However, you may find that you want to add to or qualify something in the writing that just doesn't fit into the text without being distracting. Rather than break into the thoughts being expressed in the paper, make such comments—*sparingly*—in notes that appear at the bottom of that page (footnotes) or at the end of the paper (endnotes).

Comment notes are used for

- brief elaboration, qualification, or addition to what is in the text,
- a necessary evaluative comment on a source, or
- identifying a series of sources which, if shown in parenthetical documentation, would interrupt the text of the paper.

Signal the comment note by putting a superscript arabic numeral, such as this,[1] at the place in the text where it is most relevant and after punctuation markings (except dashes). Use the same arabic numeral at the beginning of the note, then give the information.

EXAMPLE: [1] No periods or other marks are used with
                  the superscript numeral and no space is used
                  before it. However, one space always follows
                  the numeral.

Number comment notes *successively throughout a paper.*

Separate **footnotes** from the end of text on that page by four lines (two double spacings). Single-space the lines of the footnote, but if you have more than one such note on a page—which you should certainly try to avoid—double-space between them.

Endnotes are placed on a separate page headed "Notes" (centered one inch down from the top of the page) at the conclusion of the paper and before the Works Cited page. Double-space after the heading and throughout the notes on the page. Begin each note by indenting the superscript numeral five spaces from the left margin; leave a space after it and then start the words of the note, writing as far as necessary toward the right. The second and succeeding lines of each note begin at the left margin of the page.

You can see endnotes used for comment on the text of the Sample Research Paper on page 275.

Ending the Paper

Stop writing when you finish what you have to say. When you come to the end of your outline and note cards, conclude gracefully but not abruptly. Don't pad at the end, and don't try to write a sudden one-sentence "summary" of the whole paper. In particular, *don't introduce or even suggest any new ideas in the last paragraph or so of your paper*!

Good Endings

1. *If you have written an argumentive or persuasive paper, remind the audience of what you want them to do or think in order to respond to your presentation.*

> The computer has created problems of quantity, sensitivity, and variety of data about us that never existed before because never before has information been so easy and cheap to store, retrieve, and move about. If we are to retain our right of privacy, and therefore of control over our personal lives, we ought to pay attention once more to Thomas Jefferson's observation that "eternal vigilance is the price of liberty."
>
> (*from* "Computers, Government Files, and Personal Privacy" by Jason Roberts)

2. *Use a brief quotation that summarizes the ideas or attitudes you have expressed throughout the paper.*

In a 1938 speech before the National Education Association, President Franklin Delano Roosevelt said:

> Freedom to learn is the first necessity of guaranteeing that man himself shall be self-reliant enough to be free.. . . If in other lands the press and books and literature of all kinds are censored, we must redouble our efforts here to keep it free.. . . The ultimate victory of tomorrow is through democracy with education.
> (qtd. in "Censorship and Libraries" exhibit)
>> (*from* "School Libraries Should Not Ban Books" by Carol Matz)

Use a quotation only if it bears out the points you've made within your research paper and does so in a style you think especially suitable to the subject. In this case, Ms. Matz felt the quotation was particularly suitable because of the authority carried by the president's words.

3. Make some statement about your thesis instead of merely repeating it.

We have seen the Roslyn of the original story, whom
the men wanted too much to please, become the charming but
somewhat cloying girl of a later Miller story. When she
was transformed into a major character in <u>The Misfits</u>,
Roslyn grew in complexity and lost the simple definition
of innocence or sophistication that each of her "ances-
tors" had. In these three works, Miller has provided us
with an excellent view of the development of a dramatic
character from first sketches to boldly colored
completeness.

(from "Roslyn: Evolution of a Literary Character" by Judith Anndy)

The thesis of this research paper was "Arthur Miller used elements of a sophisticated mistress in one story and a childlike wife in another to develop the appealing but not fully explained character of Roslyn Taber in *The Misfits*." While the concluding paragraph alludes to that statement, it also includes other material that was presented in the paper.

4. Return to some initial generalization and show how you have proved, disproved, or enlarged upon it.

Don Quixote, then, was not simply a mad old man.
Rather, he was a person of deep humanity whose misadven-
tures stemmed mainly from attempts to help the oppressed.
Furthermore, what seemed to be his foolish dreams are
really the hopes of the sanest and least foolish people
everywhere; what seemed to be his useless persistence is
really idealism; what seemed to be his inability to cope
with his time is really the doubt and tension every human
lives with. The character Cervantes created cannot be
called "mad" unless each of us is willing to accept that
label also. For he is a composite of us all—and each of
us has within the self a bit of Don Quixote.

(from "The Madman Who Was Most Sane" by Ida Kaufman)

This concluding paragraph begins with a generalization that has pervaded the text of the research paper. The specifics that support the generalization are summaries of those that have been offered throughout the text as proof. So to end this paper, the author merely drew together the various strands already developed.

5. *Link what you have written either to something known or to what seems a future possibility.*

> Diet and exercise, then, have been shown to affect
> the longevity of various lower forms of animals. Increas-
> ingly, researchers are showing the relationship of these
> two factors to human longevity. Medical advances, too,
> are preventing or treating an assortment of diseases and
> illnesses once thought impossible to battle. Even the
> psychology of growing old is increasingly being under-
> stood, so people are learning how to cope with attitudes
> and outlooks. In short, there is a good chance that by
> the next century living to be 120 or 130 years old will
> not only be possible but will become a fact for many, many
> people.

(from "Growing Older Gracefully" by Norman Raimundo)

All the elements mentioned in the final paragraph of this paper were dealt with in earlier portions, and all of them pointed to research into the possibilities of extending life. The author of this paper decided to save the "punch line" for the final sentence by stating this prediction for the future that was mentioned in enough research sources that it could be considered common knowledge (which is why the last sentence is not documented).

6. *State a conclusion you have reached about your subject.*

> The polygraph has been called "inherently intrusive
> . . . [and the testing] invades privacy and degrades human
> dignity" (Pear). Added to that, results are often inac-
> curate and operators unreliable. The evidence <u>against</u>
> using the polygraph to screen employees in private busi-
> nesses seems overwhelming. Relatively few people are dis-
> honest. To seek them out with a lie detector does not
> justify the intimidation and heartbreak of polygraph test-
> ing for the many honest people.

(from "Polygraph Tests and Employment Practices"
by Ronnie B. Londner)

As a result of her research and writing the text of the paper, the author concluded that polygraph tests for employment should be abolished and so states her conclusion in this final paragraph. In addition, note that Ms. Londner has included a short quotation to support her conclusion—a good ending for a research paper.

Bad Endings

The ending is the last thing your audience sees and so it will leave a strong impression, despite anything else you may have written in your paper. To keep that impression good and maintain the impact of a well-written paper, avoid these bad endings.

1. **Don't bring up a new idea.** The end of a paper is the time to finish everything, not to make a fresh start.
2. **Don't stop abruptly or simply trail off.** Your paper needs a specific ending and deserves one that brings your ideas to completion.
3. **Don't ask a question.** You might get an answer you didn't count on!
4. **Don't make any statement or suggestion that needs extensive clarification.** The time to make explanations has passed.
5. **Don't fumble.** Stop when you have nothing more to say.
6. **Don't tell explicitly what you have done in the paper.** Give your audience credit for having *understood* what you did in the paper. Also, don't be so unimaginative as to write anything like "In this paper it has been shown that. . . ." The audience realizes what you have shown.
7. **Don't make a change in your style.** Keep your writing style at the end the same as it was at the beginning.

Revising Your Paper

Good writers—students, business people, hobbyists, attorneys, and everyone who makes a living by writing—make changes in wording and presentation of ideas as they write. That is one kind of revision, of tinkering with a piece of writing until it says exactly what you want it to say.

Another kind of revision comes after the first complete writing or first draft of a work. Then you may add, delete, or rearrange words and ideas. Even if you were writing from a satisfactory outline, you may find that when the whole research paper is finished, there are parts that would fit better in one place than in another.

Revision is another chance to look at what you've written and change it, to make it most precisely convey your intentions to your audience. In fact, writing is often described as a "messy process" because of constant revision.

Professional writers are seldom satisfied with their first drafts; they often rewrite extensively and then follow advice from their editors. You can emulate that working arrangement to some extent. And the more you get used to editing, the more you develop your critical facilities so you know what can profit from revision, especially in word choice, sentence structure, and accuracy.

If your instructor doesn't have classroom time available for peer reviews, you might get together with one or more classmates at a time you all have available outside of class. Either read each other's papers one at a time, making comments and suggestions as you go, or exchange papers and note on each person's draft some ways (or places) in which the writing is good and some portions that could be clarified or otherwise improved.

Revising is easiest when you approach a work as if seeing it for the first time—admittedly a difficult job if you've been working for weeks on the research paper. However, you *will* find it helpful to put the first draft away for several days—a week, if you have time—before looking at it with an eye toward making changes.

Attend to the niceties of mechanics—that is, correcting spelling, punctuation, capitalization, and paragraphing—at the last reading before typing your paper. Use a dictionary and refer to a composition handbook if you need to as a way of sticking to the conventions of edited American English that your audience will surely expect to find in your research paper.

Word Choice and Sentence Structure

Sometimes when people are engrossed in writing down their ideas, they can't find just the right word at the moment they need it. Instead of stopping and losing a train of thought, they use a second-best word. A better way of finding the right word is to mark the passage as you write; use a symbol to show that you need to improve some wording or restate a passage. If you've selected a second-best word or marked some wording for revision, now is the time to check back and find that—and any other—wording that can be changed or improved. Take time in revision to select the best words for every idea in your paper.

Remember that although *you* may know what you mean, your reader might not. Look for precision in words when you revise. And don't let sentences get away from you; revision gives you the chance to tighten them.

DRAFT SENTENCE:

```
The decision was not only about the rights of the students
in this particular case to wear armbands, but it was also
really about all other ways that students express them-
selves in schools in today's society.
```

INTENTION: The decision was about one case but it had con-
                sequences beyond that.

REVISED SENTENCE:

The decision doesn't relate only to the wearing of armbands; it was really about <u>all</u> forms of expression in the
schools.

During your research, you may learn a considerable amount of jargon, the words and phrases characteristic of a particular field and used by people knowledgeable in it. But your audience may not be as well-versed in the special "language" as you are after your research, so take care to catch any such wording and "translate" what you are writing into what your audience can understand readily.

JARGON: Soon Dorothy Liebes's trademark became her skip
                dent warps of textured and metallic yarns with
                unusual weft materials.

REVISION: Soon Dorothy Liebes's trademark became the fab-
                rics she designed of unevenly spaced textured
                and metallic yarns crossed by unusual threads or
                even by thin strips of wood or metal.

Here are some other techniques you can use to attain good writing through revision:

- Use a variety of sentence structures.
- Combine a series of short, simple sentences into one, more complex sentence.
- Use transitional words and phrases (such as "in addition," "therefore," "equally important," and "nevertheless" to connect ideas smoothly within and between sentences and paragraphs.
- Make sure modifiers are near the words they modify.
- Be sure antecedents of pronouns are clear.

These and many other aids to good writing are developed in composition and rhetoric books; consult them.

Mechanics

People expect to find the spelling, punctuation, capitalization, sentence structures, and paragraphing of the English language rather uniform in what they read. You owe it to your audience to meet those expectations. Any change from the expected is an interference to the audience, an annoyance to a reader.

Therefore, help your audience by following the conventions of edited American English and present a paper that exemplifies such customs. A check of these conventions is ordinarily the last step in revising your paper.

Make sure punctuation and capitalization are accurate. Be sure verb tenses don't shift without reason and that subjects and verbs agree in number. Use abbreviations only where permissible, and be sure those you use are accurate. (A good place to check on such matters is an English handbook or other standard guide.)

Spelling, too, is important in your final draft. Keep a dictionary handy and use it often. Check every word you're not absolutely sure about. If you work at revising with another person, ask that individual to let you know about any word that isn't spelled conventionally so you can make an appropriate change.

In short, do everything you can to be sure your audience focuses on what you have to say rather than on distracting errors of mechanics that can easily be cleared up by careful editing.

Revising on a Computer

If you compose your research paper on a computer using a word processing program, you may revise somewhat differently from those who write with pen on paper or with a typewriter. People who compose on computers usually do more revising as they write than they have done previously, and although various versions of a piece can be saved as printouts, few people bother doing so.

What most people who use computers *do* like to have for the last stages of revision is a hard copy of the final version that is saved on a disk. Editing on that printed copy, where you can see all at once what was written, and turn back and forth to different parts, is easier than trying to work with the limitation of just a few lines at a time on the screen.

One editing aid available if you compose on a computer is a "spell checker," a program that will test your spelling against the conventionally spelled words in its dictionary. The computer won't make corrections for you, but it *will* ask if you want to make a change and you have a chance to do so before you print out what you've written. Many spell checkers will also give you choices of how to spell a word it highlights. What *no* computer program can do, however, is to know whether a word fits into a given context (at least, not home computers as yet). For example "red" will be accepted because it's a word in the program dictionary, even though the proper word in the sentence should be "read."

Some computer programs analyze writing style. They will do such things as spot passive verbs (and encourage you to change them to active ones), tell you about sentence length and word choice, and give you other information that will help in revising the wording and sentence structure of what you have written.

Selecting a Title

Your research paper will be known by its title, so choose one carefully. Although some people decide on a title for their research paper when they begin it, doing so may not be a good idea. New information or a different slant in presentation may well dictate a title. Or, looking at a completed piece of writing may be the best way for you to choose a title. Generally, then, it's a good idea to save title choosing until you finish writing the text of your paper.

A title that gives readers some information about the contents of the paper is preferable to one that is general or vague. With rare exceptions, an informational title is preferable to one that is coy. But a title need not be stuffy or dull. Puns and clever wordings are possible, even desirable, if they catch the spirit of the paper they name.

However, *don't* use a question in place of a title. No matter how provocative you think one might be, it won't be informative. (Better to let the title answer the question you thought of posing.) Finally, *never* use a thesis statement as a title; it's bound to be too long and tell too much.

VAGUE: Private Clubs

IMPROVED: The Case Against Sexual Discrimination in Private Clubs

VAGUE: A Look at William Dean Howells

IMPROVED: The Concept of Work in the Novels of William Dean Howells

COY: Who's Pushing the Puffs?

IMPROVED: Changing Language in Printed Cigarette Ads

Avoid choosing a long, detailed title that gives *too much* information, particularly if you think such a title will make your work sound "academic" or "scholarly." It won't. Rather, such a title is distracting to most readers.

TOO DETAILED:

An Examination of the Setting as Metaphor in the Films of John Ford with Particular Reference to <u>Fort Apache</u>

IMPROVED: Setting as Metaphor in John Ford's Films

As these examples show, *no punctuation is used at the end of a title*. But do *capitalize the first letter of each word* in a title, except for conjunctions, articles, and prepositions. Do not underline a title or put quotation marks around it. However, do follow the conventions of underlining or enclosing in quotation marks any title that appears *within* your own title, as for the film *Fort Apache* in the example above.

Chapter 8

Documenting
Your Paper

By now you know that you *must acknowledge the sources of all material that is not original* in your research paper. That means you must tell readers where you got

- direct quotations
- borrowed ideas, including paraphrases and summaries
- visual material, such as maps, charts, diagrams, and pictures.

The only exception to this listing of what you must give credit for is information that is considered common knowledge (as explained on pages 129–30). However, if you use someone else's words to present that common knowledge, you must credit that individual.

Acknowledgment is in the form of **documentation**. That is, you tell readers **the author, title, publication information, and, if the source is in print, the** *exact page* **where you located the material.**

You also know that the documentation must be *in a prescribed form*. You already have experience in making the punctuation and spacing of your Works Cited conform to particular customs. In this chapter you will read about how to apply some special forms to documenting the text of your paper.

When you document the required material in your research paper, you not only establish your own honesty and scholarly exactness but you also give support to those ideas and conclusions that are your own. The acknowledgment also enables a reader to identify or to verify your material and, perhaps, to study further some aspect of it.

The question of *what requires documentation* and what doesn't is sometimes troublesome. A general rule to follow is: when in doubt, cite the source. It's better to have too much documentation in your paper than not enough, to be considered overzealous rather than careless.

Plagiarism—presenting another person's material as if it were your own (that is, without documentation)—is less likely if you were cautious about acknowledgment when taking notes than if you were careless in the early part of the research process. But be aware that unless you are alert while writing your paper, you might still commit plagiarism by omitting information from your note cards or by failing to include proper acknowledgment in your first draft.

The most common kind of acknowledgment you will have to make is in the text of your research paper (because many papers have no visuals). The preferred method of this book is to acknowledge sources by parenthetical documentation. Therefore, the next section will show you how to do that. Endnotes are still used, so another section of this chapter illustrates that method. The form recommended by the American Psychological Association (APA) is widely used in the social sciences and even in research in the humanities, so on pages 211–13 you can see examples of it. Other documentation systems are also presented in this chapter, in case you ever need to use them.

Parenthetical Documentation (MLA)

Parenthetical documentation is so called because you **enclose the documentation in parentheses** at the point **in your text where the reader should know the source** of information you present. That is, instead of having to look at the bottom of the page or at the end of the research paper, a reader can know immediately the source you acknowledge. It is the standard in English (and many other disciplines in the humanities) because it is recommended by the Modern Language Association [MLA].

Several qualities of parenthetical documentation are particularly helpful:

1. Typing is easy because you put in documentation as you write, without worrying about keeping numbers in order or writing part of the information in one place (the text) and part in another (the endnotes).
2. Reading is easy because the source information is part of the text and a reader needn't hunt for it on another page.

3. Documentation widely used in the social sciences and natural sciences is very similar; once you learn this style, you can readily adapt if you are required to use other documentation formats.

Parenthetical documentation gives brief and specific information—usually only the author's surname or a title plus a page number (or an act, scene, or stanza)—about a source at each point in your research paper that requires such recognition. **A Works Cited entry gives full resource information** at the end of your paper. That is, a reader consults the Works Cited to get a publication date or the name of a publisher, magazine, computer software creator, or film distributor.

The aim of parenthetical documentation is to give required information *without interrupting the flow of reading*. So, what cannot be worked sensibly into a sentence is incorporated into it within parentheses. The documentation may appear anywhere within a paragraph or a sentence—not always at the end of either—and often is best put near internal punctuation marks or where a pause in reading occurs most naturally.

Try to give your reader some indication that a passage to come is not your own work by putting the author's name or a title at the *beginning* of borrowed words or ideas. Thus, at least part of the documentation will tend to come early in sentences and paragraphs and will not allow the audience to think something is original when it isn't—a notion often encouraged by after-the-fact documentation.

Here are some examples of how you can incorporate parenthetical documentation in a text:

1. Identify the author and page in parentheses. Prefer to use an author's name (if available) for a citation because it is most convenient for a reader. Entries in the Works Cited are alphabetical, so complete information about a reference can be found most readily by locating the author.

EXAMPLE: Furthermore, the ALA/OIF notes that 300 contro-
             versies may be reported in a given year, but
             speculates that ten times as many instances of
             uncontested removals may exist (Massie 79).

2. Identify a source by title and page.   Although you may choose to use this format, doing so is generally less satisfactory than identification by author, for reasons noted directly above.

EXAMPLE: The First Amendment to the Constitution, which
             banned—author Kurt Vonnegut (<u>Meese Commission
             Exposed</u> 8) sardonically calls . . .

3. Identify the author or title in the text and put the page number in parentheses.

EXAMPLE: According to Pell (118), the pressure to ban

these works . . .

4. Use an author's last name or the title of a work if you refer to the complete work. Obviously, then, there will be no page numbers.

EXAMPLE: Ciardi's translation of <u>The Divine Comedy</u>

clearly shows the rhyme scheme of the work.

5. Use any of these formats in lieu of page numbers to give an act or scene in a play, lines or stanzas of verse, or a chapter in a book. The first number is the larger unit.

EXAMPLE: Tamburlaine crowns himself, to the acclaim of

the crowd (2.7).

or

"Not all the curses which the Furies breathe /

Shall make me leave so rich a prize as this"

(Tamburlaine 2.7).

Conventions of Parenthetical Documentation

As with other aspects of the research paper, several customs govern the documentation.

1. Omit page numbers if the source is *complete on a single page* (as in some newspapers).
2. Omit page numbers in citing *alphabetically arranged entries* in a reference work such as an encyclopedia.
3. If two authors with the same last name are among your sources, of course you will need to use *both first and last name* in the documentation.
4. Long titles may be shortened, provided they are easily identifiable. EXAMPLE: "Almost 13 Years of Book Protests . . . Now What?" may be cited as "13 Years."
5. Two arabic numerals with a period between them indicate act and scene or verse and line of dramatic and classic literary works; the first number is that of the larger unit.
6. Do not use the word "page" or any sort of abbreviation for it in documenting your sources; a number in parenthetical documentation

is assumed to be a page number. (Citations in drama or classics are easily recognizable.)

Punctuation and Spacing in Parenthetical Documentation

You know by now that documentation, including punctuation and spacing, must conform to the conventions for writing research papers. The following will serve as a guide.

1. Separate a series of sources by semicolons. However, use discretion in the amount of parenthetical information you can include without impeding the reading of your paper.

> EXAMPLE: . . . for wanting books removed from school
> library shelves (Pell 118; Books Behind
> Bars; Darling 120).

2. Allow one space before the opening parenthesis and after the closing parenthesis if documentation is within a sentence.
3. Documentation at the end of a sentence follows the last word (or the closing quotation marks) by one space. The period marking the end of the sentence is put immediately after the closing parenthesis (see examples above).
4. At the end of a long quotation (five lines or more and indented ten spaces from the left margin), begin parenthetical documentation two spaces after the period marking the conclusion of the quotation.

Special Kinds of Parenthetical Documentation

1. More than one work by an author.   Note both author's name and title OR title alone in order to indicate which work you are referring to.

> EXAMPLE: Donelson points out ("Teachers" 106) that the
> very names of some of the largest organizations
> . . .

2. Multiple authorship.   Show the names as they appear in the Works Cited. That is, use up to three authors' names or use the first author's name followed by "et al."

> EXAMPLE: The First Amendment to the Constitution, which
> banned—author Kurt Vonnegut (Carmen, et al. 8)
> sardonically calls . . .

3. Work in multiple volumes. Use the word "volume" (or the abbreviation "vol.") only when referring to a complete one. If you identify a page also, you should write the volume number, a colon, leave a space, then write the page number(s); use arabic numerals.

EXAMPLES:

Antonín Dvořák is called "Old Borax," although the source of the nickname is never explained (Huneker 2: 65–69).

or

Huneker calls Antonín Dvořák "Old Borax" (2: 65–59), although he never explains the source of the nickname.

but

The articles about New York show that he was an inveterate name–dropper (Huneker, vol. 2).

4. One work quoted within another. Sometimes you may want to track down the original source, but often doing so isn't necessary or expedient. Show that the material is quoted from a source *other than the one you used* by putting single quotation marks around the material and beginning the documentation with "qtd. in" before giving the source where you found the information. End with your resource.

EXAMPLE:

. . . ordered a trial "'means the doors to the courthouse are open. . . to explore and ventilate school board decisions . . ..'" (qtd. in Wermiel).

5. Classic works of literature. Use the same system you already read about to note acts and scenes in a play or stanzas and lines in poetry. That is, the first number cited is the larger portion of the source. The first passage cited below is in book 11, lines 15 to 44 of the Iliad.

EXAMPLE:

We know a great deal about the battle dress of the early Greeks by reading a description of Agamemnon (Iliad 11.15–44).

However, to document a specific passage from a book, *begin with the page number* on which the material is found and after a semicolon, write the chapter, part, section, or book, in which it is found, together with appropriate abbreviations, such as "ch." or "bk."

EXAMPLE: Candide finally found a place where even the
             children wore gold brocade and where their toys
             were gold, emeralds, and rubies (31; ch. 17).

6. *Different locations of information within the same work.* If you have two or more such citations, separate each by a comma and a space.

EXAMPLE: Westin points out the trends and how the speed
             of a computer is pushing them toward reality
             (158–62, 166).

7. *Documenting nonprint materials.* Follow the same method of citation as for a print resource insofar as possible. Any precise information you can provide to help locate an exact place on a record (such as the side of a multirecord set) or videotape (the number of feet), the movement of a symphony, or the number of the reel in a long film will be much appreciated.

EXAMPLES: One would hardly call realistic a song of
             farewell to an overcoat (La Boheme 4), yet it
             fits easily into the opera.

             or

             The famed farewell to an overcoat (Great Moments
             in Opera, side 3) is one of many arias from
             "realistic" operas.

             or

             The reporter finally locates Kane's former wife
             (reel 3).

Documenting Quotations

In Chapter 7, pages 178–81, you read about how to punctuate prose, poetry, and drama quotations within the text of your research paper. They also must be documented, and the general descriptions thus far in this chapter should be observed.

Fiction or nonfiction prose or dramatic dialogue of four lines or less. Incorporate into the text any quotation from a few words up to four lines. At the conclusion of the quoted material, allow one space after the closing quotation marks, put the parenthetical quotation information, and place the period immediately after.

EXAMPLE:

```
Justice Byron White cast the deciding vote
because he "concluded simply that a trial should
be held before any decisions were made about
whether or not First Amendment rights were
involved" (Wermiel).
```

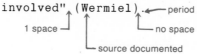

COMMENT: No page reference is given within the parenthetical documentation for this quotation because the article it is taken from is on only one page; the Works Cited list (see page 278 of the Sample Research Paper) shows that.

Use the same placement of quotation marks and parenthetical documentation if you use a quotation in the middle of a sentence.

Fiction or nonfiction prose or dramatic dialogue of five lines or more. Quotations of five or more lines of type are generally introduced by the text; often the phrasing ends with a colon so that the quotation completes a unit of thought. These are usually called "block quotes" or, by the name of the format, "block indentation."

Do *not* use quotation marks when you use a block quote. But continue typing double-spaced, as in the text of your paper, and do follow the description in Chapter 7, pages 179–80, that shows how to indent these longer quotes.

Block quotes are documented at the end. Allow two spaces after the final punctuation mark of the quoted passage, then use the parenthetical documentation. Do not use any punctuation marks after the closing parenthesis.

EXAMPLE:

```
Attorney Martha L. Black points out that
        As an essential counterpart of their right to
        freedom of expression, students may properly
        assert a claim of access to controversial liter-
        ature and freedom from school board censorship
        based on social or political taste.  (151)
```

period ending block quote   2 spaces   page number of quotation

COMMENT: The author of the passage is identified in the text that leads into the
                    quotation, so only the page number must be cited in the
                    parenthetical documentation that follows it.

Poetry of three lines or less.   When short quotations of poetry are incorporated into the text (as you read in Chapter 7, page 180), separate typographical lines are indicated by a slash or virgule (/) with a space on either
side of it at the end of each poetic line. Documentation, with a space allowed
both before and after it, usually comes at the end of the quotation.

EXAMPLE: The nonsense wording of a well-known poem,

                    "'Twas brillig, and the slithy toves / Did gyre

                    and gimble in the wabe," (Carroll 79) illus-

                    trates the structure of English.

COMMENT: This citation shows the page number in a book of poems by Lewis
                    Carroll. Another way of documenting the source is to put the poem
                    and the poet in the text and cite stanza and lines parenthetically
                    (with a period between them), as in the next example.

EXAMPLE: The wording of Lewis Carroll's poem "Jabber-

                    wocky," "'Twas brillig, and the slithy toves /

                    Did gyre and gimble in the wabe," (1.1-2)

                    illustrates the structure of English.

Poetry of four lines or more.   Document longer quotations of poetry the
same way you treat longer quotations of prose: either by putting the citation
in introductory wording or by providing parenthetical documentation two
spaces after the final period of the quotation. These customs apply whether
you indent the entire quotation ten spaces from the left margin or are quoting
a poem with unusual typography which you emulate in the text.

EXAMPLE:

Shakespeare wrote about old age in Sonnet 73:

                    That time of year thou may'st in me behold

                    When yellow leaves, or none, or few, do hang

                    Upon those boughs which shake against the cold--

                    Bare ruin'd choirs where late the sweet birds

                        sang.

or

```
Shakespeare wrote metaphorically about old age in these lines:
            That time of year thou may'st in me behold
            When yellow leaves, or none, or few, do hang
            Upon those boughs which shake against the cold--
            Bare ruin'd choirs where late the sweet birds
                sang. (Sonnet 73)
```

Documenting Maps, Charts, Graphs, and Tables

Honesty requires that you acknowledge the sources of all visual materials you didn't create yourself. That means if you use a map, chart, table, graph, diagram, picture, or any similar item in your research paper, you must document it within the paper and show its full source in the Works Cited.

Figure is the term by which all other illustrative materials—charts, graphs, photos, figures, drawings, and so on—are called. Each is labeled "Fig." and given a consecutive arabic numeral throughout your research paper. That designation appears, together with a title or caption that includes the source, *below the figure.*

```
EXAMPLE:    Fig. 2.  Roth, Corporate Ladder, Private
            collection.
```

This documentation begins at the left margin directly under the figure and may extend as many lines as required, all going from one margin to the other of the paper. Complete information about this documentation is found, of course, in the Works Cited.

A **table** is captioned, together with an arabic numeral showing its order in your paper, *at the top and above the title* (if there is one) of the item. Provide documentation *beneath the table,* as the accompanying illustration shows. That is, after the word "Source" and a colon, give the place from which you got the table.

Table 1

Odds of Repeating Head on Coin Flip

Number of Flips   Odds Against All Heads

Number of Flips	Odds Against All Heads
1	2 to 1
2	4 to 1
3	8 to 1
4	16 to 1
5	32 to 1
6	64 to 1
7	128 to 1
8	256 to 1
9	512 to 1
10	1,024 to 1
11	2,048 to 1
12	4,096 to 1

Source: Rodney Stark. <u>Sociology</u>, 2nd ed. Belmont: Wadsworth, 1987: 78.

Since complete information about the source appears in the Works Cited, an alternate form is to use the same kind of documentation you do for text material; that is, give the source name or title and the page number on which you discovered it.

ALTERNATE
FORM: Source: Stark 78.

Using Comment Notes As Well As Parenthetical Documentation

Sometimes you have additional or explanatory material to add to the text or you want to make some comment on what you have written in your research paper, but adding to the text would impede the flow of reading. As you read in Chapter 7, pages 181–82, you may use comment notes *in addition to the parenthetical documentation* in your paper. Pages 251–52 in Chapter 10 explains how to prepare the page on which they appear within your research paper; such notes are put immediately after the text. See an example of comment notes in the Sample Research Paper on page 275.

Endnotes

Endnotes give documentation at the end of the research paper (hence, their name). Text citations and endnotes **work in pairs between the text and the page of documentation;** a *superscript number provides the coordination.* Put superscript numbers (used sequentially throughout the paper) immediately after each borrowed idea or a quotation in the text and use the corresponding numbers to give the complete documentation on the page of endnotes.

Endnotes give four pieces of information about the source you used: *author, title, publication information, and the actual page or pages* the information was on—in that order. (Naturally, variations are made for nonprint sources.) The forms you use, although similar to those on the Works Cited page, have some slight differences, which will be illustrated on pages 204–11 in this chapter.

There is also a difference in the format of a citation depending on whether it is a first reference or a subsequent reference to a source. (The following examples are divided according to those categories.)

All the information you need for documenting sources is already on your Works Cited cards; you only need to make some adaptations. The chief differences between them are these:

Information	*In Endnotes*	*In Works Cited*
Three units: author, title, publication info.	Separated by commas or parentheses	Separated by periods
Author's name	Written in usual order	Surname, then given name
Publication information for books	In parentheses	No parentheses
Page numbers	Given for each note entry	None given for books

Another difference between the two is that **endnotes are typed in paragraph indentation form;** that is, the first line of each note is indented five spaces from the left margin but succeeding lines each begin at that margin. (Works Cited, you recall, are always written in hanging indentation.)

Begin a page of endnotes by typing "Notes" at the center of a page, one inch down from the top. (Put your name and the successive page numbers 1/2 inch down and ending at the right margin.) Double-space between the heading and the first line of notes, and continue double spacing throughout the endnotes.

Note Numbering System

The points at which endnotes are required to give information are marked with superscript arabic numerals successively throughout the research paper. (Occasionally, very long papers with several chapters or divisions begin numbering anew in each unit, but you will probably not need to use that system.)

The numbers on both notes and their text counterparts are put in superscript—type set 1/2 line above the text line. You can stop typing and turn the roller half a line to accommodate the text line. Most computer word processing programs have a signal that controls superscript numbers, but you must use a printer that supports the feature.

Within the text, put the note numbers at the end of a phrase, clause, or sentence. Allow a single space before beginning the documentation information. *Never* use a period or other mark before or after superscript numerals, either in the text or in the endnotes.

First References: Books

The basic form for the first reference of a book begins with the author's name one space after the note number. Put a comma after the name, allow one space, and write the title of the book (underlined, of course), then another space. Enclose the publication information in parentheses: the place of publication followed by a colon and a space, the name of the publisher—in the shortened form as explained on pages 66–67—then a comma, a space, and the date of publication. Allow one space after the closing parenthesis and write the exact page (or pages) from which you obtained information, but do not use any word or abbreviation with it. End the documentation note with a period. The whole reference is typed double-spaced and with paragraph indentation, as illustrated on the following pages:

                                    ┌──────── 1 space ────────┐
                                    ↓   ↓   ↓   ↓   ↓
[1] James A. Michener, <u>Legacy</u> (New York: Random, 1987) 45.
                            comma ┘   colon ┘ comma ┘   period ┘

The same customs prevail for documentation endnotes as for Works Cited with regard to using only the names of cities (not states), using shortened forms of publisher's names, and using abbreviations if you can't find some items of the publication information (see "Conventions," pages 62–69).

The following examples show some of the various kinds of first references for books in endnotes. (A complete list of Works Cited forms is in Chapter 9, pages 220–39. To write endnotes, make the necessary adaptations if what you need isn't shown here.)

BOOK BY TWO OR THREE AUTHORS

[2] Kenan Heise, and Mark Frazel, <u>Hands on Chicago:</u> <u>Getting Hold of the City</u> (Chicago: Bonus, 1987) 23.

BOOK BY MORE THAN THREE AUTHORS

[3] Elise F. Jones, et al., <u>Teenage Pregnancies in</u> <u>Industrialized Countries</u> (New Haven: Yale UP, 1987) 124–25.

ORGANIZATION OR INSTITUTION AS AUTHOR

[4] Union of Concerned Scientists, <u>Empty Promises: The</u> <u>Growing Case Against Star Wars</u> (Boston: Beacon, 1986) 186.

BOOK IN COLLABORATION

[5] Willard Scott with Daniel Paisner, <u>America Is My</u> <u>Neighborhood</u> (New York: Simon, 1987), 46–48.

BOOK WITH SINGLE EDITOR OR COMPILER OF A COLLECTION

[6] Jon Bryant, ed., <u>A Companion to Melville Studies</u> (New York: Greenwood, 1986) 52.

ANTHOLOGY WITH NO EDITOR GIVEN

[7] <u>Annual Survey of American Poetry, 1986</u> (Great Neck: Roth, 1987) 22–25.

WORK IN AN ANTHOLOGY

8 Susan Grayson, "Rousseau and the Text as Self," <u>Narcissism and the Text: Studies in Literature and the Psychology of Self</u> (New York: New York UP) 78–79.

INTRODUCTION [FOREWORD, AFTERWORD, PREFACE] BY OTHER THAN AUTHOR

9 Bernard Stonehouse, foreword, <u>The Arctic and Its Wildlife</u>, by Bryan Sage (New York: Facts, 1986) 9.

WORK IN SEVERAL VOLUMES

10 Oliver Wendell Holmes, <u>Complete Works of Oliver Wendell Holmes</u>, 13 vols. (Justin: Am. Biog. Service, 1987) 10: 135–37.

TRANSLATED BOOK

11 Albert Camus, <u>American Journals</u>, trans. Hugh Levick (New York: Paragon, 1987) 57.

EDITION OF A BOOK

12 Audrey J. Roth, <u>The Research Paper: Process, Form, and Content</u>, 6th ed. (Belmont: Wadsworth, 1989) 198.

REPUBLISHED BOOK

13 Ernest Hemingway, <u>A Farewell to Arms</u> (1929; New York: Macmillan, 1987) 133.

First References: Periodicals

The first time you give an endnote reference to a periodical, the form to use is almost exactly like that for a Works Cited entry *except* that commas (each followed by one space) replace periods in the entry and the author's name is given in usual (rather than reverse) order. Also, the *exact page* you used for specific information is given.

Begin each entry with the superscript number to match the one you used in the text for the acknowledgment, and observe paragraph indentation and double spacing throughout.

The following examples show how to record selected kinds of first references of periodicals in endnotes. If you use endnotes but don't find models here, make the necessary adaptations from the examples of periodicals for the Works Cited listing on pages 227–29.

MAGAZINE ARTICLE BY KNOWN AUTHOR, PAGINATION BY ISSUE

[14] Lawrence Zuckerman, "Now She's Queen for a Daily," Time 23 May 1988: 51.

MAGAZINE ARTICLE BY KNOWN AUTHOR, CONTINUOUS PAGINATION

[15] Thomas J. Abercrombie, "The Persian Gulf: Living in Harm's Way," National Geographic 173 (1988): 650–51.

BOOK OR FILM REVIEW IN A MAGAZINE

[16] Paul Gray, "A Testament to Civility," rev. of New and Collected Poems, by Richard Wilbur, Time 9 May 1988: 84.

NEWSPAPER ARTICLE BY KNOWN AUTHOR

[17] Joseph Pereira, "For Hard-Pressed Students, Financial Options Abound," Wall Street Journal 11 Dec. 1987, eastern ed.: sec. 2:33.

NEWSPAPER EDITORIAL, NO AUTHOR SHOWN

[18] "Fees for the Roads," editorial, Miami Herald 21 May 1988, final ed.: A22.

BOOK OR FILM REVIEW IN NEWSPAPER

[19] Robert Berry, "Latest 'Friday' Not the Bloody Mess Expected," rev. of <u>Friday the 13th Part VII--The New Blood</u>, dir. John Carl Buechler, <u>Atlanta Constitution</u> 18 May 1988: 3F.

First References: Other Print Sources

Follow the same general set of rules and customs that apply to books and periodicals when you record other print sources in endnotes. Separate units of information by commas and single spaces, and type entries double-spaced and in paragraph indentation. Mainly, keep endnotes as uncluttered as possible.

The following examples will serve as guidelines for you to record other print sources as references in endnotes. If you need to record a reference source not shown here, adapt it from the Works Cited on pages 220–39.

DOCUMENT FROM AN INFORMATION SERVICE

[20] Adrienne Chute, "Meeting the Literary Challenge," ERIC 1987, ED 284549.

PAMPHLET BY KNOWN AUTHOR

[21] Mary Doyle, <u>Involuntary Smoking--Health Risks for Nonsmokers</u> (New York: Public Affairs, 1987) n.p.

The designation "n.p." signifies that there are no page numbers in this pamphlet. In the interests of scholarship, you cannot simply count pages and supply one!

PERSONAL OR UNPUBLISHED LETTER

[22] Sharon Lee, letter to the author, 22 Nov. 1987.

GOVERNMENT PUBLICATIONS

[23] Department of the Interior, National Park Service, <u>Environmental Assessment: Modify Wastewater Treatment</u>

Plant, South Rim: Grand Canyon National Park, Arizona
(Washington: GPO, 1985) 21-23.

First References: Nonprint Sources

You may have found that computer programs, films, paintings, interviews, radio or television programs, records, or other nonprint media extend the range and kind of resources supplying you with information for your research paper. When you quote from these sources or borrow ideas from them, readers will want to know the important elements of each source, so you feature them in the documentation for each medium.

Record the necessary information by following the models here (based on the Works Cited examples on pages 220–39) or by adapting what you have already recorded on your preliminary Works Cited cards. In most cases that means substituting commas for periods and giving names in conventional order. The endnotes continue to be double-spaced and recorded with paragraph indentation; leave one space after each comma in the entry.

PERSONAL OR TELEPHONE INTERVIEW

[24] Judith A. Matz, personal interview, 4 Aug. 1988.

[25] Nancy Tuck Davis, telephone interview, 12 Nov. 1988.

WORKS OF ART

[26] Pierre-Auguste Renoir, <u>San Marco</u>, Minneapolis Institute of Arts, Minneapolis.

[27] Hanukah Lamp from Poland, Jewish Museum, New York.

[28] Constantin Brancusi, <u>Sleeping Muse</u>, Metropolitan Museum of Art, New York.

LECTURE

[29] Clifford Lynch, "Response Time Measurement in Information Retrieval Systems," American Library Association, San Francisco, 27 June 1987.

COMPUTER SOFTWARE

30 Alan Bird, Timeout Quickspell, vers. 1.5, computer software, Beagle Bros., 1987.

MATERIAL FROM A COMPUTER SERVICE

31 Fred M. Hechinger, "Report Shows School Censorship is Growing," New York Times 27 Oct. 1981: C5 (DIALOG file 111, item 0404580).

RADIO OR TELEVISION PROGRAM

32 You and the Law, writ. and prod. Alan Roy, ABC Special Report, WSVN Miami, 10 Oct. 1988.
33 "School's Out!" writ. Norman Raymond, Lookin' Local dir. by Martin Matts, KWPC Belmont, 2 Sept. 1988.

FEATURE-LENGTH FILM

34 Dir. Orson Welles, Citizen Kane, RKO, 1941, reel 3.
35 Ball of Fire, dir. Howard Hawks, prod. Samuel Goldwyn, MGM, 1941.

SHORT FILM, FILMSTRIP, VIDEOTAPE, OR SLIDE PROGRAM

36 Rudy Diaz, filmmaker, Duane Hanson, U of Miami, 1984 (16 mm. color sd., 19 min.).

LIVE THEATRICAL OR MUSICAL PERFORMANCE

37 Chuck Berry, and Bo Diddley, Chastain Park Amphitheatre, Atlanta, 21 May, 1988.

PHONOGRAPH RECORD, ALBUM, OR AUDIOTAPE

38 Michael Jackson, Bad, Epic CD, EK40600, 1987.

Subsequent References

Once you have recorded the full information about a source, you can shorten the citation the next time you refer to the work and **give only the author or title and a page number** for printed sources. Author or title and any identifying location, if possible, suffices for nonprint materials.

The number of additional references you make to a work already documented in full does not matter, nor does the location of the subsequent reference in the numerical listing of the endnotes.

Typical subsequent references look like this:

[8] Pell 89.

[9] Donelson, "13 Years" 95.

The following examples show how a series of first and subsequent references might appear.

[1] Martha L. Black, "The Student's Right to Know," Censorship and Education, ed. Eli M. Oboler (New York: Wilson, 1981) 151–52.

[2] Eva Pell, The Big Chill (Boston: Beacon, 1984) 26.

[3] Black 154.

[4] Black 161.

[5] "Justice Brennan Follows ALA's Line in Island Trees Case," American Libraries 13 (1982): 444.

[6] Pell 85.

[7] "Justice Brennan" 444.

The abbreviations "ibid." (meaning "in the same place"), "op. cit" (meaning "in the work cited"), and "loc. cit." (meaning "in the place cited") are no longer used in any kind of research paper documentation.

American Psychological Association (APA) Documentation

The forms of documentation you have been reading about and have seen as illustrations in this book are those usually used in the humanities; they are based on the recommendations of the largest subject-matter professional association in those disciples, the MLA [Modern Language Association]. However, several other academic disciplines have their own preferred way of documenting sources within the text of a paper and in the Works Cited (or List of Sources or Bibliography or the equivalent).

The American Psychological Association's *Publication Manual of the American Psychological Association,* 3rd ed. (Washington: APA, 1983) is the standard for most of the social sciences as well as for other fields, including research in the humanities. It is an author and date system. Although the APA system differs somewhat from the MLA system, you will find it easy to use if called upon to do so.

APA Reference Citations in Text

The APA system calls for **parenthetical documentation** within the text of the research paper. However, to each citation of **author's name (or a title) and page number of a work is added** *the date of its publication.* The full publication information for both print and nonprint sources is given in References at the end of the research paper. (The correct forms are illustrated in Chapter 9, pages 239–43.)

Acknowledging ideas or short quotations.   APA considers that **a short quotation contains fewer than 40 words.** If the quotation or passage to be cited occurs at the end of a sentence, put the documentation before the period. If the quotation or other borrowed idea is in the middle of a sentence, put the parenthetical documentation immediately after what needs to be cited, then continue the sentence. If you want to let readers know the source of an idea or quotation so that they don't think it's your own, put the parenthetical documentation as an introductory notation. The examples that follow illustrate such placements.

1.   The citation information for a **complete work** consists of the author's name or the title of a work and date of the publication.

EXAMPLE: Celebrating Censored Books (1985) is a unique
             turn-around because it . . .

             or

             A unique turn-around is in another book (Karol-
             ides and Burress, 1985) that provides . . .

2.   **Anonymous works** are acknowledged by title (or a shortened form of it) and the date of publication. Readers can, of course, find the complete title in the References listing.

EXAMPLE: The vote to reinstate the books . . . a divisive
force in the local community ("Island Trees,"
1982).

3. **The specific acknowledgment of a page or chapter** in APA documentation calls for *preceding those numbers with an abbreviation* of pages with a "p." and of chapters by a "ch."

EXAMPLES: Darling (1983) notes that since there is a great
division of responsibility . . . in procedures
for handling complaints against books (p. 121).

      or

      Darling (1983, p. 121) notes that since . . .

      or

      There is a great division of responsibility
(Darling, 1983, p. 121) . . .

4. If a work has **two or more authors,** cite the names of all authors the first time you mention the work. After that, name both authors if there are only two. If there are three to five authors, cite all names the first time but subsequently use only the surname of the first author and then "et al." (without the quotation marks, of course). If you should ever use a work by six or more authors, both the first and subsequent citations are by surname of only the first author followed by "et al.," an abbreviation of the Latin *et alii,* which means "and others."

5. Should you have occasion to document works by **two or more authors with the same last name in the same parentheses,** obviously you have to signal the reader which author you are referring to (if they are not coauthors). Give the dates of publication in chronological order, separated by commas.

6. **Two or more works by the same author(s) published in the same year** are shown by assigning each a lowercase letter, alphabetically by title, to distinguish them in parenthetical documentation. (Use the same letters when you cite those works in a Reference listing; see page 240.)

Other Documentation Systems

Handbooks and style manuals for various disciplines give the preferred forms of documenting ideas and quotations; they are used particularly by those who publish in the fields. For example, the *Style Manual* 3rd ed. (1978), published by the American Institute of Physics, bears, on the title page, the notation "for Guidance in the Preparation of Papers for Journals Published by the American Institute of Physics and its Member Societies" (and is being revised as this book goes to press). The Council of Biology Editors publishes the *CBE Style Manual: A Guide for Authors, Editors, and Publishers in the Biological Sciences,* 4th ed. (1983), and the American Mathematical Society has *A Manual for Authors of Mathematical Papers,* 7th ed. (1980).

The next few sections of this chapter show some other methods of documenting sources, though not necessarily in English or the humanities.

Footnotes

The familiar footnotes that used to fill the bottom margins of research papers are almost never used now. They are so called because they are notes at the "foot" or bottom of the page. (Many kinds of documentation are still carelessly called "footnotes" when, in fact, they are not.)

Footnotes may either give the documentation for borrowed words and ideas or they may contain your own comments about the text that are put separately to avoid interrupting the flow of the paper. The **forms for using footnotes** are the same as those for endnotes, so refer to pages 204–10 in this chapter.

Type footnotes in single spacing on the page where you make the acknowledgment; begin them two double spaces (that is, four lines) below the end of the text on the page. Use sequential **superscript numbers** at the point in the text where each is needed and coordinate each with a footnote. If you use footnotes in a paper you are typing, you will have to count lines carefully in order to get the proper spacing.

Some computer programs are available that allow for footnotes. Or, you can preview the set-up of a computer page and make adjustments for the footnotes before you print.

Author and Date System

This system is essentially the same as the APA documentation. That is, in crediting a source the author (or title) and date of publication are of primary importance. If the reference is to a particular page, that is also listed, usually after a comma that follows the date. This documentation should be as near as possible to the text it documents, whether that location is the middle or either end of a sentence. If the documentation concludes a sentence, put it after the final word but before the period.

Use the APA examples on pages 211–13 as a guide for any author and date documentation system. For example, if you have two or more works by the same author that are published in the same year, assign a lowercase letter to each publication; use the same letter in the Works Cited listing to maintain the differentiation.

EXAMPLE:　David's investigations showed that the instal-
　　　　　　lation was adequate (1988a, 28) but that both
　　　　　　natural and induced vibration weakened the
　　　　　　structure considerably (1988b, 4).

See page 244 in Chapter 9 for the way to enter sources noted in the author and date documentation in a Works Cited listing.

Full In-Text Documentation

Another possibility for documenting sources is to give complete information in the text of your paper. Because it is fairly cumbersome and interrupts the flow of reading, the method is seldom used. However, full in-text documentation might be convenient if you have only a few sources to acknowledge.

In this system, enclose within parentheses the documentation information you do not mention in the text and put the publication information in square brackets within the parentheses.

EXAMPLES:　This decision, Gerald S. Snyder indicates (<u>The
　　　　　　Right to be Informed: Censorship in the United
　　　　　　States</u> [New York: Messner, 1976] 130–32),
　　　　　　offered the most clear-cut definition of stu-
　　　　　　dents' constitutional rights that has been
　　　　　　handed down from the courts.

　　　　　　or

　　　　　　Judith Krug, Director of the American Library
　　　　　　Association's Office for Intellectual Freedom,
　　　　　　stated that the most important victory was
　　　　　　access to the courts in school-related First
　　　　　　Amendment disputes and that students can chal-
　　　　　　lenge the personal values of school board mem-

```
bers ("Justice Brennan Follows ALA's Line in
Island Trees Case" [American Libraries 13
(1981)] 444).
```

If you use such full in-text documentation, it may not be necessary to prepare a separate bibliography or list of Works Cited because the information in either case will only be redundant. Check with your instructor for guidance.

Numbering Sources

This system is widely used in the natural sciences such as medicine and health-related fields, chemistry, physics, computer science, and mathematics, as well as in technological writing. Documentation in the text is **an arabic numeral, underlined, followed by a comma, a space, and then by an exact page reference;** the whole is enclosed within parentheses.

Each **numeral is then coordinated with a numbered entry in a list of Works Cited at the end of the paper.** Resources, then, are *listed in the order in which they are cited in the text* rather than alphabetically.

EXAMPLES:
```
Justice Abe Fortas, in his decision on Tinker,
said, "School officials do not possess absolute
authority over their students" (1, 132).
```

or

```
This organization launched the "Right to Read"
campaign, which sent famous authors across the
nation to speak about books and First Amendment
rights (2, C11).
```

The Works Cited for these two sources would be written this way:

```
1. Snyder, Gerald S. The Right to Be Informed: Censorship
     in the United States. New York: Messner, 1976.
2. Kakutani, Michiko. "The Famous Will Gather to Read the
     Forbidden." New York Times 5 Apr. 1982: C11.
```

Note that although there is a period after the number in the Works Cited, none is used in the parentheses within the text.

Chapter 9

Preparing the Works Cited

Until recently, people who wrote academic research papers relied almost entirely on written sources. Therefore, the word *bibliography* (meaning a list of information sources in print) was commonly used at the end of a paper to show readers the researched material the paper was based on. But since students (and others) began using such nonprint resources as films and records, the literal meaning of "bibliography" no longer applies. Now a variety of untraditional sources is available, including those generated by computer. The customary word is no longer accurate, though it's a habit many people still cling to.

Works Cited is a term that fits with the parenthetical documentation you read about in the last chapter. The sources you need to cite within your paper are acknowledged in the text. Now, at the conclusion, you provide *complete documentation about the works you have already referred to.* (Be sure you list *every* source that you drew from; use revision time to check the paper against note cards.)

Less frequently used is the heading *Works Consulted,* which is a listing that shows all the sources you consulted and from which you *actually got information* in preparing your research paper. However, you may not have had occasion to cite all those works within the text.

Never list any material that you looked at but found irrelevant or insufficient for your purposes. You are obligated to refer a reader of your research paper *only* to resources directly related to information on your subject because one function of either the Works Cited or Works Consulted list is to tell [not "lead"] readers which sources directly helped your own research.

If you provide annotations (explained in Chapter 10, pages 253–54) for the sources listed, you may use the heading *Annotated List of Works Cited* or *Annotated List of Works Consulted,* depending on which kind of list you are providing.

What to Include

The Works Cited list gives complete information about the resources you mention within the text so that anybody who wants to look at what you used can find the same sources. In order that they can, you must provide full documentary evidence.

The information included in the Works Cited list is exactly what you wrote on your preliminary citation cards—so it's already available to you. All you need do is put it in alphabetical order.

Information about *books* has three units: the author's name, the title of the work, and the publication information (location and name of the publisher, plus the publication date). Follow punctuation rules and other details in Chapter 4, pages 62–66.

Periodical citations contain the same three units of information. However, the publication information shows pages on which an entire article appears. Remember that for journals with continuous pagination you also record volume numbers and that for newspapers you also record the edition and section in which the information appeared.

Nonprint and computer materials citations, in addition to author and title, show information helpful to someone seeking the same source: tape width or speed, director, distributor, and so on. Sometimes a performer's name takes precedence, or a title appears before the name of its author. The listing of forms in this chapter shows many different resources and explains the various styles that may be used.

Conventions to Follow

A number of customs are observed in the way you present the list of Works Cited. Some of them, such as how to record the title of a film included in the title of a book, or not distinguishing a hardbound from a softbound book, were presented earlier and should already be on the preliminary citation cards. Remember that you will be using *hanging indentation* throughout! (That is, the first line of an entry begins at the left margin; subsequent lines are each indented five spaces from that margin.) Here are some other conventions not previously noted.

1.   Start the list of Works Cited on a new page at the conclusion of the text of your research paper.

2.   Number the Works Cited page(s) successively following the text of your research paper.   That is, if the last page of the text was 16, the first page of the Works Cited will be 17. Follow the custom of previous pages by putting the numeral after your name and 1/2 inch down from the top right-hand corner of the page.

3.   Center the heading Works Cited (or Annotated List of Works Cited or whichever title describes your list) *one inch down from the top of the page.*

4.   Double-space between the heading and the first entry—as well as throughout the list.

5.   List entries alphabetically according to the last name of the author (or that of the first author given, if there is more than one person). **If no author's name is shown,** begin with the title of the work and use the first word (except for the articles *A*, *An*, or *The*) to determine the alphabetical placement. **Omit titles or honorifics** (Dr., Sir, or O.B.E.), even if they are shown with the author's name in the source you used.

6.   If there are several entries by the same author, use the name in the first entry only. Substitute **three spaced hyphens in place of the name for subsequent works** by that person. Put these entries in alphabetical order by titles.

7.   The only time page numbers within a book are recorded is if your citation is to a particular part of it, such as a work in an anthology or collection or an introduction. See the proper forms in the following section.

8.   Never use the word "page" or an abbreviation for it.

9.   Never number the entries in a list of Works Cited.

Use the Works Cited in the Sample Research Paper on pages 276–78 as an illustration of the conventions listed above and on succeeding pages.

Standard Forms for Works Cited

Books

Remember that the three kinds of information cited for books are intended to give readers the facts about author, title, and publication. The examples that follow are guides to the forms, most of which should already be on your preliminary Works Cited cards. Since *spacing* after periods, commas, and colons *is important,* use these sample entries as a check on your own work.

BOOK BY SINGLE AUTHOR

```
Michener, James A.  Legacy.  New York: Random, 1987.
```

Note that the period after the middle initial serves as the period ending the author unit. There is one space after the colon and another after the comma.

BOOK BY TWO OR THREE AUTHORS

```
Heise, Kenan, and Mark Frazel.  Hands on Chicago: Getting
     Hold of the City.  Chicago: Bonus, 1987.
Stokes, John, Michael R. Booth, and Susan Bassnett.  Bern-
     hardt, Terry, Duse: The Actress in Her Time.  New
     York: Cambridge UP, 1988.
```

Only the name of the first author shown on the title page of the book is given in reverse order (that is, last name, a comma, then the first name). The "and" before the name of the second or third author is preceded by a comma, though those names are in usual order.

BOOK BY MORE THAN THREE AUTHORS

```
Jones, Elise F., et al.  Teenage Pregnancy in Industrial-
     ized Countries.  New Haven: Yale UP, 1987.
```

The Latin abbreviation "et al." (for *et alii* or, in English, "and others") is used instead of writing a string of names. The period after the abbreviated word suffices as the period to end the author unit.

ORGANIZATION OR INSTITUTION AS AUTHOR

Union of Concerned Scientists. <u>Empty Promise: The Growing Case Against Star Wars</u>. Boston: Beacon, 1986.

BOOK IN COLLABORATION

Scott, Willard, with Daniel Paisner. <u>America Is My Neighborhood</u>. New York: Simon, 1987.

If the title page shows that the book is by someone "as told to" or "with the collaboration of" someone else, use those words rather than the "with" in this model.

ANONYMOUS BOOK

<u>AIDS Plague</u>. New York: Gordon, 1987.

Since the author of this book is unknown, the item is entered into the Works Cited by the first word of the title.

AUTHOR'S NAME ABSENT FROM BOOK
BUT KNOWN FROM ANOTHER SOURCE

[Dynner, Eugene.] <u>Camera Techniques</u>, 2nd ed. Miami: Travelogue, 1988.

The square brackets indicate interpolation by the writer. In this case, the person who prepared the list of Works Cited was able to determine the actual or probable author, although that name wasn't on the title page of the book.

BOOK BY PSEUDONYMOUS AUTHOR
BUT REAL NAME SUPPLIED

Holt, Victoria [Eleanor Hibbert]. <u>Secret for a Nightingale</u>. Garden City: Doubleday, 1986.

Note that the author's real name is in usual first-name first order and that the period concluding the author unit is after the brackets containing the real name.

BOOK IN WHICH ILLUSTRATOR
OR PHOTOGRAPHER IS IMPORTANT

```
Zollinger, Jean Day, illus.  Whales: The Nomads of the
     Sea.  Text by Helen Ronay Sattler.  New York: Loth-
     rop, 1987.
```

or

```
Sattler, Helen Ronay.  Whales: The Nomads of the Sea.
     Illus. Jean Day Zollinger.  New York: Lothrop, 1987.
```

An abbreviation is used for "illustrator" in either form. If the illustrator is featured on the title page of the book, or if your research paper centers on book illustrators or art work (or on this particular person), use the first form shown. Use the second version if the book is more important than the illustrator in your research.

Use *photo.* to show that the visuals in a book are the work of a *single photographer* whose name appears on the title page.

```
Muench, David, photo.  Desert Images: An American Land-
     scape.  Text by Edward Abbey.  New York: Chantecleer-
     Harcourt, 1979.
```

BOOK CONDENSATION OF A LONGER WORK

```
Hall, Richard.  Yankee.  Cond. from Yankee.  Pleasant-
     ville: Digest, 1988.
```

The word "condensed" is abbreviated as shown. If the author of the original work is different from the person who wrote the condensation, note that name before the original book title.

BOOK WITH SINGLE EDITOR
OR COMPILER OF A COLLECTION

```
Bryant, Jon, ed.  A Companion to Melville Studies.  New
     York: Greenwood, 1986.
```

Put a comma after the author's name and let the period after the abbreviation for "editor" stand as the period concluding the author unit. The abbreviation *comp.* is used if the word "compiler" rather than "editor" appears on the title page of the book.

BOOK WITH TWO OR MORE EDITORS OR COMPILERS

Carver, Raymond, and Tom Jenks, eds. <u>American Short Story Masterpieces</u>. New York: Delacorte, 1987.

Follow the customs of multiple authorship if a book is the work of several editors or compilers.

ANTHOLOGY WITH NO EDITOR GIVEN

<u>Annual Survey of American Poetry, 1986</u>. Great Neck: Roth, 1987.

BOOK EDITED BY OTHER THAN AUTHOR OF CONTENTS

Van Doren, Mark. <u>The Selected Letters of Mark Van Doren</u>. Ed. George Hendrick. Baton Rouge: Louisiana State UP, 1987.

WORK OF AUTHOR CONTAINED IN COLLECTED WORKS

Hemingway, Ernest. <u>The Complete Short Stories of Ernest Hemingway</u>. New York: Scribner's, 1987.

BOOK BEARING AN IMPRINT OF A PUBLISHER

Michaels, Joanne, and Mary Barile. <u>The Hudson Valley and Catskill Mountains</u>. New York: Crown—Harmony, 1988.

An imprint identifies a group of books a publisher brings out. Show the imprint before the hyphen and the publishing company after it.

SEVERAL-VOLUME WORK UNDER GENERAL TITLE, WITH EACH VOLUME HAVING SEPARATE TITLE

August, Paul Nordstrom. <u>Brain Function</u>. New York: Chel-
    sea, 1988. Vol. 2 of <u>Encyclopedia of Psychoactive</u>
    <u>Drugs</u>, Series 2. 3 vols. to date. 1987– .

BOOK IN SERIES EDITED BY OTHER THAN AUTHOR

Debner, Claudia Biolke. <u>Chemical Dependency</u>. Ed. David
    L. Bender, and Bruno Leone. Opposing Viewpoints
    Series. St. Paul: Greenhaven, 1985.

WORK IN SEVERAL VOLUMES

Holmes, Oliver Wendell. <u>Complete Works of Oliver Wendell</u>
    <u>Holmes</u>. 13 vols. Justin: Am. Biog. Service, 1987.

The page number and specific volume used will appear in the parenthetical documentation in the text of the research paper. This entry in the Works Cited shows the total number of volumes in the work; obviously, you need not have used all of them.

TRANSLATED BOOK BY KNOWN AUTHOR

Camus, Albert. <u>American Journals</u>. Trans. Hugh Levick.
    New York: Paragon, 1987.

List the book by author if references in your paper are to that person or work. However, if the translator is the subject of your paper or figures importantly in it, put that person's name first, as in the following example.

Levick, Hugh, trans. <u>American Journals</u>. By Albert Camus.
    New York: Paragon, 1987.

The abbreviation for translator is always *trans.*, but it is capitalized only when it appears before the person's name. "By" precedes the author's name if it appears after the title.

TRANSLATED BOOK
WITH AUTHOR'S NAME INCLUDED IN TITLE

<u>Poems of Fernando Pessoa</u>. Trans. Edwin Honig and Joan M.
    Brown. New York: Ecco, 1987.

EDITION OF A BOOK

Roth, Audrey J. <u>The Research Paper: Process, Form, and
    Content.</u> 6th ed. Belmont: Wadsworth, 1989.

Some editions carry designations such as "rev." (revised) or "alt." (alternate); use in the Works Cited whichever wording is on the title page of the book, as in the example below.

American Fuchsia Society Staff. <u>Fuchsia Judging School
    Manual and AFS Judging Rules</u>, rev. ed. Eureka: Am.
    Fuchsia, 1986.

PRIVATELY PRINTED BOOK

Cameron, Dini, and Peter Cornelisse. <u>The Dyer's Comple-
    ment.</u> Ashton, ON: Self-published, 1988.

This book was published by the authors. If the book is privately printed by contract with a publishing company, write the publication information as you would for any commercially printed work. The location of Canadian cities is given by province; Ashton is in Ontario.

REPUBLISHED BOOK OR MODERN
REPRINT OF OLDER EDITION

Hemingway, Ernest. <u>A Farewell to Arms</u>. 1929. New York:
    Macmillan, 1987.

Note that the date of original publication stands by itself with two spaces before it and two spaces after the period concluding it. The name of the original publisher (if different from the new one) is not shown.

Portions of books.   If your reference source was only a part of a book—a poem or introduction, for example—rather than the complete book, the author of just that section begins the Works Cited entry. Also, in addition to author, title, and publication information, *the page numbers on which this part appears* are added to the citation, beginning two spaces after the copyright date.

POEM IN ANTHOLOGY

```
Rose, Wendy.  "Learning to Understand Darkness."  That's
     What She Said.  Ed. Rayna Green.  Bloomington: Indi-
     ana UP, 1984.  201.
```


ARTICLE, CHAPTER, STORY, OR ESSAY
IN A COLLECTION NOT BY THE AUTHOR

```
Grayson, Susan.  "Rousseau and the Text as Self."  Narcis-
     sism and the Text: Studies in Literature and the Psy-
     chology of Self.  Eds. Lynne Layton and Barbara Ann
     Shapiro.  New York: New York UP, 1986.  78-96.
```


INTRODUCTION [FOREWORD, AFTERWORD,
PREFACE] BY OTHER THAN AUTHOR

```
Stonehouse, Bernard.  Foreword.  The Arctic and Its Wild-
     life.  By Bryan Sage.  New York: Facts, 1986.  9.
```

Use whichever descriptive heading (of those above) is used in the book you are recording in the Works Cited.

SIGNED ARTICLE IN REFERENCE BOOK

```
Reilly, John C., Jr.  "Antisubmarine Warfare."  McGraw-
     Hill Encyclopedia of Science and Technology.  1987 ed.
```

Volume and page numbers are omitted from alphabetically arranged reference sources. If an author's initials, but not whole name, appear with an article, check (usually near the front of a volume) for a list of names that the initials stand for.

UNSIGNED ARTICLE IN REFERENCE WORK

```
"Angola."  Countries of the World.  1988 ed.
```

Periodicals

The three units of information recorded for each periodical article are author, title, and publication information—including the page numbers on which the article appears. Your preliminary Works Cited cards will also show a volume number for continuously paginated journals or magazines, an edition of a newspaper, or other information particular to periodicals. The examples that follow are guides to the forms, most of which are probably already on your preliminary Works Cited cards. Since *spacing* after periods, commas, and colons *is important*, use these sample entries as a check on your own work.

The headlines of newspaper articles are considered their "titles." Authorship is shown in a byline, unless you are citing a letter to the editor, which is signed at the end. **A wire service** such as AP or UPI **is** *never* **considered an author**.

MAGAZINE ARTICLE BY KNOWN
AUTHOR, PAGINATION BY ISSUE

```
Zuckerman, Lawrence.  "Now She's Queen for a Daily."  Time
      23 May 1988: 51.
```

This article is complete on one page.

```
Nyson, Herberg.  "Sidney Poitier Is Back."  Ebony May
      1988: 31+.
```

This article begins on page 31 and continues on several, but not successive, pages. Use a "+" to show the additional pages.

MAGAZINE ARTICLE BY KNOWN
AUTHOR, CONTINUOUS PAGINATION

```
Abercrombie, Thomas J.  "The Persian Gulf: Living in
      Harm's Way."  National Geographic 173 (1988):
      648-71.
```

Because this publication numbers its pages successively throughout a publication year, the citation shows the volume after the title and the year in parentheses. Note that the hundreds digit in page numbering is not repeated.

MAGAZINE ARTICLE BY UNKNOWN AUTHOR

```
"Doctors' Fee Controls Pressed."  Modern Maturity Apr.-
     May 1988: 89.
```

MAGAZINE EDITORIAL

```
Stine, Annie.  "Scarcely Watched Trains."  Editorial.
     Sierra Mar./Apr. 1988: 16-19.
```

This editorial has a title. Often, however, editorials don't have titles, as in the example below:

```
Charp, Sylvia.  Editorial.  T.H.E. Journal May 1988: 8.
```

BOOK OR FILM REVIEW IN MAGAZINE

```
Gray, Paul.  "A Testament to Civility."  Rev. of New and
     Collected Poems, by Richard Wilbur.  Time 9 May 1988:
     84+.
```

The name of the person writing the review or the title of the review comes first in this citation. "Rev." indicates a review. If the review is neither titled nor shows authorship, begin with: Rev. of . . . .

NEWSPAPER ARTICLE BY KNOWN AUTHOR

```
Pereira, Joseph.  "For Hard-Pressed Students, Financial
     Options Abound."  Wall Street Journal 11 Dec. 1987,
     eastern ed., sec. 2: 33.
```

The abbreviation "sec." here signifies that the article is in section 2 of the paper. If section numbers or letters were part of the paging, a colon would have been placed after the edition and just the page number used (as in the following example). Otherwise, follow the information for the preliminary Works Cited cards designating newspaper articles, as explained on pages 65–66.

NEWSPAPER ARTICLE BY UNKNOWN AUTHOR

"U.N. Finds Missing Files in Archives." <u>Miami Herald</u> 11
    Dec. 1987, final home ed.: A5.

NEWSPAPER EDITORIAL

"Fees for the Roads." Editorial. <u>Miami Herald</u> 21 May
    1988, final ed.: A22.

If the editorial is signed, begin with the author's name.

BOOK OR FILM REVIEW IN NEWSPAPER

Berry, Robert. "Latest 'Friday' Not the Bloody Mess
    Expected." Rev. of <u>Friday the 13th Part VII—The New
    Blood</u>, dir. John Carl Buechler. <u>Atlanta Constitution</u>
    18 May 1988: 3F.

A book review follows the same format.

THEATER OR DANCE REVIEW IN NEWSPAPER

Gussow, Mel. "Bill Irwin's Adventures as a Post–Modern
    Hoofer." Rev. of <u>Largely/New York</u> by Bill Irwin.
    <u>New York Times</u> 17 May 1988: C15.

A theater review is handled essentially the same way. A dance director or choreographer's name might be used. The author of a play or the director might also be cited.

NEWSPAPER SUPPLEMENT IN MAGAZINE FORM

Achenbach, Joel. "A Single Step." <u>Tropic</u> in <u>Miami Herald</u>
    24 Apr. 1988: 8+.

Other Print Sources

DOCUMENT FROM AN INFORMATION SERVICE

Chute, Adrienne. "Meeting the Literary Challenge." ERIC,
     1987. ED 284549.

The name of the information service and an accession number is added to the
usual citation form. The service may be named as publisher if the material
was not published before, except that it is unnecessary to state a location for
ERIC [Educational Resources Information Center] or other government
information services.

UNPUBLISHED THESIS OR DISSERTATION

Byrd, Susan Gray. "A Comparison of the Relationship of
     the Locus of Control and Study Habits to the Level of
     Achievement on a Unit of Library Instruction in
     Freshman Community College English Classes." Diss.
     Nova University, 1986.

Even though a dissertation—and its title—may be book length, the title is
put in quotation marks rather than being underlined. Allow two spaces before
and after the dissertation designation. The degree-granting institution is named
before the date.

Putman, Lesley Jane. "Tannins and Other Polyphenols in
     Sorghum: Separation, Identification and Polymeriza-
     tion." <u>DAI-B</u> 48 (Apr. 1988): 2961-B. Purdue Univer-
     sity, 1987.

This entry shows that the resource is an abstract from *Dissertation Abstracts*
(DA) or *Dissertation Abstracts International (DAI)*. The above abstract is from
Volume B—The Sciences and Engineering. Leave a space after that designation
and before the volume number. The page on which the abstract is recorded
follows the date of the volume.
     Treat a published dissertation as a book, with title underlined, but give
the publication information after the identification of the work as a dissertation.

MIMEOGRAPHED, DITTOED, OR PHOTOCOPIED REPORT

Kahn, Sue, and Jim Preston.   "Reading Across the Curricu-
      lum." Mimeo. Miami: n.p. [1988].

The letters "n.p." show that no publisher is given. The date, although not printed on the mimeographed report, is known and is therefore put in brackets.

PAMPHLET BY KNOWN AUTHOR

Doyle, Mary.   Involuntary Smoking—Health Risks for Non-
      smokers. New York: Public Affairs, 1987.

PAMPHLET BY UNKNOWN AUTHOR

Using Records in the National Archives for Genealogical
      Research. National Archives General Information
      Leaflet No. 5. Washington: GPO, 1986.

PERSONAL OR UNPUBLISHED LETTER

Lee, Sharon.   Letter to the author. 22 Nov. 1987.

The personal letter is presumed to be in the possession of the person to whom it was addressed.

Nightingale, Florence.   Letter to Sir Arthur Landrow. 3
      Feb. 1898. Sheffield Historical Society, Sheffield,
      England.

Include the museum or archives where an unpublished letter is located.

PUBLISHED LETTER

Rosner, Hy. "'Elder Corps' is Vital." Letter. Miami Her-
      ald 21 May 1988, final ed.: A22.

This letter has been given a "title" or heading by the editor of the newspaper.

Nadel, Lawrence. Letter. <u>AAA World</u>. May/June 1988: 4.

Vitanza, Victor J. "A Comment on 'Protocols, Retrospec-
     tive Reports, and the Stream of Consciousness.'"
     Letter. <u>College English</u> 49 (1987): 926–28.

Letters in magazines may be given titles by the editor (as in the second
example above) or they may not (as in the first example above). These two
samples also illustrate the difference between a letter published in a periodical
with paging by issue (the first one) and one published in a periodical with
continuous pagination. Both follow the general format of articles in those
publications, except for identifying the material as a letter.

GOVERNMENT PUBLICATION

Cong. Rec. 17 June 1988: S8179.

Only the date and page number are required for citations from the *Congressional Record*. Note that the letter before the page number signifies whether
it is the record of proceedings of the House of Representatives (shown by an
H before the page number) or of the Senate (shown by an S before the page
number).

United States. Cong. House. Subcommittee on Courts,
     Civil Liberties, and the Administration of Justice of
     the Committee on the Judiciary. <u>Audio and Video</u>
     <u>First Sale Doctrine: Hearings</u>. 98th Cong., 1st and
     2nd Sess. S. Res. 32 and H. Res. 1027 and 1029.
     Washington: GPO, 1985.

Department of the Interior, National Park Service. <u>Envi-</u>
     <u>ronmental Assessment: Modify Wastewater Treatment</u>
     <u>Plant, South Rim: Grand Canyon National Park, Ari-</u>
     <u>zona</u>. Washington: GPO, 1985.

Show the title of the government agency issuing the document as author if
there is no person's name so designated. The number and session of Congress
are listed, and publications are abbreviated according to whether they are
resolutions (Res.), reports (Rep.), or documents (Doc.) emanating from the

Senate (S) or the House of Representatives (H) together with the number of the document.

GPO means "U.S. Government Printing Office," the federal publisher of official documents.

Use the examples above as a guide to citing publications by state governments, by the United Nations, or by other countries.

PUBLISHED INTERVIEW

```
Dalai Lama.   "The Dalai Lama."   Interview.   With Liz Nick-
     son.   Life June 1988: 21+.
```

Ordinarily, the last name, then the first name of the person interviewed begins the citation; this is an unusual case because the individual is known only by his title. The identification of the article as an interview follows the heading it was given in the magazine. If the interview is untitled, state that it is an interview but don't use quotation marks around the word. If the interview was published in a book, treat it as if it were a chapter in the book; if the entire book is an interview, put the title and publication after the interviewer's name. If the interview was published in a newspaper or magazine (as this example was), follow the interviewer's name with the usual periodical publication information.

Nonprint Sources

CARTOON OR ILLUSTRATION

```
Schulz, Charles.   "Peanuts."   Cartoon.   Miami Herald 19
     May 1988: D10.
Bergen, Candice.   Photograph.   Life Apr. 1988: 6.
```

Put the title of a cartoon or illustration in quotation marks; however, *do not* consider a picture caption as a title.

PERSONAL OR TELEPHONE INTERVIEW

```
Matz, Judith A.   Personal Interview.   4 Aug. 1988.
Davis, Nancy Tuck.   Telephone Interview.   12 Nov. 1988.
```

QUESTIONNAIRE, SURVEY, OR POLL YOU DEVELOP

```
Questionnaire.  15 Dec. 1987.
Jay Stevens.  Survey.  8 June 1988.
```

Use the name of a particular respondent your information came from if you know it. Otherwise, your reader will assume that the questionnaire or survey was answered anonymously. If you had a number of signed responses to an inquiring document, arrange them alphabetically by surname and use just the first one with *et al.*, as in `"Adams, Pat, et al."`

WORKS OF ART

```
Renoir, Pierre-Auguste.  San Marco.  Minneapolis Institute
     of Arts.  Minneapolis.
Hanukah Lamp from Poland.  Jewish Museum.  New York.
Brancusi, Constantin.  Sleeping Muse.  Metropolitan Museum
     of Art.  New York.
```

If your reference to a work of art is not the original piece but a photograph of it, then after the location information, cite the illustration number, slide number, or page number of the place (or book) where you saw the picture.

```
Benin Kingdom, Edo peoples, Nigeria.  "Equestrian Figure."
     Private collection.  Illus. 45 in African Art in the
     Cycle of Life.  By Roy Sieber and Roslyn Adele
     Walker.  Washington: National Museum of African Art,
     1987.
```

This particular citation is not attributed to an individual artist, nor does it have a formal name. Thus, the makers of the sculpture and the title it is given in the book are used as the initial part of this citation.

```
Rodin, Auguste.  Meditation.  Musée Rodin, Paris.  Illus.
     5.6 in Rodin Rediscovered.  Ed. Albert E. Elsen.
     Washington: National Gallery of Art, 1981.
```

This citation of an illustration of a statue includes its sculptor, title, and location, as well as information about the book in which the author of the term paper found it.

RADIO, TELEVISION, OR RECORDED INTERVIEW

Tuck, Susan. Interview. <u>Know Your Community</u>. WFCM,
Miami. 27 Apr. 1988.

LECTURE

Lynch, Clifford. "Response Time Measurement in Information Retrieval Systems." American Library Association. San Francisco, 27 June 1987.

RECORDED SPEECH OR LECTURE

Herndon, James. "Teaching and Its Discontents." National
Council of Teachers of English 71052–011, 1986.

RECORDING OF THE SPOKEN WORD

Cain, James F. <u>The Postman Always Rings Twice</u>. 2 audio
cassettes. Read by Fred Curchack and Mollie Boice.
Prod. by Amy Glazer. Book of the Road, Sebastopol,
CA, 1984.

SPEECH OR LECTURE

Ferguson, Marilyn. Opening General Sess. NCTE Convention. Los Angeles, 20 Nov. 1987.

If the speech or lecture is untitled, acknowledge it by citing the occasion
before the location and date.

COMPUTER SOFTWARE

Bird, Alan. <u>Timeout Quickspell</u>. Vers. 1.5. Computer
software. Beagle Bros., 1987. Apple IIe, 128K,
disk.

If other information is important, such as the computer for which the software is designed, the number of kilobytes, or the operating system (CP/M, for example), list it in order beginning two spaces after the period following the date. Separate the items by commas.

MATERIAL FROM A COMPUTER SERVICE

```
Hechinger, Fred M.   "Report Shows School Censorship is
     Growing."  New York Times 27 Oct. 1981: C5.   DIALOG
     file 111, item 0404580.
```

Record the source as you would any other printed material, except that after the usual concluding period, put the name of the computer service and the file designation or item or accession number. If you later find and use this material in another form, such as microfilm, use the format in the Works Cited for the one actually consulted.

RADIO OR TELEVISION PROGRAM

```
You and the Law.   Writ. and prod. Alan Roy.   ABC Special
     Report.   WSVN, Miami.   10 Oct. 1988.
```

If there is a narrator, use the abbreviation "Narr." before that person's name, and put a period after it. This citation indicates the program was produced or distributed by a national network, so its designation is immediately before the call letters of the local station on which it was viewed.

```
"School's Out!"  Writ. Norman Raymonds.   Lookin' Local.
     Dir. by Martin Matts.   KWPC, Belmont.   2 Sept. 1988
```

The writer and director of this program from a series is known and therefore shown in the citation. Often you see something on TV and can't get that information. Then use the following form.

```
"The Neutral Zone."  Start Trek: The Next Generation.
     WPIX, Miami.   22 May 1988.
```

FEATURE-LENGTH FILM

```
Welles, Orson, dir.   Citizen Kane.   With Welles, Joseph
     Cotten, and others.   RKO, 1941.
```

Feature-length films are usually listed by their directors. If the author of the screenplay, an actor, or another person connected with the film is of major importance in your research, put that name first and give the name of the director after the title of the film.

Moorehead, Agnes, actress. <u>Citizen Kane</u>. Dir. Orson
    Welles. With Welles, Joseph Cotten, and others.
    RKO, 1941.

Mankiewicz, Herman J., and Orson Welles, screenwriters.
    <u>Citizen Kane</u>. Dir. Orson Welles. With Welles,
    Joseph Cotten, and others. RKO, 1941.

The producer's name may be given, as may those of composers, lyricists, or others connected with the production of the film who are important to note in your research; put them after the name of the film or the director, whichever is second. You may note if film is on videocassette after the date (see Figure 24 on page 101).

<u>Ball of Fire</u>. Dir. Howard Hawks. Prod. Samuel Goldwyn.
    Screenplay by Charles Brackett and Billy Wilder.
    Photography by Gregg Toland. Music by Alfred Newman.
    With Gary Cooper, Barbara Stanwyck, Dana Andrews.
    MGM, 1941.

SHORT FILM, FILMSTRIP, VIDEOTAPE, OR SLIDE PROGRAM

Diaz, Rudy, filmmaker. <u>Duane Hanson</u>. Dir. Rudy L. Diaz.
    U of Miami, Coral Gables, 1984. 16 mm. color sd.,
    10 min.

Physical characteristics of the film are noted after the date. The maker of a short film is often of prime importance, so list that person (or persons) first. Otherwise, begin with the name of the film or the name of the director, depending on which is more important in your research paper. If the producer must be credited, do so after the name of the director.

Simon, Tom, prod. and dir. <u>Before the First Word</u>. Video-
    cassette. WNET in assoc. with Learning Designs.
    Chicago: Encyclopaedia Britannica Educational, 1982.
    color sd., 29 min.

If a videocassette comes in just one format, note it just before the time (that is, "VHS" or "U-matic 3/4 in."). This videocassette is available in several formats, so none needs to be listed. Note, however, the full production and distribution information given.

<u>National Defense</u>. 2 filmstrips, 2 audiocassettes. Writ-
        ten by Kate Griggs. Photo ed. Wendy Davis. Pren-
        tice-Hall Media, 1982. Each 84 fr. color; 1 7/8,
        mono, 27 min.

The medium is generally stated after the title and before other information about filmstrips, slide programs, and so on.

LIVE THEATRICAL OR MUSICAL PERFORMANCE

<u>Tosca</u>. By Giacomo Puccini. Production by Bliss Hebert.
        Cond. Willie Anthony Waters. With Peter Puzzo, Eliz-
        abeth Holleque. Greater Miami Opera. Dade County
        Auditorium, Miami. 19 Jan. 1988.
<u>La Cage Aux Folles</u>. Dir. Arthur Laurents. By Harvey
        Fierstein. Music by Jerry Herman. With Gene Barry
        and George Hearn. Palace Theater, New York. 21 Mar.
        1984.

Most citations of performances begin with the title and contain the names of important people associated with the production, such as the director, author, performers, and so forth. Each unit ends with a period followed by two spaces. The theater and city of performance constitute another unit, as does the date.

Berry, Chuck, and Bo Diddley. Chastain Park Amphitheatre,
        Atlanta. 21 May 1988.

Performances of musicians or other individuals not within a show title are listed by feature performer.

BROADCAST OR TELECAST
OF MUSICAL PERFORMANCE

<u>Turandot.</u> By Giacomo Puccini. With Placido Domingo, Eva
        Marton, Leona Mitchell. Prod. by Franco Zeferelli.

```
Cond. James Levine.  Metropolitan Opera.  WPBT,
Miami.  27 Jan. 1988.
```

Follow the custom for other performances and films of beginning the citation with the element that is primary in your research paper. After the names of people important to the performance, give the network (such as CBS), the station call letters on which you heard or saw the program, the location of the station, and the date of broadcast. In general, follow the form you would use for a radio or television program.

PHONOGRAPH RECORD, ALBUM, OR AUDIOTAPE

```
Jackson, Michael.  Bad.  Epic, EK40600, 1987.
```

No differentiation is made among LP, CD, or cassette except by the producer's number of the individual recording. The one shown here, for instance, is a CD; had the cassette of the album been used as a resource, the number OET40600 would have conveyed that information.

```
Brahms, Johannes.  Piano Concerto #2 in B# Major, op. 83.
     Sviatoslav Richter. Cond. Erich Leinsdorf.  Chicago
     Symphony Orch.  RCA Papillon, GD 86518, 1988.
```

Although record titles are underlined (as in *Bad*), the titles of musical compositions are not if the identification is by form and key.

APA Reference Forms

The APA [American Psychological Association] equivalent of the Works Cited listing is called "References," and that word is typed at the center of the first line of a new page to begin the list.

Start the first line of each entry at the left margin, but indent the second and succeeding lines of each entry *three spaces* from that margin. Type the list *double-spaced* and in *alphabetical order by author's last name, or by title of source used* if the work is anonymous. (Titles beginning with *A, An,* or *The* are typed that way, but alphabetizing is by next word.)

Each entry in the Reference list contains four units, in this order:

the author,
the date of publication,
the title,
the publication information (that is, location and name of the publisher).

The units end with periods and are *separated from each other by a single type-writer space*. Of course, there are variations for nonprint references.

Only proper nouns and the first word of a title (and of a subtitle) are capitalized. No quotation marks are used in a list of References. Book and periodical titles are underlined. Months are written out in full.

The following list summarizes some of the other customs you are expected to adhere to in the APA reference style.

1. *The Author*

   1.1 **Give the surnames and initials of all authors,** no matter how many there are. Use commas between the names and an ampersand (&) before the last name.

   1.2. If a book is the work of **one or more editors,** enclose the abbreviation Ed. or Eds. in parentheses after the name of the last editor.

2. *The Date of Publication*

   2.1. **Enclose the year of publication in parentheses.** For magazines and newspapers, put a comma after the year, then the month—written out in full—and the date.

3. *The Title*

   3.1. **Two or more works by the same author(s) are listed in the order of publication. Repeat the name of the author(s) for each entry. If those works were** published in the same year, assign each a small letter—based on alphabetizing the titles—that appears next to the date of each piece of work.

   EXAMPLE: Michaels, D. (1988a). Living in the
                 21st Century . . .
                 Michaels, D. (1988b). Mastering
                 Welding . . .

   3.2. If a book appears in any **special edition such as revised, alternate, or subsequent edition,** enclose that information in parentheses after the title and put a period after it.

4. *Publication Information*

   4.1. **Unless the city is well-known, show the state in which a publisher is located,** using the standard two-letter Postal Service abbreviations. A colon separates the location from the name of the publisher.

   4.2. An **article or chapter within a book** is treated simply as an article through the first three units: author, date, and title. Then, add the word "In" and give the author or editor's name, the book title, then parentheses enclosing the abbreviation "pp." with the page numbers on which it appears. Finally, give the publisher's location and name, followed by a period.

4.3. **Omit such words as "Company" or "Incorporated"** but do spell out the names of university presses and of publishing companies.

4.4. A **journal article in a periodical with continuous pagination** shows the name of the publication and the volume number (each underlined but separated by a comma), then a comma and the page numbers of the article, followed by a period.

EXAMPLE: <u>College English</u>, <u>49</u>, 902–910.

4.5. A **journal article in a periodical with *pagination by issue*** adds the number of the issue in parentheses after the volume and the comma comes after that addition.

EXAMPLE: <u>Computers and Composition</u>, <u>5</u>(2), 39–50.

4.6. **Magazine and newspaper articles** show all the page numbers on which the entry appears, preceded by an abbreviation of either p. (if the article is on only one page) or pp. (if it is on several, even discontinuous, pages). If pages are not continuous, show all pages but separate them by commas in this way:

pp. 12, 25, 30–32.

Print Resources

The following are some selected examples of the APA system of noting reference works.

BOOK BY SINGLE AUTHOR

Hamilton, I. (1988). <u>In search of J. D. Salinger</u>. New York: Random House.

BOOK BY TWO OR MORE AUTHORS

Stokes, J., Booth, M. R., & Bassnett, S. (1988). <u>Bernhardt, Terry, Duse: The actress in her time</u>. New York: Cambridge University Press.

BOOK EDITED OR COMPILED

Carver, R., & Jenks, T. (Eds.). (1987). <u>American short
    story masterpieces</u>. New York: Delacorte Press.

EDITION OF A BOOK

Roth, A. J. (1989). <u>The research paper: Process, form, and
    content (6th ed.)</u>. Belmont, CA: Wadsworth.

CHAPTER IN A BOOK

Grayson, S. (1986). Rousseau and the text as self. In L.
    Layton, & B. A. Shapiro (Eds.). <u>Narcissism and the
    text: Studies in literature and the psychology of
    self</u>. (pp. 78–96). New York: New York University Press.

This entry illustrates that when the names of editors are not in the author
position, they are not inverted; they are also preceded by the word "In." Also,
note that the first word of the subtitle is capitalized. Because the reference is
to only a portion of the book, the pages on which it appears are written after
the title of the book and with the indication that they are pages.

MAGAZINE OR JOURNAL ARTICLE
WITH CONTINUOUS PAGINATION

Abercrombie, T. J. (May 1988). The Persian Gulf: Living in
    harm's way. <u>National Geographic</u>, <u>173</u>, 648–671.

MAGAZINE ARTICLE WITH PAGINATION BY ISSUE

Zuckerman, L. (1988, May 23). Now she's queen for a daily.
    <u>Time</u>, p. 51.

NEWSPAPER ARTICLE BY KNOWN AUTHOR

Spears, G. (1988, May 27). Elderly must bear new Medicare
    costs. <u>The Miami Herald</u>, pp. 1A, 16A.

This entry illustrates an article on discontinuous pages.

Nonprint Resources

FEATURE-LENGTH FILM

```
Welles, O. (Director), Mankiewicz, H. J., & Welles, O.
    (Writers). (1941). Citizen Kane [Film]. R.K.O.
```

SHORT FILM

```
Sorkin, A., & Kahn, T. (Filmmakers), Kah, T. (Director).
    (1977). Scarcity and planning [Film]. Los Angeles:
    Walt Disney Educational Media.
```

COMPUTER SOFTWARE

```
Bird, A. (1987). Timeout quickspell [Computer program].
    San Diego: Beagle Bros. (vers. 1.5; Apple IIe, 128K).
```

AUDIO RECORDING

```
Herndon, J. (1986). Teaching and Its Discontents. (Cas-
    sette Recording No. 73063-011). Urbana, IL: National
    Council of Teachers of English.
```

REFERENCE SOURCE

If you use the APA form and need a model not shown in this brief section, consult the *Publication Manual of the American Psychological Association,* 3rd ed., Washington, DC: APA, 1983.

Works Cited Form
in Author and Date System

For the sake of consistency, if you use the author and date system for documentation, you must also use it in the Works Cited listing. The form is similar to that of the Works Cited used with APA documentation, except there are **no parentheses around the dates and the first letter of each word in a title is capitalized.** Also, *two spaces* follow each period.

EXAMPLES: Hamilton, Ian. 1988. <u>In Search of J. D. Sal-</u>
        <u>inger</u>. New York: Random.

Michaels, David. 1988a. "Living in the 21st
        Century." <u>Buildings</u> Feb.–Mar.: 27–30.

Michaels, David. 1988b. "Mastering Welding for
        Jewelry Repairs." <u>Ornament</u> Spring: 18+.

Chapter 10

Final Presentation

Your paper is written, the revisions made, and now you are ready to do the last few tasks to make a final copy of your paper and put it in presentation form. Follow the few guides in this chapter and your paper will make the best possible impression on your audience (and on the instructor who will grade your work).

Not all of the sections in this chapter will apply to you. For example, business, technical, and scientific research works sometimes have a synopsis or abstract of the study included with the presentation. You may not need them. But you will certainly want to study about page numbering and proofreading. If you read through the entire chapter, you will see what possibilities exist for various kinds of research papers.

Check the **Sample Research Paper,** beginning on page 257, as an example of details that have been explained throughout the book and as a model for your own paper. You will find two kinds of commentary in the margins of that paper:

- Information about **form** is printed in turquoise.

- **Content** notes commenting on the substance and organization are printed in black.

For example, you can read about the heading for the first page of your text on pages 247–48 and see an example of it, together with a marginal explanation of spacing, on page 259.

Sections in this chapter follow the order of your working process at this stage, as well as of the parts of the research paper, from typing/word processing to fastening pages together.

Typing/Word Processing

To type your paper (and you should always do so unless specifically permitted to handwrite), choose a standard serif or sans-serif type, never a script or other fancy typeface. Use *only black type,* never any color on your work. Make sure the type is clean and that the ribbon prints a dark, clear image.

Use standard 8½ × 11-inch white typing paper of a good quality for your research paper. "Erasable" paper is not recommended because it smudges easily and is hard for your instructor to write comments on. Onionskin or other thin paper is too hard to handle and makes reading difficult. Never submit a photocopy.

If you have written and revised your research paper on a computer, your work can be printed out quickly. Try to make your final hard copy on a letter-quality printer, a laser printer, or a daisy wheel printer. If you use a dot-matrix printer, be sure the letters are legible and that the ribbon is printing dark enough to make reading easy. (Get a new ribbon, if necessary, before printing the paper.) Use plain white paper of good weight. (Pin-feed paper is all right to use if the perforated edging tears off cleanly.)

Follow these spacing customs:

- Double-space all text, including long quotations and Works Cited entries.
- Type (or print) on only one side of each page.
- Leave one-inch margins all around the text. (Set a computer to print justified lines only if your instructor permits.)
- Indent the beginning of each new paragraph five spaces from the left margin.
- Long quotations (four or more lines) are indented ten spaces from the left margin.

Accent marks or other symbols you can't type or print should be added afterwards. Do so neatly in black ink, using a fine or medium-point pen.

Page Numbering

Number **all pages** of the text, appendixes, Works Cited, and so on, **consecutively** in the upper right-hand corner, 1/2 inch down from the top. The first page of your paper is labeled "1"; beginning with page 2, write your last name before the number. (Use your first initial, also, if there is another person in the class with the same last name as yours.) Do *not* add periods, abbreviations, or any other marks. Check spacing so the *line will end* one inch from the right edge of the paper.

Should you have several pages of front matter before the text, such as an outline, preface, or synopsis, number those pages with consecutive small roman numerals (i, ii, iii); write your name, also, beginning with the second page. (See how the outline on pages 257–58 preceding the Sample Research Paper applies this numbering.)

Proofreading

An author is responsible for the accuracy of all work, so even though spelling and punctuation variations may be typing errors, they will not be so judged when people read your paper. Therefore, it's imperative to **correct any errors**.

Read each page carefully before removing it from the typewriter. Then you can white-out minor errors and retype letters or words as needed and still keep lines even. If something short has been omitted, type it in directly above the line where it should have been and use a caret (∧) to show where the insert goes. Retype pages on which there are long insertions or changes. Never write in the margins of your paper and don't crowd lines so much that they're unreadable.

Take time to proofread your entire research paper before turning it in because you may catch additional errors when you look at the whole work. If you find any errors previously overlooked, you can correct them—very carefully and neatly—in black ink.

Most people who work on computers prefer to do their proofreading from a hard copy rather than from the screen; typos and other errors seem to be more apparent on the printed page. Make any final corrections on the disk before a last printout.

First Page

The first page of your text will contain all the necessary identification if you are following the MLA style recommended throughout this book. (If you are requested to use an alternate format with a separate title page, see Appendix C on page 296.)

In the upper left-hand corner of your paper, one inch down from the top and one inch in from the left side of the paper, type the following information (double-spaced):

your name

the name of your instructor

the course number for which you wrote the paper (you may also be asked
to note the sequence number of your section)

the date the paper is due

Double-space again and **center the title** of your paper. Use capital letters
to begin each word except articles, conjunctions, and short prepositions.
Underline or put in quotation marks the titles of books, films, or short stories
as is customary. However, *do not* put your title in all capitals, enclose it within
quotation marks, underline it, or put a period at the end.

EXAMPLES: `School Libraries Should Not Ban Books`

             or

             `Story into Film: "Pickets" and `<u>`A Time Out of War`</u>

If your title requires more than one line of type, double-space between them.

Use a quadruple space (two double spaces) between the end of your title
and the beginning of the text of the paper—the only change from double
spacing you will need in the entire typing of the paper.

Begin the text with the usual five-space indentation from the left margin
for the first paragraph. If you begin with a long quotation without introduction, however, follow the indentation you would use anywhere else in the
paper: all lines are indented ten spaces from the left margin.

Outline

The outline from which you wrote your research paper is often included with
the presentation text so an instructor can see the content and organization of
your paper before reading it. Since the outline comes before the first page of
the text, which bears the paper's identifying information, repeat that information on the first page of your outline. That is, observing standard margins
and double spacing, put your name, instructor, course, and date, at the top
left corner. Use small roman numerals to number pages in an outline, even if
there is only one such page.

Double-space all typing (or printing) in the outline and adhere to the
same margins as in the text of the paper.

Center the title of your paper and follow it with a quadruple space before
writing the thesis statement (so labeled and double-spaced) and then the
outline. (See an example on page 257.)

You do not need to label this page as an outline, because anybody looking
at it can see that it is one.

Preface or Statement of Purpose

Few undergraduate papers require a preface or a statement of purpose. However, if you are asked to include either in the final presentation of your research work, you should know what they are. **A preface is a brief introduction,** usually no more than half a page, **telling what the audience will find in the paper.** The preface precedes the text, but follows a table of contents (if you include one).

A **statement of purpose tells what you propose to do or show in the text that follows.** Sometimes it also tells the reason you undertook the research being reported—that is, the purpose you hoped to achieve by doing it.

Center the word "Preface" or "Purpose"—without the quotation marks—one inch down from the top of the paper; type it in capitals and lowercase letters. Double-space between that title and the text as well as between lines on the page. Otherwise, follow all the conventions already described, including small roman numerals and your name in the top right-hand corner of the page, regular paragraph indentation, and standard margins.

Synopsis or Abstract

Neither a synopsis nor an abstract (the words are often used interchangeably) is usually included with an undergraduate paper of the length this book discusses, though it might be expected with some research done in the natural or social sciences. Include either of these only if you are specifically told to do so—and instead of a Preface or a Statement of Purpose.

The **synopsis or abstract tells what is found in more detail within the text.** Both *differ from the preface* because they give more information about content. The synopsis or abstract is also likely to stress the purpose for which research was undertaken. Neither is longer than one page.

Center the heading "Synopsis" or "Abstract" (but without the quotation marks shown here) in capital and lowercase letters, one inch down from the top of the paper. Number the page with small roman numerals, type everything on it in double spacing, and observe one-inch margins around the text.

This page usually comes after a title page and before other introductory material to the paper itself.

The Text

Follow the information about writing your paper in Chapter 7 and the conventions of documenting it you read about in Chapter 8. Take one last look before submitting your paper to make sure that you have acknowledged all material that isn't original, that pages are numbered consecutively, and that you have been consistent in using the preferred documentation system.

Underlining in typing or writing means that if the words were set in type they would be italicized—the custom for titles of many works, foreign words or phrases, or words you want the reader to note particularly.

If you are printing your research paper from a computer disk, don't get fancy with boldface or multiple typeface changes, even if your computer and printer support such variations. Just keep the text readable.

Illustrative Materials: Charts, Tables, Graphs, and Pictures

Put illustrative materials as close as you can to the portion of the text they illustrate; doing so makes your research paper easy to read and understand. Since visual representations of complex ideas are often helpful to readers, plan on using whatever will fit your subject. A map to show population change, a graph to illustrate the relation between interest rates and employment, a table to show attendance at professional football games, some bars of music, an original drawing or photograph—all these are the kind of illustrative materials you can use with your research paper.

Don't depend on finding just the right visual; create your own. You can draw, photograph, or create a montage of cutouts. Many computer programs either contain visuals, format them for you, or enable you to draw them yourself.

A **table** is so labeled in capital and lowercase letters *above* the visual and is followed by an arabic numeral; tables are numbered successively throughout your research paper. On a second line, a caption in capital and lowercase letters tells what the table shows. Both the label and the caption begin at the left margin of your paper. The table itself should be typed double-spaced.

EXAMPLE:

```
Table 18.4

Changes in agricultural productivity, 1800–1980.

Product                                   1800    1900    1980

WHEAT
Hours of labor per acre (yearly)          56.0    15.0     2.8
Hours of labor per 100 bushels           373.0   108.0     9.0
Yield per acre (in bushels)               15.0    13.9    31.4
CORN
Hours of labor per acre (yearly)          86.0    38.0     3.6
Hours of labor per 100 bushels           344.0   147.0     4.0
Yield per acre (in bushels)               25.0    25.9    95.2

Source: U.S. Census, 1975, 1981
```

Figures are photographs, drawings, graphs, charts, and maps; they are abbreviated "Fig." and assigned successive arabic numerals throughout your paper. In addition, each is given a title or caption, in capital and lowercase letters, set flush with the left margin. Both label and title or caption are placed *below* illustrative materials. For examples, look at the drawings in this book, especially of sample preliminary citation cards in Chapter 4.

Cite the sources of any tables or figures that are not original. Do so immediately below the illustration by writing the word "Source" followed by a colon and the required documentation.

Think how frustrating it would be for a reader to follow a graph line without knowing what that line represented. So, as a final check, be sure all the components of any illustrative materials are labeled.

Comment Notes

As explained in Chapter 7, pages 181–82, you may have comments that you decide to put at the end of the text of your paper as endnotes. These are brief elaborations, comments on the text, or a series of sources that would interrupt the text if written as parenthetical documentation.

Follow the format explained in the next section regarding the heading of pages and other matters of recording endnotes. See an example of how such comment notes are used in the Sample Research Paper on page 275.

Endnotes

If you are not using in-text parenthetical documentation, you will have numbered all material that needs documentation or other comment, as explained in Chapter 8, pages 203–11, with successive superscript numbers throughout the text of your paper. You then must supply the explanation for each by matching the superscript numbers and listing all such material in endnotes.

Endnotes begin on a new page immediately after the research paper text concludes. Center the title "Notes" (without the quotation marks) one inch from the top and put your name and page number in the usual right-hand location; remember that these are successive page numbers continuing from the text. Typing continues to be double-spaced.

Each note begins with the appropriate superscript (or "superior") arabic numeral (without periods or underlining) indented five spaces from the left margin; skip one space and then type the required information. Second and subsequent lines begin at the left margin. That is, you will be using *paragraph indentation*.

Make a final check to be sure the note numbering in endnotes corresponds to those in the text of your paper.

Works Cited

If you have been following the recommendations of this book and using parenthetical documentation, only an author's name and a page number or some equally concise designation appears in the text of your paper to document a source. The complete information your audience needs is in the listing of Works Cited at the end of your research paper.

The forms to use for each item in this list have been described in detail in Chapter 4, so your sources should be recorded accurately on the preliminary citation cards you will work from. Further help in forms, including many conventions, was given in Chapter 9.

The listing of Works Cited (or of Works Consulted) is always in alphabetical order by author's last name or by title (except for articles) of anonymous works. Use three spaced hyphens rather than repeat an author's name, and alphabetize the works by title. Wire services are *not* authors of works and are never recognized in a citation.

Never number the items in a Works Cited list. Nor should you note exact page numbers you consulted within a book, except for a single essay or other short work within a collection.

Begin this list on a new page at the end of the text of your research paper, but continue the page numbering, together with your name, in the top right corner. Center the heading "Works Cited" one inch from the top of this page, double-space, and begin typing the entries. Continue using double spacing within and between each item you cite. Remember that you will be using *hanging indentation* for each item; that is, begin the first line at the left margin, and succeeding lines for an entry are each indented five spaces from that margin.

If you require more than one Works Cited page, continue with the page numbering but do not use a heading. For an example of the proper form for your Works Cited, see pages 276–78 of the Sample Research Paper.

Notice that this is a *composite list of all sources cited* and is not divided by medium. Longer papers and books sometimes divide sources into Primary Sources and Secondary Sources, or into groups such as Books, Periodicals, Computer Software, Films, and so on. However, all student research papers should use a single, alphabetized list of works.

Annotation

An annotation is a short statement that tells what is important or characteristic about a source. Customarily, an annotation is not a complete sentence, though it begins with a capital letter and ends with a period. Annotations are brief; one or two remarks suffice.

If you are asked to make annotations, begin each one two spaces after the period ending the citation. Head the new page on which the entries begin "Annotated List of Works Cited" (or "Annotated List of Works Consulted"), centered and one inch from the top. Continue the page numbering system with your name at the top right corner. Follow the conventions for a Works Cited page with all items double-spaced and in hanging indentation form. No title is necessary on subsequent pages because the form shows the content.

Annotations are particularly helpful to anyone who wants to decide whether or not to consult a source you have used in preparing your research paper. Since they tell something of the contents of each source or make some other comment, a reader can decide what is of special interest.

If you know you will have to supply annotations to the works you cite in your paper, you should write comments on the citation card for each source as you use it. The questions you answer in evaluating your source materials (see pages 112–15) will also help you think of comments you might want to make in annotation. Each example in the following list shows a kind of

comment you might make in an annotation. You may also combine the various
sorts of comments.

1. State the general content of a source.

> Supports the author's contention that <u>Painted Veils</u>
> was written in only six weeks.

2. Make a judgment about the source.

> Particularly clear explanation of the legal basis of
> the suit.

3. Point out valuable properties or qualities of the source.

> Contains photographs by the author.

4. Note the viewpoint or bias of the author.

> Lacks suggestions for or allowances for alternate
> solutions.

5. Tell something about the author of the source.

> Author is professor who has published widely on
> intellectual harm caused by book banning.

Look at the annotated bibliographies in some of the sources you use for your
research work, and you may discover additional kinds of information an
annotation may contain.

The Works Cited listing in the Sample Research Paper is not an annotated
one, but here are examples of what some of the entries would be like if it
were.

Black, Martha L. "School Library Censorship: First Amend-
    ment Guarantees and the Student's Right to Know."
    <u>Censorship and Education</u>. Ed. Eli M. Oboler. New
    York: Wilson, 1981: 150–57. Author is staff attorney
    in a Federal District Court.

<u>Books Behind Bars: A Selection of "Banned" Books</u>. Miami:
    Public Library, 1987. Catalog of special exhibit of
    books banned in various communities in U.S. and
    elsewhere.

"Censorship and Libraries." Traveling exhibition spon-
    sored by American Library Association. Miami–Dade
    Main Library Auditorium, Miami. 18 June 1987.
    Exhibit is touring U.S. March 1985 to Oct. 1987.

Appendix

An **appendix contains additional illustrations or other materials that amplify the text without interrupting it.** That is, use it for showing a series of charts or tables or other materials that are useful to readers' understanding without breaking their concentration as they read the text of your paper. If they are not necessary within the text, they can safely be presented in an appendix.

This book has several appendixes (an alternate form of the word is appendices). The first one, which lists some reference works available in libraries, is related to the content of Chapter 4 but isn't absolutely necessary to read at that point in the research process; you can consult it then or at another time, so it's an appendix.

If your paper requires an appendix (or several of them), give each a different designation with capital letters, as they are in this book; put them immediately after the text and before the Notes or Works Cited.

Head the first one "Appendix A" and center it one inch down from the top of the paper. (Subsequent appendixes should show the same heading but with different letter designations.) Continue with successive page numbers as you do throughout the text and other material in your research paper.

Fastening Pages

Use a paper clip at the top left-hand corner to fasten together the pages of your completed research work. A paper clip is easy for a reader to remove and thus frees the pages to turn. Or, a reader may want to put the Works Cited page alongside of the text for handy reference. Since all pages are numbered and contain your name, the paper can readily be assembled again.

Some instructors want to have papers submitted in one of the many kinds of inexpensive covers or binders that protect your work as well as hold it together. Others prefer to have papers stapled together.

Ask your instructor which method of fastening pages is preferred!

Typing a Research Paper in APA Style

Observe many of the same customs in typing a research paper using the APA style of documentation as you would using the MLA style described throughout this book. That is, double-space throughout the paper and indent each paragraph five spaces from the left margin. Allow only one space after a comma, semicolon, colon, or period in the documentation or the References listing. The following list gives typing information that differentiates the APA style from others.

1. *A title page* is provided for the research paper. Center the title of the paper and, under it, your name. At the bottom margin and in all capital letters, center a "running head" that could be used to identify your paper. Put a shortened form of the title of the paper at the upper right corner and, double spaced below it, the number "1" (without quotes, of course).

    Because this is a paper for a class rather than one being submitted for publication in a journal that uses APA style, you will have to provide some additional information so your instructor can identify your paper readily. Therefore, about three-fourths of the way down your paper, and with an even right margin, put the name of the course for which the paper is being submitted, the sequence number if requested, the name of your instructor, and the date the paper is submitted.

    Appendix C on page 296 shows the format of this title page.

2. *Margins* should be 1-1/2 inches at the top, bottom, and each side.

3. *Pages are numbered consecutively on the top right corner of each one.* Put a **shortened form of the title** 1-1/2 inches down from the top of each page and, **double-spaced below it, the page number.**

4. *Quotations of more than 40 words are typed as a block indent;* that is, indent each line *five spaces* from the left margin established for the page. Should a new paragraph be required, indent the first line of it another five spaces from the left margin of the block.

5. *The usual order for a research paper in APA style* is this: title page, abstract, text, references, appendixes.

Sample Research Paper

On the following pages is a research paper written by a student. It includes the outline, the paper itself, an example of comment notes, and a Works Cited listing.

In the margins of each page you will see two kinds of comments:

■ Comments printed in **turquoise** are about **form**.

■ Comments printed in *black* are about *content*.

Use them as a guide to preparing your own research paper for final presentation.

Carol Matz
Professor Sharona   Double space.
ENG 102
June 10, 1988
        School Libraries Should Not Ban Books
                                     Quadruple space.

1" THESIS: Removing books from school libraries ——1"——
              limits students' free access to ideas   Double space.
              and information.
                                     Quadruple space.

    I.   Principles of free access
         A.   Meaning of intellectual freedom
         B.   Impediment of censorship
   II.   Censorship in past
         A.   Banned books
         B.   Who attempts censoring
         C.   "Reasons" for book removal
         D.   Frequency of censorship attempts
  III.   Major litigation
         A.   President's Council
         B.   Minarcini and Chelsea victories
         C.   Pico v. Island Trees
              1.   Source of case   Indent five spaces
              2.   Supreme Court decision   from capital
              3.   Reactions and implications   letters.
   IV.   First Amendment philosophy
         A.   "Right to receive information"
         B.   Tinker v. Des Moines
              1.   Background
              2.   Opinion

1"

1"

Matz ii

Use lowercase
roman numerals
for pages of
outline.

V. Future prevention of censorship

    A. Policy formation of schools

    B. Organizations battling censorship

    C. Implications of denying access

Double space

Carol Matz

Professor Sharona

ENG 102

June 10, 1988

School Libraries

Should Not Ban Books

Through most of human history, waving the banners of religious and philosophical righteousness, authority has invoked censorship to stifle free expression. Here in the United States, where the very success of our form of government depends on the participation of informed citizens, the issue of censorship becomes a very frightening one. A constitutional republic, such as ours, can only exist with an electorate that has unrestricted access to ideas and information—so it can be fully informed and make wise decisions.

The education of the future electorate of our country starts in the public schools. In the past few decades, the practice of banning books from public school libraries has become prevalent. This practice denies students, our future electorate, what they need most: ready access to all kinds of thinking represented in books. Such censorship comes at a time when many of their ideas are being formed, that is, while they are in school. Because such intellectual freedom is essential, our government is threatened when access to that basic freedom is removed.

Last name and page number.

Double space.

Center title.

Quadruple space.

Indent all paragraphs five spaces.

1"

Type entire paper double space.

Begins with background.

Sets tone of writing.

Transition to focus of the paper.

Thesis of the paper.

1"

Sample Research Paper

Last name and page number on each page.

Beginning of II of outline.
Author's name is part of text.

Parenthetic documentation after summary.

Citation prepares reader to know information source.

Free expression, as guaranteed by our Constitution, can only flourish in a society that is taught to value intellectual freedom. Libraries are the embodiment of intellectual freedom, and the best lesson in free expression that can be taught to students involves the protection of their school libraries, which are a major source of their intellectual freedom.

Censorship in America has been a problem in the past 200 years. Kraus notes that as our country moves away from being a "melting pot" and becomes more diversified, demands are being made to the schools to impart values to students. As we become more culturally pluralistic, more questions are raised about what values should or shouldn't be taught in schools and what the role of the school should be in society (343). The most recent trend toward censorship is viewed by some as a reflection of the growing political conservatism of the country. However, others see it as less a political matter than a social one, a kind of reaction to the "confusions" of the 1960s.

Whatever the reasons may be for the recent trend toward censorship, our schools are definitely feeling the full force of its impact. The traveling exhibit "Censorship and Libraries" showed that everything from mythology to dictionaries can be removed. In 1979, books on Greek mythology were removed from an Arizona school library because they contained two drawings of bare-breasted goddesses. In that same year, two sex education books in an Oregon school library were removed because of explicit anatomical drawings. In 1982, a California school returned 146 volumes of the <u>American Heritage Dictionary</u> to the publisher because the principal noted thirteen "inappropriate words," among them "French kiss."

> Book title is underlined.

These are only a few examples of book banning in our public schools. <u>Books Behind Bars</u> lists many award-winning novels that have been banned, including George Orwell's <u>1984</u>, Ralph Ellison's <u>The Invisible Man</u>, Margaret Mitchell's <u>Gone with the Wind</u>, and Alice Walker's <u>The Color Purple</u>. Professor Ken Donelson ("Almost 13 Years" 98), drawing conclusions from his 1984 survey, reports that the most frequently banned authors are John Steinbeck and Judy Blume, both award-winning novelists. Donelson also shows that many banned books are considered literary classics and include works by Shakespeare, Dickens, and Twain.

> Shortened title of article.
> Date of information helps audience focus on time.

According to Pell (118), the pressure to ban these works from our school libraries is coming primarily from right-wing extremist groups and individuals. The majority of would-be censors come in the name of God and Country; their crusade is to root out all evil, the subversive, and to save their children's minds from the devil and Communism. Donelson points out in "Teachers" (106) that the very names of some of the largest organizations active in the crusade to ban books from school libraries

> Parenthetic documentation.

> Integrating author and shortened title in text.

Matz 4

reflect that belief, for among them are groups
called Churches United for Decency, Save Our
Children, and Parents for God, Home, and
Country.

Such groups are not the only ones who try

Variation in wording.

to ban books. Donelson further shows that some
forms of censorship have come from within.
Librarians wanting to avoid conflict have set
up reserved or closed shelves. Or, they have

Quotation marks show special uses of familiar words.

withdrawn books from shelves and listed them as
"lost" or "stolen" (106–08). These measures

Author shows own ideas.

may have been taken to avoid the censors, yet
they are acts of censorship themselves!

Variation in wording.

In the same article, Donelson points out
that censors also exist on the left, making
attempts to wipe out such wrongs as sexism and
racism. They are just as wrong in attempting
censorship because

Quotation of five or more lines is a block quote; indent block quotes ten spaces.

> Once the door is open to anyone to
> censor, then it cannot be closed
> because one kind of censorship is said
> to be good and another is said to be
> bad. All censors would argue that they

Documentation is placed after period in block quote.

> censor for good and moral reasons.
> (109)

Several writers have explored some of the
many "reasons" censors give for wanting books

Several sources cited as group; documentation in series is separated by semicolons.

removed from school library shelves (Pell 118;
<u>Books Behind Bars</u>; Darling 120). Predominantly
right-wing groups and individuals have made
claims that works are pro-Communist,
unpatriotic, contrary to prevailing religious
beliefs, vulgar, too sexual, too "adult" for

students, or that they don't promote traditional
family roles. In addition, Hechinger points out
that many communities are trying to purge school
libraries of what they call "secular humanist"
books, including those on Darwin's theory of
evolution, which are not in accordance with the
"creationist" views.

Here is a list extracted from <u>Books Behind
Bars</u> of some of the most widely banned classics
and the "reasons" students have been denied
access to them:

> Maya Angelou, <u>I Know Why the Caged
> Bird Sings</u>--displays "bitterness
> and hatred against whites"
>
> Ray Bradbury, <u>The Martian Chronicles</u>--
> uses God's name in vain
>
> William Golding, <u>Lord of the Flies</u>--
> "implies man is little more than
> an animal"
>
> J.D. Salinger, <u>Catcher in the Rye</u>--
> it's "vulgar and perverse"
>
> John Steinbeck, <u>Grapes of Wrath</u> and <u>Of
> Mice and Men</u>--both for their use
> of "vulgar language"

Indent block quote ten spaces.

Hanging indentation highlights information that is enumerated.

These and other banned books were not just the
targets of attack in isolated incidents in the
past. In fact, many books have been banned
simultaneously around the country in reaction to
the publicized banning of particular books.

Censorship is visibly on the rise. In the
decade from 1965 to 1975, over 500 censorship
cases were reported to have occurred in public
school libraries (Nolte 213). Massie reports

Parenthetical documentation at end of sentence.

Matz 6

that the American Library Association's Office
for Intellectual Freedom says that in the half
decade between 1975 and 1980, there have been

<u>three times as many attempts</u> as in the preceding
decade. Furthermore, the ALA/OIF notes that 300
controversies may be reported in a given year,
but speculates that ten times as many instances
of uncontested removals may exist (79). Thomas
Emerson writes that in the American Civil

Liberties Union's 1982 national survey on
censorship, over 50% of high school librarians

reported pressure from the censors (191).

From the early 1970s to the present, this
pressure has been felt strongly enough to bring
the issue of censorship in school libraries into
the courts. Most litigation efforts during this
period have involved cases in which school
boards were accused of banning books from their
libraries, not because of lack of shelf space or
relevance but because of "morally objectionable"
material. The amazing thing is that the cases
involved books previously evaluated as being
worthy of acquisition under operating criteria
of book selection!

The earliest opinion handed down by the
courts in that decade was in the 1972 case

<u>President's Council, Dist. 25 v. Community
School Board</u>. In this decision, the District
Court of Appeals upheld the removal of Piri

Thomas's <u>Down These Mean Streets</u> (an
autobiography of a Puerto Rican growing up in
Spanish Harlem) from junior high school
libraries in District 25 of New York City. The

Matz 7

court ruled on the grounds that reviewing a decision of the school board contradicted the ruling of <u>Epperson v. Arkansas</u>. The <u>Epperson</u> ruling stated that the court couldn't intervene in "resolution of conflicts which arise in daily operation of school systems and which do not directly and sharply implicate basic constitutional values" (North 135). In the <u>President's Council</u> case, the court reduced the issue to one of merely shelving a book, stating that the banning of Thomas's book did not involve any constitutional issue.

Documentation at end of quotation that ends a sentence.

Four years later, the first small victory occurred in the fight against school library censorship. In <u>Minarcini v. Strongsville [Ohio] City School District</u>, the Court of Appeals for the Sixth Circuit ruled against the school board's removal of Joseph Heller's <u>Catch 22</u> and Kurt Vonnegut's <u>Cat's Cradle</u>. The Office for Intellectual Freedom's case summaries report that the court upheld students' "right to receive information," and that the judge went on to further state that school libraries are an "important privilege" created for the students—a privilege that isn't to be withdrawn by the whim of the school board (147). In 1978, relying on the <u>Minarcini</u> precedent, a judge ruled in the <u>Right to Read Defense Committee of Chelsea v. School Committee of the City of Chelsea</u> [MA] that the school committee's attempt to ban a poetry anthology [because of one poem in it] couldn't pass First Amendment standards already established by the Supreme Court and

State in which case took place is identified by author.

Documentation in middle of paragraph.

Author's interpolation in square brackets.

Sample Research Paper

lower court rulings.

    Shortly after the <u>Minarcini</u> and <u>Chelsea</u> victories, the most important case involving school library censorship started to make its way through the courts. This case, <u>Pico, et al. v. Island Trees [NY] Union Free School District No. 26</u> was brought to court by several students, led by Steven Pico, who challenged the removal of nine books from the school library by the

Superscript number corresponds with "Notes" at end of paper.

school board in March 1976.[1] The board removed the books because, it stated, they were "anti-American, anti-Christian, anti-Semitic, and just plain filthy," and justified the removal on

Short quotations are written as part of text.

grounds of its "duty, or moral obligation, to protect the children in our schools from this

Ellipses show omission in quotation.

moral danger . . ." (qtd. in North 134). According to North, these books were removed by the board even though a board-appointed committee recommended their educational suitability and relevance (134).

    In 1979 a district court judge ruled in favor of the school board, relying on the <u>President's Council</u> precedent. In 1980 the case was appealed to the U.S. Court of Appeals, Second Circuit; the district court's decision was reversed and it was remanded for trial, since the court found that the student plaintiffs stated a suitable claim for violation of First Amendment rights. On that basis, in 1981 the Supreme Court agreed to review the case.

    On June 25, 1982, the Supreme Court, with a 5-4 vote, affirmed the Court of Appeals ruling, but was unable to agree on a majority opinion. The decision was split, but the plurality opinion said the case should be tried to see whether the school board acted to inhibit the spread of ideas it disagreed with or only removed the books because of "vulgarity." Justice Byron White cast the deciding vote because he "concluded simply that a trial should be held before any decisions were made about whether or not First Amendment rights were involved" (Wermiel).

Short quotation is part of text.

Article is on single page so no page number is needed.

Justice Brennan's written opinion with the majority vote expresses the idea that students should have the "right to receive information" and that the issue of the Pico case is one of the school board's intention to deny the right of access to ideas it disagrees with. However, Emerson notes that the opinion doesn't clarify the standards or guidelines the courts should use in making decisions of whether violations of First Amendment rights occur, except proof of intent to deny access to students (193–94).

First digit of page number is omitted rather than repeated.

Since the Supreme Court decision, no trial has taken place in the Pico v. Island Trees case. The nine books in question were reinstated by the school board on a 6–1 vote. However, this vote had a clause to its ruling: librarians have to send notes to parents whose children check out any of these books, because the board still sees them as objectionable. The vote to reinstate the books occurred because their removal became quite a divisive force in the local community ("Island Trees").

Matz 10

The <u>Pico v. Island Trees</u> case seems to have
raised more questions than it answered. It did
establish the relevance of the First Amendment
in this issue, but did not clarify the extent of
its application. Furthermore, as Kraus points
out (344–45), the case raised the issue of
acquisition versus retention. The <u>Pico</u> case
only directly affects the removal or retention
of books in a school library and does not
address the guidelines for acquisition of new
books. It fails to consider the point at which
book selection may border on book
censorship. It doesn't consider whether refusal
to acquire a book because of its ideas or
content contradicts Justice Brennan's analysis
of the students' "right to receive information."
Nor does it consider whether limits should be
placed on acquisition and retention and, if so,
whether the school board or the courts should be
the authority to make those limits.

In contrast to the idea that the <u>Pico</u> case
was nothing more than a tainted victory in the
issue of school library censorship, some view
the overall outcome as a success. Judith Krug,
Director of the American Library Association's
Office for Intellectual Freedom, stated that the
most important victory was access to the courts
in school-related First Amendment disputes and
that students can challenge the personal values
of school board members ("Justice Brennan"). A
New York attorney who filed a friend-of-the-
court brief on behalf of the Association of
American Publishers feels that the fact the

Source identified
by title.

Matz 11

court ordered a trial "'means the doors to the courthouse are open . . . to explore and ventilate school board decisions . . ..'" (qtd. in Wermiel).

Single quote marks for a quotation within a quotation.

The important point in these cases, and the reason they have been reviewed here, is that by establishing precedent, they could very well affect the outcome of future school library censorship cases. There has now been judicial recognition of a "right to receive information," which means that students are guaranteed rights to read and think for themselves. If this right is included in the First Amendment, and First Amendment rights are applicable to students, then students have their rights to intellectual freedom guaranteed by the Constitution. That is, students <u>do</u> have the right to free access to information in library books.

Transitional phrasing.

Beginning of IV of outline.

The First Amendment to the Constitution, which banned—author Kurt Vonnegut (<u>Meese Commission Exposed</u> 8) sardonically calls "the fundamental piece of obscenity from which all others spring," simply states

> Congress shall make no law respecting an establishment of religion, or prohibiting the free exercise thereof; or abridging the freedom of speech, or of the press, or the right of the people to peaceably assemble, and to petition the Government for a redress of grievances.

Constitution is common knowledge.

According to Landy (199), several recent cases decided by the Supreme Court indicate that the "right to receive information" is included

Superscript
indicating note
after paper.

in the First Amendment.[2] Their outcomes say
that receiving information and ideas is
constitutionally guaranteed regardless of any
judgments on social value. To show how
intricate the issues are, Attorney Martha L.
Black points out that

> The First Amendment guarantees that
> government cannot interfere with the
> free exchange of ideas without showing
> a serious threat to national
> security. This protection has /
> traditionally been extended to freedom
> of speech or expression. . . . As an
> essential counterpart of their right
> to freedom of expression, students may
> properly assert a claim of access to
> controversial literature and freedom
> from school board censorship based on
> social or political taste. (150–51)

Transitional
wording.

One more case reference shows how the First
Amendment is applicable to minors attending
public schools. It is the 1969 landmark
decision in the case <u>Tinker v. Des Moines
Independent Community School District</u>.

The case was initiated in 1965 when a group
of Iowa high school students decided to wear
black armbands in school to protest the Vietnam
War and the school administration decided to
oust temporarily any students who did so. Some
students wore the armbands, though they knew
about the warning. When five students were
suspended from school as a result, their parents

filed a complaint with the U.S. District Court,
claiming that their children's right to free
expression was violated. The court upheld the
school's action, stating that the administration
was only taking measures for the sake of
discipline. The case was appealed in the Court
of Appeals for the Eighth Circuit and again the
plaintiffs lost. In 1969 it was appealed yet
again, this time to the Supreme Court, which
ruled that First Amendment rights <u>are</u> applicable
to students. This decision, indicates Snyder
(130–32), offered the most clear-cut definition
of students' constitutional rights that has been
handed down from the courts.

Spread of pages
shows information
is a summary.

     <u>Tinker</u> is important because it related to
<u>all</u> forms of freedom of expression in the
schools. Justice Abe Fortas stated this in his
decision on the case:

> state-operated schools may not be
> enclaves of totalitarianism. School
> officials do not possess absolute
> authority over their students.
> Students in school as well as out of
> school are 'persons' under our
> Constitution.. . . .

Quotation begins
with lowercase
letter because it's
the middle of a
sentence.

>   In our system, students may <u>not</u>
> [emphasis added] be regarded as
> closed-circuit recipients of only
> that which the State chooses to
> communicate. They may not be confined
> to the expression of those sentiments
> that are officially approved. (qtd.
> in Snyder 132)

New paragraph in
block quote
indented three
spaces.
Research paper
author's comment
in square
brackets.

Author didn't read
the decision, but
read about it in
this source.

Matz 14

These cases have been cited here at some length to point out that the "right to receive information" is guaranteed by the First Amendment and is applicable to students in public schools. Since the Constitution <u>does</u> protect that right of students, school library censorship directly violates it.

Because of the growing wave of censorship affecting our school libraries, actions are being taken by both groups and individuals to aid in preventing censorship. Perhaps the most important preventive measures come from within the schools themselves. Darling calls attention to a great division of responsibility regarding school libraries (librarians, principals, teachers, school board), which makes it easier for censors to attempt book removal with a degree of success. Therefore, schools and school principals are starting to consider forming strict policies regarding book selection and procedures for handling complaints against books (121).

In addition, many prestigious organizations have actively campaigned to prevent book banning, especially in school libraries. The American Association of School Librarians has prepared material to give schools some guidelines for the prevention of censorship. It encourages schools to develop <u>written</u> policies on book selection which include procedures for the review of challenged material. It asks that these policies be made familiar to the staff, administration, and community through

Matz 15

newsletters, PTAs, and so on. Furthermore, the guidelines explain how to handle complaints and inform the schools of the various organizations they can turn to for help if necessary.

Other organizations have mobilized to oppose censorship by helping to raise public awareness and providing legal assistance. Pell writes that the American Civil Liberties Union's lawyers are at the forefront of many legal battles involving library censorship. The Office for Intellectual Freedom of the American Library Association publishes a newsletter on the subject, tracks current cases, and provides statistics on censorship cases. The American Library Association's Freedom to Read Foundation provides financial and legal assistance, along with its lobbying and fundraising efforts (147).

Another group active in battling censorship is an author's group called P.E.N. This organization launched the "American Right to Read" campaign, which has sent famous authors, including John Irving, Erica Jong, and E. D. Doctorow, across the nation to speak about books and First Amendment rights (Kakutani).

> Article is on one page so no page number needs to be shown.

The National Council of Teachers of English (which has a Committee Against Censorship) distributes a unique project published by one of its affiliates that aids in preventing censorship. It is a volume of individual "reviews" of some of the most frequently banned books in public schools; it is called <u>Celebrating Censored Books</u>. These reviews or essays, written mostly by university professors,

> Authors identified to give weight to citation.

provide rationales for the use of these books in the schools. The academic values of these books are explained to help arm those who are fighting against new censorship attempts.

Concluding section of outline restates author's position.

In all, censoring books by removing them from public school libraries denies students their right to intellectual freedom. These students must have free access to ideas and information in order to make well-informed decisions as adults--adults who will form the electorate that will make decisions about how the country is run and who will value free expression as guaranteed by the Constitution.

In a 1938 speech before the National Education Association, President Franklin Delano Roosevelt summed up the situation:

Paper ends with apt quotation.

> Freedom to learn is the first necessity of guaranteeing that man himself shall be self-reliant enough to be free. . . . If in other lands the press and books and literature of all kinds are censored, we must double our efforts here to keep it free. . . . The ultimate victory of tomorrow is through democracy with education. (qtd. in "Censorship and Libraries" exhibit)

Source of quotation follows final period of block quote.

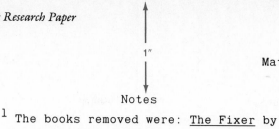

Continue page numbers from paper.

Center title.

Superscript number, followed by one space.

Double-space throughout.

Note contains information that interrupt the flow of text.

Note number corresponds with number in text of paper.

Notes

[1] The books removed were: <u>The Fixer</u> by Bernard Malamud, <u>Slaughterhouse–Five</u> by Kurt Vonnegut, <u>Soul on Ice</u> by Eldridge Cleaver, <u>The Naked Ape</u> by Desmond Morris, <u>Down These Mean Streets</u> by Piri Thomas, <u>Best Short Stories by Negro Writers</u> edited by Langston Hughes, <u>Go Ask Alice</u> (anonymous), <u>A Hero Ain't Nothin' But a Sandwich</u> by Alice Childress, and <u>A Reader for Writers: A Critical Anthology of Prose Readings</u> edited by Jerome Archer.

[2] These "right to receive information" cases include <u>Lamont v. Postmaster General</u>, <u>Red Lion Broadcasting v. FCC</u>, and <u>Stanley v. Georgia</u>.

Continue page
numbering.

Center title.

Double-space
throughout.

Indent five spaces
(hanging
indentation).

Type with spacing
on Works Cited
cards.

←——— 1" ———→

A nonprint source.

Dashes indicate
same author as
previous work.

1"

Works Cited

American Association of School
         Librarians. "What Can a School Library Media
         Specialist Do To Preserve Intellectual
         Freedom?" Chicago: AASL, n.d.

Black, Martha L. "The Student's Right to
         Know." Censorship and Education. Ed. Eli
         M. Oboler. New York: Wilson, 1981: 150-69.

Books Behind Bars: A Selection of "Banned"
         Books. Miami: Miami-Dade Pub. Lib., 1987.

Carmen, Arlene, et al. The Meese Commission
         Exposed. New York: Nat. Coalition Against   ←—— 1"——
         Censorship, 1987.

"Censorship and Libraries." Sponsored by
         American Library Association. Miami-Dade
         Main Library Auditorium, Miami. 18 June
         1987.

Darling, Richard L. "School Libraries and
         Intellectual Freedom." Intellectual
         Freedom Manual, 2nd ed. Comp. by Office
         for Intellectual Freedom. Chicago: Am. Lib.
         Assoc., 1983: 120-22.

Donelson, Ken. "Almost 13 Years of Book
         Protests . . . Now What?" School Library
         Journal Mar. 1985: 93-98.

- - -. "Teachers and Librarians as
         Censors." Censorship and Education. Ed.
         Eli M. Oboler. New York: Wilson, 1981:
         104-110.

Emerson, Thomas I. "Academic Freedom." Our
         Endangered Rights. Ed. Norman Dorsen. New
         York: Pantheon, 1984: 179-202.

1"

Matz 19

Hechinger, Fred K. "The Essence of Censorship
in the Schools." New York Times 27 Oct.
1981: C5.

"Island Trees School Board Lifts Seven Year Book
Ban." Library Journal 107 (1982): 1694.

"Justice Brennan Follows ALA's Line in Island
Trees Case." American Libraries 13 (1982):
444.

Kakutani, Michiko. "The Famous Will Gather to
Read the Forbidden." New York Times 5 Apr.
1982: C11.

Karolides, Nicholas J., and Lee Burress,
eds. Celebrating Censored Books. Racine:
WI Council of Teachers of Eng., 1985.

Kraus, Larry L. "Censorship: What Island Trees
v. Pico [sic] Means to Schools." Clearing
House 57 (1984): 343–45.

Landy, Alex P. "The Chelsea Case." Censorship
and Education. Ed. Eli M. Oboler. New
York: Wilson, 1981: 189–206.

Massie, Dorothy C. "Censorship in the
Schools." Censorship and Education. Ed.
Eli M. Oboler. New York: Wilson, 1981: 78–
86.

Nolte, M. Chester. "Official Constraints on
Indecent Words." Censorship and
Education. Ed. Eli M. Oboler. New York:
Wilson, 1981: 206–32.

North, William D. "School Library Censorship
and the Courts." Intellectual Freedom
Manual, 2nd ed. Comp. by Office for
Intellectual Freedom. Chicago: Am. Lib.
Assn., 1983: 133–43.

Articles have no
authorship shown.

Article in
periodical with
continuous
pagination.

Book with two
authors.

[sic] signifies
author of paper is
aware of error in
title of this legal
case.

Article in a book
edited by another
person.

Shorten
publishers'
names.

Organization as author.

Office for Intellectual Freedom. <u>Censorship</u>
<u>Litigation and the Schools</u>. Chicago: Am.
Lib. Assn., 1983.

Entire book is listed, not pages used.

Pell, Eva. <u>The Big Chill</u>. Boston: Beacon,
1984.

Snyder, Gerald S. <u>The Right to Be Informed:</u>
<u>Censorship in the United States</u>. New York:
Messner, 1976.

Wermiel, Stephen. "Justices Fail to Resolve
School Boards' Constitutional Authority to
Ban Books." <u>Wall Street Journal</u> 28 June
1982: 9.

Appendix A

Selected List of Reference Works Available in Libraries

To list all the reference materials available in even a moderate-sized library is impossible! Reference books are constantly being updated and new titles are being added. Periodicals begin or cease publication. New information and retrieval systems are being installed as computers are used ever more extensively. So as soon as any list is compiled for a book like this, it is out of date. (Besides, if such a list were complete it would be far, far longer than this entire book!)

What follows, then, is a *selected* listing of sources found in most libraries and likely to help students in preparing research papers. The titles of most volumes here are self-explanatory, so full citations and annotations are omitted. If you do your research in a particularly large library or in one devoted to a special subject, be prepared to find many, many additions to this list.

Most materials named here are either published as books or are indexes of published periodical articles. Computer information retrieval services can direct you to hundreds of thousands of items in minutes. And it is also possible to locate unpublished documents, for example, by consulting the ERIC [Educational Resources Information Center] index compiled by government-funded centers that gather, catalog, and reproduce such materials for educators. Furthermore, media centers and audiovisual departments also usually have extensive lists of catalogs and sources of information that are not included in this listing; the same is true of computer centers.

Every business, profession, and hobby has at least one (and usually several) journal, magazine, or newspaper published for people concerned with it—publications ranging from the *American Waterworks Association Journal* to *Volume Feeding Management.*Obviously, to list all such periodicals is unnecessary and impossible. The library in which you do your research certainly has a listing of those to which it subscribes and has the facilities for locating the periodicals you need to consult.

The following selected list is offered only as a guide to the many materials available. It is by no means complete or exhaustive in any category. If publication of a title is regular, the beginning date is noted next to it; otherwise, the latest publication date, as of this book printing, is shown. The list is divided into five main groups with numerous subgroups:

    I. General Reference Works
        A. General
        B. Atlases
        C. Biographies
        D. Dictionaries
        E. Encyclopedias
        F. Periodical Indexes

   II. Science and Technology
        A. General
        B. Agriculture
        C. Biology
        D. Chemistry
        E. Computer Technology and Electronic Data Processing
        F. Energy
        G. Engineering
        H. Environmental Studies
         I. Geology
         J. Medicine
        K. Physics and Mathematics

  III. Social Sciences
        A. General
        B. Business
        C. Criminology
        D. Economics
        E. Education

    F. Geography
    G. History
    H. Political Science
    I. Psychology
    J. Sociology

IV. Humanities
    A. Art and Architecture
    B. Literature
    C. Music and Dance
    D. Philosophy and Religion

V. Vocational Studies
    A. Aviation
    B. Broadcasting
    C. Fashion Careers
    D. Travel, Motel, Tourism Management
    E. Interior Design
    F. Medical and Allied Health Careers
    G. Office Technology

I. General Reference Works

A. General

Britannica Book of the Year. Since 1938
Dissertation Abstracts International. Since 1967 (Formerly
    Dissertation Abstracts. Since 1938)
Europa Year Book: A World Survey. 2 vols. Since 1959
Facts on File: World News Digest. Since 1940
Familiar Quotations. 1980
Guide to Popular U.S. Government Publications. 1986
Home Book of Proverbs, Maxims and Familiar Phrases. 1949
Information Please Almanac. Since 1947
Monthly Catalog of United States Government Publications.
    Since 1895
The Reader's Adviser. 6 vols., 1988
The Reader's Encyclopedia. 1965
Statesman's Year-Book. Since 1864
Statistical Abstract of the United States. Since 1878
World Almanac and Book of Facts. Since 1868
Year Book of the United Nations. Since 1948
United States Government Manual. Since 1935
Vertical File Index. Since 1935

B. Atlases

Atlas of American History. 1978
Atlas of Early American History. 1976
Columbia Lippincott Gazeteer of the World. 1962
Commercial Atlas and Marketing Guide. Since 1876
The National Atlas of the United States of America. 1970
National Geographic Atlas of the World. 1981
Rand McNally Cosmopolitan World Atlas. 1981
The Times Atlas of the World. Comprehensive Edition, 1981

C. Biographies

American Men and Women of Science. 7 vols., 1982
Biography Almanac. 2 vols., 1983
Biography and Genealogy Master Index. 1987
Biography Index: A Cumulative Index to Biographical Material in Books and Magazines. Since 1946
Chambers' Biographical Dictionary. 1986
Current Biography. Since 1940
Dictionary of American Biography. 21 vols., 1958
Dictionary of National Biography. 22 vols., 1885–1971
Dictionary of Scientific Biography. 16 vols., 1980
Directory of American Scholars. Since 1942
International Who's Who. Since 1936
McGraw-Hill Encyclopedia of World Biography. 1973
The National Cyclopaedia of American Biography. 69 vols. Since 1891
New Century Cyclopedia of Names. 3 vols., 1954
The New York Times Biographical Edition. Since 1969
Twentieth Century Authors. With suppl., 1942
Who Was Who in America. 7 vols., 1981
Who's Who. Since 1848
Who's Who in America. Since 1899

D. Dictionaries

Acronyms, Initialisms and Abbreviations Dictionary. 1988
Black's Law Dictionary. 1979
Black's Medical Dictionary. 1977
The Concise Oxford Dictionary of English Etymology. 1986
Dictionary of American English on Historical Principles. 4 vols., 1938–1944
Dictionary of Astrology. 1985
Dictionary of Business Terms. 1987
Dictionary of Educational Acronyms, Abbreviations and Initialisms. 1982

Dictionary of Electronics. 1987
Dictionary of Psychotherapy. 1986
Dorland's Illustrated Medical Dictionary. 1985
International Dictionary of Medicine and Biology. 3 vols., 1986
Oxford English Dictionary. 13 vols. and suppl., 1933
Random House Dictionary of the English Language. 1966
Roget's International Thesaurus. 1984
Webster's New World Dictionary of Synonyms. 1984
Webster's Third New International Dictionary. 1961

E. Encyclopedias
Academic American Encyclopedia. 21 vols., 1987
Collier's Encyclopedia. 24 vols., 1988
Encyclopaedia Britannica. (Britannica 3), 32 vols., 1987
Encyclopedia Americana. 30 vols., 1987
Random House Encyclopedia. 1983
World Book Encyclopedia. 22 vols., 1988

F. Periodical Indexes
Applied Science and Technology Index. Since 1958
Art Index. Since 1929
Bibliographic Index: A Cumulative Bibliography of Bibliographies.
   Since 1938
Book Review Digest. Since 1905
Business Periodicals Index. Since 1958
Education Index. Since 1929
General Science Index. Since 1978
Humanities Index. Since 1974
Index to Book Reviews in the Humanities. Since 1960
Industrial Arts Index. 1913–1957 (Superseded by *Applied
   Science and Technology Index* and *Business Periodicals Index.*
   Since 1958)
International Index to Periodicals. 1907–1964 (Superseded by
   Social Sciences and Humanities Index. Since 1965)
International Nursing Index. Since 1966
MLA [Modern Language Association] *International
   Bibliography.* Since 1963
The Music Index. Since 1949
New York Times Index. Since 1851
Nineteenth Century Readers' Guide, 1890–1899. 1945
Poole's Index to Periodical Literature, 1802–1906. 1945
Public Affairs Information Service Bulletin. Since 1915
Readers' Guide to Periodical Literature. Since 1900
Social Science Index. Since 1974

Social Sciences and Humanities Index. 1965–1974 (Superseded
   by *Social Sciences Index* and *Humanities Index.* 1974)
Technical Book Review Index. Since 1917
United States Catalog: Books in Print. Since 1928
Vertical File Index. Since 1935

II. Science and Technology

A. General
Dictionary of Science. 1986
Dictionary of Scientific Biography. 1980
A Guide to the History of Science. 1952
McGraw-Hill Dictionary of Scientific and Technical Terms. 1984
McGraw-Hill Encyclopedia of Science and Technology. 20 vols.,
   1987
Van Nostrand's Scientific Encyclopedia. 1983

B. Agriculture
Bibliography of Agriculture. Since 1942
Biological and Agricultural Index. Since 1916
Guide to Sources for Agricultural and Biological Research. 1981
Index to Publications of the U.S. Department of Agriculture.
   Since 1901
Yearbook of Agriculture. Since 1894

C. Biology
Biological Abstracts. Since 1926
Biological and Agricultural Index. Since 1916
*Dictionary of Scientific Terms in Biology, Botany, Zoology,
   Anatomy, Cytology, Embryology, Physiology.* 1960
Encyclopedia of the Biological Sciences. 1981
Gray's Anatomy. 1980
Grzimek's Animal Life Encyclopedia. 1975
Grzimek's Encyclopedia of Evolution. 1976
Guide to the Literature of the Life Sciences. 1972
Progress in Biophysics and Biophysical Chemistry. Since 1950
   (Now *Progress in Biophysics and Molecular Biology*)

D. Chemistry
Chemical Abstracts. Since 1907
Chemical Publications: Their Nature and Use. 1982
The Condensed Chemical Dictionary. 1981

Encyclopedia of Chemistry. 1984
Handbook of Chemistry and Physics. Since 1914
Lange's Handbook of Chemistry. 1985
McGraw-Hill Dictionary of Chemistry. 1984
Van Nostrand Reinhold Encyclopedia of Chemistry. 1984

E. Computer Technology and Electronic Data Processing
Computer-Readable Databases. 2 vols., 1985
Datapro Directory of Microcomputer Software. Since 1981
Dictionary of Computing. 1986
A Dictionary of Minicomputing and Microcomputing. 1982
Encyclopedia of Computer Science and Technology. 16 vols., 1975
Prentice-Hall Standard Glossary of Computer Technology. 1984
Software Catalog. Since 1983

F. Energy
Energy Handbook. 1984
Energy Research Abstracts. Since 1976
McGraw-Hill Encyclopedia of Energy. 1981
Sourcebook on Atomic Energy. 1979

G. Engineering
Annual Book of ASTM Standards. 66 vols., 1983
Applied Science and Technology Index. Since 1958
Engineering Encyclopedia. 2 vols., 1963
Engineering Index. Since 1884
McGraw-Hill Dictionary of Electrical and Electronic Engineering.
   1984
Standard Handbook for Civil Engineers. 1983
Sweet's Catalog. 1986
U.S. Government Research Reports. Since 1946.

H. Environmental Studies
Conservation Dictionary. 1985
Dictionary of the Environment. 1977
Environment Abstracts. Since 1971
Pollution Abstracts. Since 1970

I. Geology
Bibliography and Index of Geology. Since 1933
Bibliography of North American Geology. Since 1906
Glossary of Geology. 1980
McGraw-Hill Dictionary of Earth Sciences. 1984
McGraw-Hill Encyclopedia of Earth Science. 1978
Minerals Yearbook. Since 1933

J. **Health**
   Complete Home Medical Guide. 1985
   Cumulative Index to Nursing and Allied Health Literature.
      Since 1977
   Nutrition and Health Encyclopedia. 1985
   Sourcebook on Food and Nutrition. 1982

K. **Medicine**
   Index Medicus. Since 1927
   The Merk Manual. Since 1899
   Physicians' Desk Reference. Since 1947

L. **Physics and Mathematics**
   Annual Review of Nuclear and Particle Science. Since 1952
   Barlow's Tables. 1958
   *Dictionary of Named Effects and Laws in Chemistry, Physics and
      Mathematics.* 1970
   Encyclopaedic Dictionary of Physics. 9 vols., 1961
   Handbook of Chemistry and Physics. Since 1914
   Handbook of Mathematical Science. 1978
   McGraw-Hill Encyclopedia of Physics. 1983
   Prentice-Hall Encyclopedia of Mathematics. 1982
   Reviews of Modern Physics. Since 1929

III. **Social Sciences**
   A. **General**
      Dictionary of the Social Sciences. 1964
      An International Encyclopedia of the Social Sciences. 17 vols.,
         1968
      Public Affairs Information Service. Since 1915
      A Reader's Guide to the Social Sciences. 1970
      Social Science Encyclopedia. 1985
      Social Sciences Index. Since 1974
      Sources of Information in the Social Sciences. 1973

   B. **Business**
      Business Information Sources. 1985
      Business Periodicals Index. Since 1958
      Commodity Year Book. Since 1939
      Dictionary of Business and Management. 1983
      Dun and Bradstreet Reference Book of Corporate Management.
         Since 1967

Dun's Business Month. Since 1893
Encyclopedia of Business Information Sources. 1983
Foreign Commerce Yearbook. Since 1933
Moody's Manual of Investments. Since 1929
Standard and Poor's Corporation Records. Since 1928
Standard and Poor's Register of Corporations, Directors and Executives, United States and Canada. Since 1928
Survey of Current Business. Since 1921
Thomas' Register of American Manufacturers. Since 1905
Wall Street Journal Index. Since 1958

C. Criminology
Crime in the U.S. Since 1930
Criminal and Civil Investigation Handbook. 1981
Criminal Justice Abstracts. Since 1977
Criminal Justice Periodical Index. Since 1975
Encyclopedia of American Crime. 1982
Encyclopedia of Crime and Justice. 4 vols., 1983
Use of Criminology Literature. 1974

D. Economics
Dictionary of Business and Economics. 1984
Encyclopedia of Economics. 1982
Information Sources in Economics. 1984
McGraw-Hill Dictionary of Modern Economics. 1983
World Economic Survey. Since 1945

E. Education
Current Index to Journals in Education. Since 1969
Dictionary of Education. 1982
Digest of Educational Statistics. Since 1962
Directory of American Scholars. Since 1942
Education Index. Since 1929
Encyclopedia of Education. 10 vols., 1971
Encyclopedia of Educational Research. 1982
ERIC Resources in Education. Since 1966
International Encyclopedia of Higher Education. 1977

F. Ethnic Studies
Dictionary of Race and Ethnic Relations. 1984
Ethnic Almanac. 1981
Handbook of North American Indians. Since 1978
Minority Organizations. Since 1978
Sourcebook of Hispanic Culture in the United States. 1982

G. Geography
Climates of the States. Since 1974
Encyclopedic Dictionary of Physical Geography. 1985
Geo-Data, The World Almanac Gazeteer. 1983
Modern Dictionary of Geography. 1986
National Geographical Index. Since 1899
The Weather Almanac. 1977
World Survey of Climatology. Since 1969

H. History
American Destiny. 10 vols., 1975
American Historical Review. Since 1895
Cambridge Ancient History. 12 vols., 1923–1939
Cambridge History of Latin America. 1984
Cambridge Medieval History. 8 vols., 1911–1936
Concise Dictionary of World History. 1983
Dictionary of American History. 8 vols., 1976
Dictionary of Historical Terms. 1983
Dictionary of the History of Ideas. 1973
Encyclopedia of American History. 1976
Historical Abstracts. Since 1955
*History of American Life: A Social, Cultural, and Economic
    Analysis.* 13 vols., 1929–1944
New Cambridge Modern History. 14 vols., Since 1957
*The New Larned History for Ready Reference, Reading, and
    Research.* 12 vols., 1922–1924

I. Political Science
American Political Science Review. Since 1906
Congressional Record. Since 1873
Dictionary of Political Thought. 1982
Documents on American Foreign Relations. Since 1939
Encyclopedia of American Political History. 3 vols., 1984
Index to Legal Periodicals. Since 1909
International Handbook of Political Science. 1982
Municipal Year Book. Since 1934
Political Handbook of the World. Since 1927
Public Affairs Information Service Bulletin. Since 1915
Statesman's Yearbook. Since 1864

J. Psychology
American Journal of Psychology. Since 1887
Encyclopedia of Occultism and Parapsychology. 1978
Encyclopedia of Psychology. 4 vols., 1984

Encyclopedic Dictionary of Psychology. 1983
Handbook of Parapsychology. 1977
Man, Myth and Magic. 1970
Mental Measurements Yearbook. Since 1938
Psychological Abstracts. Since 1927
Psychological Bulletin. Since 1904
Understanding Human Behavior. 24 vols., 1977

K. Sociology

American Journal of Sociology. Since 1895
American Sociological Review. Since 1936
Encyclopedia of Sociology. 1981
Social Forces. Since 1922
Social Science Abstracts. 5 vols., 1929–1933
Social Work Year Book. Since 1929
Sociological Abstracts. Since 1953

L. Women's Studies

Directory of Financial Aids for Women. 1988
Rights of Women. 1983
Women's Annual. Since 1981
Women in Popular Culture. 1982
Women's Studies Abstracts. Since 1972

IV. Humanities

A. Art and Architecture

American Art Directory. Since 1898
Art Index. Since 1929
Encyclopedia of World Art. 16 vols., 1959
Illustrated Dictionary of Art and Artists. 1984
Macmillan Encyclopedia of Architecture. 4 vols., 1982
New International Illustrated Encyclopedia of Art. 24 vols.,
    1967
The Oxford Companion to Art. 1970
Who's Who in American Art. Since 1937

B. Literature

Abstracts of English Studies. Since 1958
American Authors, 1600–1900. 1938
American Literature. Since 1929
Book Review Digest. Since 1905

British Writers. 8 vols., 1984
Cambridge Guide to English Literature. 1983
Cambridge History of American Literature. 3 vols., 1972
Cambridge History of English Literature. 15 vols., 1907–1933
Columbia Dictionary of Modern European Literature. 1980
Contemporary Authors. Since 1962
Contemporary Literary Criticism. Since 1973
Dictionary of Literary Biography. Since 1978
Dramatic Criticism Index. 1972
Essay and General Literature Index. Since 1900
Fiction Catalog. Since 1908
Granger's Index to Poetry. 1986
Guide to English and American Literature. 3rd ed., 1976
Handbook to Literature. 1980
Humanities Index. Since 1974
Literary History of the United States. 2 vols., 1974
Macmillan Home Book of Proverbs, Maxims and Phrases. 1965
Magill's Critical Survey of Drama. 6 vols., 1985
Magill's Critical Survey of Long Fiction. 8 vols., 1983
Magill's Critical Survey of Poetry. 8 vols., 1982
Magill's Critical Survey of Short Fiction. 7 vols., 1981
McGraw-Hill Encyclopedia of World Drama. 5 vols., 1984
Masterpieces of World Literature in Digest Form. 1968
Masterplots. 11 vols., 1976
New Guide to Modern World Literature. 1985
Oxford Companion to American Literature. 1983
Oxford Companion to Classical Literature. 1986
Oxford Companion to English Literature. 1985
Oxford Companion to French Literature. 1961
Play Index. 6 vols., 1949–1982
PMLA [Publications of the Modern Language Association].
    Since 1921
*Poetry Explication: A Checklist of Interpretation Since 1925 of
    British and American Poems Past and Present.* 1980
Princeton Encyclopedia of Poetry and Poetics. 1975
The Reader's Encyclopedia. 1965
Short Story Index. 5 vols., 1950–1973. Supp. Since 1974
Twentieth Century Literary Criticism. Since 1978
Twentieth Century Short Story Explication. Since 1977
Writer's Handbook. Since 1936

C. Music and Dance
Dance Encyclopedia. 1967
The Encyclopedia of Dance and Ballet. 1977
Encyclopedia of Folk, Country and Western Music. 1983
The International Cyclopedia of Music and Musicians. 1985

Music Index. Since 1949
New Grove Dictionary of American Music. 4 vols., 1986
New Grove Dictionary of Music and Musicians. 20 vols., 1980
New Grove Dictionary of Musical Instruments. 3 vols., 1984
New Oxford Companion to Music. 2 vols., 1983
New Oxford History of Music. 2 vols., 1983

D. Philosophy and Religion

Bible Atlases and Concordances (A variety of titles is available)
Concise Encyclopedia of Western Philosophy and Philosophers.
  1975
Dictionary of the History of Ideas. 4 vols., 1973
Dictionary of Philosophy and Psychology. 3 vols., 1949
Encyclopaedia Judaica. 16 vols., 1972
Encyclopaedia of Religion and Ethics. 13 vols., 1959
Encyclopedia of Islam. 5 vols., 1954–1983
Encyclopedia of Philosophy. 8 vols., 1967
Encyclopedia of Religion. 16 vols., 1986
The Golden Bough: A Study in Magic and Religion. 12 vols.,
  1907–1915
History of the Church. 10 vols., 1987
International Bibliography of the History of Religions. Since
  1954
Interpreter's Dictionary of the Bible. 4 vols., 1962
Jewish Encyclopedia. 12 vols., 1939–1944
Journal of Philosophy. Since 1904
New Catholic Encyclopedia. 15 vols., 1967
A New Dictionary of Christian Theology. 1983
New Larousse Encyclopedia of Mythology. 1969
New Schaff-Herzog Encyclopedia of Religious Knowledge.
  13 vols., 1949–1950
Philosopher's Index. Since 1967
Philosophical Review. Since 1892
A Reader's Guide to the Great Religions. 1977
Religion Index One: Periodicals. Since 1949
Research Guide to Philosophy. 1983
Sacramentum Mundi: Encyclopedia of Theology. 6 vols.,
  1968–1970
World Philosophy. 5 vols., 1982
Yearbook of American Churches. Since 1916

V. Vocational Studies

  A. Aviation

*Above and Beyond: The Encyclopedia of Aviation and Space
  Sciences.* 1967

Aviation Space Dictionary. 1980
International Encyclopedia of Aviation. 1977
Jane's All the World's Aircraft. Since 1909
World Aviation Directory. Since 1940

B. **Broadcasting and Mass Media**
  Broadcast Communications Dictionary. 1978
  Broadcasting Around the World. 1981
  Broadcasting Cablecasting Yearbook. Since 1982
  Broadcasting Yearbook. Since 1982
  Communication Abstracts. Since 1978
  Facts on File Dictionary of Telecommunications. 1983
  Longman Dictionary of Mass Media and Communication. 1982
  Telecommunications Systems and Services Directory. Since 1983
  Television and Cable Factbook. Since 1946
  Who's Who in Television and Cable. 1983

C. **Fashion Careers**
  Costume and Fashion: A Concise History. 1983
  Dressmaking Explained. 1985
  Fairchild's Dictionary of Fashion. 1975
  Fashion Encyclopedia. 1982
  New Encyclopedia of Textiles. 1980

D. **Hotel, Motel, Tourism Management**
  Encyclopedia of World Travel. 2 vols., 1979
  Fodor's Travel Guides. (By country) Since 1936
  Hotel and Motel Redbook. Since 1886
  Hotel and Travel Index. Since 1938
  Tours and Visits Directory. 1981

E. **Interior Design**
  Antique Collector's Guide. 1981
  The Dictionary of Interior Design. 1966
  The Encyclopedia of Furniture. 1965
  Interior Design. Since 1932
  Studio Dictionary of Design and Decoration. 1973

F. **Medical and Allied Health Careers**
  Dorland's Illustrated Medical Dictionary. 1981
  Drugs of Choice. Since 1958
  Handbook of Nursing. 1984
  Index Medicus. Since 1927
  Medical School Admission Requirements. 1988–1989

Physicians' Desk Reference. Since 1947
Textbook of Medicine. 1982

G. Office Technology
Complete Secretary's Handbook. 1983
Office Automation. 1982
Professional Secretary's Handbook. 1984
Secretary's Standard Reference Manual and Guide. 1978
Webster's New World Secretarial Handbook. 1981

H. Recreation and Physical Education
Campground and Trailer Park Directory. Since 1984
Encyclopedia of Crafts. 3 vols., 1980
Language of Sport. 1983
Official Rules of Sports and Games. 1986
Physical Education Index. Since 1978
Recreation and Outdoor Life Directory. 1983

Appendix B

Reference Words and Abbreviations

Knowing the words and abbreviations often found in reference and scholarly materials will make searching for and recording information easier. You may want to use some of them in your own note taking or perhaps in writing the text of your research paper. However, you should know that there is a trend *away* from using foreign (mostly Latin) terms. Even the once-popular "ibid." and "op. cit." are no longer recommended for documentation. Nevertheless, some of the many reference words are in the following list:

abbr.	abbreviation
abr.	abridged
adapt.	adapted by, or adaptation
anon.	anonymous
biblio.	bibliography
biog.	biography
c or ©	copyright
c. or ca.	*circa* ("about")—used with approximate dates
cf.	*confer* ("compare with")
ch. or chap.	chapter
col., cols.	column(s)
comp.	compiled by, or compiler
diss.	dissertation
ed., eds.	edited by or edition or editor(s)
e.g.	*exempli gratia* ("for example")

enl.	enlarged
esp.	especially
et al.	*et alii* ("and others")—[always abbreviate]
etc.	*et cetera* ("and so forth")
ex.	example
f., ff.	following page(s)
fig., figs.	figure(s)
fn.	footnote
fwd.	foreword
ibid.	*ibidem* ("in the same place")
i.e.	*id est* ("that is")
illus.	illustrated or illustrations or illustrator
introd.	introduction
l., ll.	line(s)
ms., mss.	manuscript(s)
NB	*nota bene* ("mark well")—take notice
n.d.	no date of publication available
n.p.	no publisher available; no place of publication given
n.p., n.pag.	no pagination available
op. cit.	*opere citato* ("in the work cited")
p., pp.	page(s)
pass.	*passim* ("throughout")—here and there throughout the work
pref.	preface
pseud.	pseudonym
pub. or publ.	publisher or published by or publication
qtd.	quoted in
rept.	report, or reported by
rev.	revised by or revision; reviewed by or review—[spell out the word if confusion is possible]
rpt.	reprint or reprinted by
sic	so, or thus
supp.	supplement
tr. or trans.	translator or translated by or translation
v. or vide	see, consult
viz.	*videlicet* ("namely")
vol., vols.	volume(s)

Appendix C
APA Form Title Page

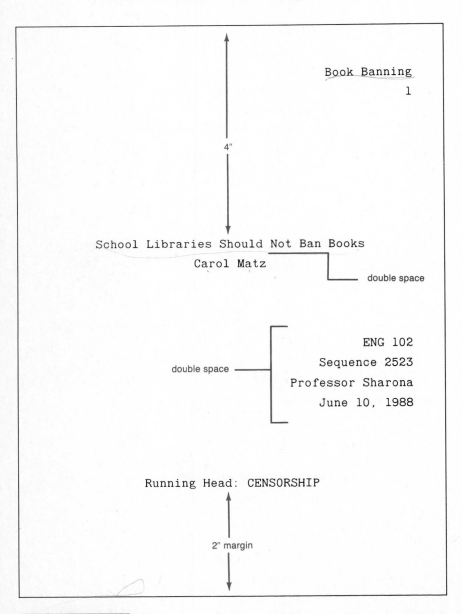

Book Banning

1

4"

School Libraries Should Not Ban Books

Carol Matz

double space

double space

ENG 102

Sequence 2523

Professor Sharona

June 10, 1988

Running Head: CENSORSHIP

2" margin

Index